PRAISE FOR
THRIVING WITH ANXIETY

"David H. Rosmarin is an accomplished clinician, educator, and scientist, whose pioneering academic work highlights the relevance of spirituality to mental health. *Thriving with Anxiety* is an accessible and artful book that stands to improve the lives of those with psychiatric illness by both combating stigma and expertly providing evidence-based strategies to a wide audience."

—Scott L. Rauch, MD
President and psychiatrist in chief at McLean Hospital;
professor of psychiatry at Harvard Medical School

"*Thriving with Anxiety* is a guide that offers a new and empowering perspective on anxiety. Dr. Rosmarin challenges the conventional notion of anxiety from a feeling of fear to a tool that helps deepen compassion, self-awareness, and relationships. By looking inward, readers are encouraged to utilize anxiety to transcend their internal barriers into a life of connection, acceptance, and resilience."

—Bobby Berk
Emmy-nominated TV host and author of *Right at Home*

"In times when stress and anxiety are at an all-time high, *Thriving with Anxiety* can provide an important antidote and relief. Drawing on his research and experience, David H. Rosmarin has created a vital masterpiece."

—Tal Ben Shahar, PhD
New York Times bestselling author of *Happier: Learn
the Secrets to Daily Joy and Lasting Fulfillment*;
Harvard instructor on positive psychology;
cofounder of the Happiness Studies Academy

"As a person who has lived with anxiety my whole life, I had never seen it through the many lenses this book offers. I couldn't put the book down! It opened up a whole new world to me of the profound gifts that anxiety also offers. Instead of viewing it as a curse, it offers a reframe for self-discovery and personal growth that has already had a deep impact on my life."

—Tessa White
The Job Doctor and author of *The Unspoken Truths for Career Success*

"*Thriving with Anxiety* will teach you to not just learn to live with anxiety but to recognize how anxiety can help you to enjoy the life you want to live. All too often, anxiety is viewed negatively, as something to be avoided. Ironically, it's the constant struggle to avoid anxiety that keeps it alive. This book illustrates the differences between helpful anxiety and anxiety that gets in the way. It will show you how to change your relationship with anxiety, how to learn to embrace anxiety, and how to harness your anxiety to soar to new heights in your relationships and your life!"

—Martin M. Antony, PhD
Former president of the Canadian Psychological Association;
professor of psychology at Toronto Metropolitan University;
author of *The Shyness and Social Anxiety
Workbook* and *The Anti-Anxiety Program*

"*Thriving with Anxiety* offers a counterintuitive yet scientifically grounded approach to the treatment of anxiety-related disorders. With increasing prevalence of anxiety across the age spectrum, in part related to the impact of the COVID-19 pandemic and the uncovering of existing, common, and unaddressed mental health challenges, there has never been a time when Dr. Rosmarin's wisdom and guidance is so critically needed."

—Brent P. Forester, MD, MSc
Chief and chairman of the department
of psychiatry at Tufts Medical Center;
Dr. Frances S. Arkin Professor of Psychiatry
at Tufts University School of Medicine

"In *Thriving with Anxiety*, Dr. Rosmarin guides readers to a deeper understanding on the nature of anxiety, thus releasing us from self-blame, struggles with inadequacy, and feelings of shame. He engages our inner CEO to embrace and thrive, even while anxious. We move from being taken hostage by anxiety against our will to grabbing hold of the opportunities that anxiety presents to enhance connection throughout our lives."

—Lisa Miller, PhD
New York Times bestselling author of *The Spiritual Child*;
founder of the Spirituality, Mind, Body Institute (SMBI);
professor of psychology at Columbia University

"Rosmarin's work on anxiety, spirituality, and mental health and well-being constitute fundamental contributions. In *Thriving with Anxiety* he applies his extensive knowledge, understanding, and clinical experience to help people thrive amidst the many challenges of contemporary life."

—Tyler VanderWeele, PhD
Director of the Harvard University Human Flourishing Program;
professor of epidemiology in the Harvard School of Public Health

"*Thriving with Anxiety* is the silver lining inside anxiety that will enable you to turn a potential breakdown into a breakthrough that will change your life."

—Mark Goulston, MD
Bestselling author of *Just Listen: Discover the Secret
to Getting Through to Absolutely Anyone*

"*Thriving with Anxiety* takes a brilliant approach to transcending our limits by coming to terms with and accepting who we are. From this sense of heightened self-awareness and inner peace comes the ability to truly know others and accept them for who they are. This fresh perspective on emotional and behavioral health is especially timely in light of Gen-Z/Zoomers' isolation from living in a world of digital technology. Yet all generations suffer from anxiety to some degree, and embracing it to become more self-aware, to connect more effectively with others, and to reach our full potential is the noble purpose of this much-needed book."

—Paul Falcone
Bestselling author, speaker, and consultant in
human resources and leadership

THRIVING
WITH
ANXIETY

9 TOOLS TO MAKE
YOUR ANXIETY WORK FOR YOU

DAVID H. ROSMARIN, PHD

HARPER HORIZON

ISBN 978-1-4003-2834-5 (Ebook)
ISBN 978-1-4003-2785-0 (HC)

Library of Congress Control Number: 2023938080

Printed in the United States of America
23 24 25 26 27 LBC 5 4 3 2 1

This book is dedicated to my wonderful colleagues at Center for Anxiety and McLean Hospital / Harvard Medical School, who teach others how to thrive with anxiety each and every day.

CONTENTS

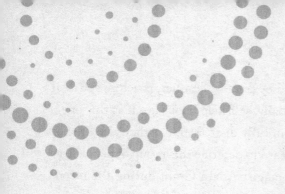

PREFACE

Who Is This Book For?

From my experiences in the past twenty years of clinical work, it seems to me that all people fall into one of four broadly defined groups of emotional and behavioral health: flourishing, languishing, distressed, and severely distressed. More accurately, all people at any moment can be categorized into one of these four groups, and over a lifespan we may go from one group to another at different points in time.

The first group consists of those who are *flourishing*. Not to be confused with thriving, which can occur at any point along the continuum,* people who are flourishing are doing well in their lives across the board. They generally feel good about themselves, and they are not overwhelmed by any major life difficulties or physical ailments. Most individuals who are flourishing still need some support to remain in this

---

* As we shall see throughout this book, even people who are distressed or severely distressed can learn how to thrive. By contrast, *flourishing* is a more global term representing one's overall level of well-being.

category, but this can be provided by friends, families, coaches, spiritual or religious mentors, and, potentially, self-help books (such as this one).

The second group are not clinically distressed, but they also are not flourishing. The best term I've heard to describe this group of people was notably used by Wharton psychologist Adam Grant during the recent pandemic on the pages of the *New York Times*: *languishing*.[1] Folks in this category are, as Grant put it, "feeling meh . . . joyless and aimless," and thus struggling to maintain a sunny disposition in the context of their life stressors. Individuals who are languishing need all of the above supports that the flourishing can benefit from, but they generally need more of them. They also may benefit from a support group, a mental health well visit, or even ad hoc consultation (a session once in a while) with a mental health professional to monitor their feelings and behaviors and come up with some more advanced strategies.

The third and fourth groups are clinical territory. These individuals presently need to come to mental health professionals, such as myself, for help on a regular basis. Group three includes people who are *distressed*. They are significantly affected by symptoms of one or more mental disorders, such as anxiety, depression, alcohol or drug use, or the like. However, they are generally able to function day-to-day and take care of themselves, with a minimal amount of support (for example, weekly therapy; one or two basic psychiatric medications). They aren't happy campers by any stretch, but when push comes to shove, they get out of bed, go to work, shower and brush their teeth with reasonable regularity, and they are not at significant risk for harming themselves (through suicide or self-injury).

Group four is *severely distressed*. These individuals need a high level of professional care to function or stay safe. They usually need intensive therapy multiple times per week, advanced psychiatric medications under active management, and possibly residential care or psychiatric hospitalization. Of course, the goal of these treatments is to help rehabilitate and support recovery so patients can move into the distressed, languishing, or even flourishing categories. Fortunately, this is a common trajectory.

As noted previously, *all four groups of people need guidance, support, and help in the area of emotional well-being.* Even those who are flourishing need support in order to remain in their coveted category. Further, as I already noted, people can and generally do fluctuate between these categories over the lifespan. I've seen many severely distressed patients—individuals who needed psychiatric hospitalization—go on to flourish. Conversely, I've seen many individuals flourish for years or even decades before disaster struck, at which point they descended into distress or even severe distress. As the Greek philosopher Heraclitus taught, no one can step in the same river twice, for even if it's the same river they are not the same person. In essence, change is the only constant.

The contents of this book are appropriate for individuals in all four groups. Individuals who are flourishing often have some anxiety, and they can benefit from learning how to harness it to be more self-aware, be more connected with others, and achieve more of their potential. Those who are languishing also stand to benefit from this book. Often the self-judgment that comes with "feeling meh" makes it harder to function, and this book will show how anxiety is not only normal but often a great sign of inner strength.

As for those who are distressed and severely distressed, on the one hand this book has plenty of content that is relevant, practical, and helpful. Readers will learn about anxiety in new and different ways. The only caveat is that this book alone is unlikely to provide sufficient support for those who are distressed or severely distressed without concurrent professional help such as psychotherapy or pharmacotherapy. After all, no book can be a replacement for individualized, professional mental health care.

In sum, all of us can benefit from these strategies for thriving with anxiety, but some may need additional support as well.

INTRODUCTION

How to Thrive in a New Age of Anxiety[*]

About a decade ago, after more than ten years of university study and fellowship, I had begun a faculty position at Harvard Medical School—a job I had always dreamed of—when an astonishing opportunity came my way. I had the chance to start an anxiety center in New York City, but it would require commuting two days a week by train from Boston to Manhattan—an eight-hour door-to-door round trip. Still, it was too good an opportunity to ignore, so I put my reservations on hold. I found an office in Midtown Manhattan and set up a travel schedule to spend one to two days a week there, while also teaching and doing research in Boston.

Soon after, though, a problem arose that I had not anticipated. While I had built a name for myself in Boston, I was not known in New York.

---

* This book contains dozens of patient stories from my clinical practice. All names and identifying details have been changed to protect privacy. Furthermore, in most instances, descriptions are composites of many cases that have been simplified to reflect general concepts and approaches.

My prestigious academic affiliation and all those expensive years of training I had completed seemed to mean nothing. I could barely get any referrals, and initially I had just one patient. And that patient paid a reduced rate, which didn't even cover the cost of my weekly travel, let alone office expenses. Bills and stress piled up, and so did some bad habits. I was eating greasy food from take-out restaurants, my time for exercising dwindled, and I was losing sleep because of my brutal commute. Each Wednesday, I left my home in Boston at six in the morning and returned after midnight on Thursday. After several months, I started to feel the burden of this arrangement.

This whole scenario took me *way* out of my comfort zone. But when I discussed the situation with my mentors and my wife, they all said it was early yet, and I should stick with the plan. Still, it was beginning to feel like not only an incredible burden but also a huge risk. I had signed a yearlong lease on my office, already expended on furniture, and had built a website to attract a clientele—but nobody was coming. One morning after my Boston–New York commute, I was walking out of Penn Station to go see my lone patient that day when I received an unexpected email that he was canceling his session. A wave of anxiety swept over me. This was followed quickly by a sense of self-criticism for being hypocritical, followed by a surge of catastrophic thinking. *Whoa!* I thought. *I'm supposed to be helping people overcome their anxiety—and I'm feeling anxious myself! How will I ever be successful? I must be headed for failure!*

At that moment, I realized that I needed to practice what I was preaching. *David, of course you're feeling anxious!* I said to myself, almost blurting it out in the middle of the street. *You decided to take on a big challenge, and right now it is a genuinely stressful situation. In fact, if you weren't feeling anxious during a challenge, then it's probably not worthwhile in the first place! You are dreaming big, and it's inevitable that you're going to hit some thorny issues along the way. Be humble and accept the challenges head-on! It's okay if it's not going your way. Just because you're not successful out of the gate doesn't mean you're not going to flourish down the road. Let go of your need for control, and don't let your anxiety get in the way. You have a goal. You have a dream! This is something you want to do, and you don't need to let your anxiety stop you. You can transcend it. Your anxiety is normal. You know deep down that these limits are not real—only perceived—and you don't need to give up just because the going is tough.*

By the time I got to my office, I already felt immensely better than I had in weeks. Since my patient had canceled, I took the time to reflect on what had just occurred. Instead of ignoring my anxiety or trying to block it out, I had used it to thrive. What had started out as a near-panic attack had turned into a moment of internal connection. My self-talk had shifted from criticism and catastrophizing to acceptance and encouragement.

In the weeks that followed, I experienced continued thriving when my anxiety would surge, not because my practice had taken off—as it was still just beginning—but because of some critical changes I decided to make. I started that week by finding a nicer restaurant that served healthier foods in a relaxed atmosphere. The next week, I packed my gym clothes and began exercising each Thursday morning in New York. More importantly, rather than shouldering all the stress of my professional life on my own, I connected with other people. I spoke to my wife, mentors, and some friends at length about my anxiety and how I was feeling. At first it felt embarrassing as an *anxiety specialist* to acknowledge that I myself was struggling. But opening up to others increased my sense of connection with them. I also surrendered to my anxiety and accepted that while I could choose to do my best, any success I might have would be determined by forces beyond my control, and I would likely feel anxiety for some time to come. By recognizing that anxiety is natural for those who strive for monumental achievements, I began the process of identifying, accepting, and ultimately transcending my limits.

Looking back on that day, I realize that it crystalized an entire philosophy toward dealing with mental health struggles: *we can thrive with anxiety.* What I had seen as hypocrisy was, in fact, a wake-up call telling me that one need not rid oneself of anxiety to live a happy and productive life. On the contrary: having anxiety can teach us about ourselves, deepen our relationships with others, and enable us to transcend our internal barriers to achieve our deepest dreams and goals in life. Anxiety can be a great blessing, if we learn how to deal with it and use it to thrive.

I believe that many current approaches to anxiety fall short because they are predicated entirely on the medical model. Typically, people seek to eliminate—or at least reduce—their anxiety. Of course, no one wants to live an anxious life, but the best tools for living with anxiety involve learning to be self-compassionate, connect with others, and increase our capacity to tolerate adversity, discomfort, and uncertainty.

During the past decade, my New York practice has grown to service more than one thousand unique patients each year. Our expanding staff of over seventy people now occupies four offices in New York and two more in Boston. And the data we collect from our patients and therapists have confirmed what I learned myself many years ago: we can live vibrant and productive lives with anxiety. Indeed, we can harness the power of anxiety to thrive and flourish.

The New "Age of Anxiety"

According to the National Institute of Mental Health, prior to the COVID-19 pandemic of 2020, approximately one in three American adults experienced an anxiety disorder at some point in their lives (almost one in five, at any point in time). Among teens, the situation was even more dire: almost one in three American adolescents experience an anxiety disorder *each year.*[1] As alarming as these prevalence rates are, the bigger concern is the growing *severity* of anxiety. Even before the pandemic, a substantial number of people were suffering with clinically significant levels of anxiety that were genuinely debilitating to the point of not being able to work.[2] In many cases, anxiety can also be associated with what is known in the therapeutic world as *nonsuicidal self-injury*, which can include cutting, burning, and other forms of self-harm.[3] Along these lines, the total age-adjusted suicide rate in the US increased 35.2 percent from 1999 to 2018.[4] Needless to say, all of these figures are substantially higher today. The World Health Organization reports that our anxiety across the globe has risen by 25 percent since 2020.[5]

Interestingly, the first half of the twentieth century has been called the "age of anxiety," in part because of the viciousness of two world wars, genocides, and the use of nuclear weapons on civilian populations.[6] However, objectively speaking, from the turn of the twenty-first century to today (even before the pandemic), our anxiety is higher than any other time in history.[7] In fact, "normal" healthy children in the United States today have higher levels of anxiety than hospitalized psychiatric patients from the mid-1950s![8]

Let us pause to ask a basic question: Why is our society more anxious today when overall levels of security, safety, and financial stability are far better than they were in the mid-1900s? Yes, serious social and economic disparities exist throughout large segments of America. But the average person has far more technology, information, educational opportunites, and access to basic medical care today than we did one hundred years ago. So why has our anxiety exploded to such high levels, when our stressors seem to have lessened?

One answer is the very reason I'm writing this book: *We have turned anxiety into something to be gotten rid of because we make the mistake of fearing anxiety itself. We need to interpret our anxiety not as something to overcome but as something that can potentially enhance our lives.* At a basic level, anxiety is a little like a smoke alarm. If the alarm goes off because you left the burner on under a skillet after you finished cooking, it's not a bad thing—it's a good thing! The alarm alerts us that we have a problem to deal with, and as long as we heed the sound of that alarm early enough and take appropriate action (in this example, turn off the burner), we can be perfectly fine. However, if we jump up and down and start cursing at ourselves for letting the alarm go off, or if we overreact to the alarm, we are making a bad situation out of a potential positive. Worse yet, if we disconnect the alarm because the constant blaring is disturbing and upsetting—well, we may end up burning down the house!

Fear of Anxiety

When Amelia describes the first onrush of anxiety, she says it feels like a hurricane that keeps mounting in intensity. That's because the stormy winds of anxious feelings are followed by a torrent of guilt and shame. "I judge myself for feeling anxious," she says to me. "I'm already nervous about my job, but then I get concerned that I have a disease, that I'm not strong enough and I won't be able to handle things. I start worrying that people will think I'm insecure and even crazy!"

Simply seeing anxiety as something we shouldn't have and need to get rid of *increases* our anxiety. For some, it's more like an avalanche than a hurricane, as the initial shock of recognition shakes loose ensuing layers of mental and emotional debris until the person fears being suffocated.

Amelia's anxiety *about* the fact that she is anxious supercharges the initial anxiety exponentially. Although she has a secure job in a public relations firm, Amelia has been socially anxious for many years, since she was in college. She used to cope with her social anxiety by drinking, but then she developed an alcohol problem. She cut way back on her drinking, which has been beneficial for her, but at the same time she never dealt with her anxiety. "Now whenever I'm in a social situation, I can't stop thinking that everyone notices that I'm feeling anxious," she says. "And that makes me feel even more anxious." As a result, she withdraws and avoids going out much. Amelia interprets her anxiety as an indication that she's not socially competent, that she won't be funny, that people will know there's something wrong with her. That perpetuates a classic cycle: she is more likely to avoid social situations, which in turn heightens her anxiety because she never learns that she is more socially skilled than she thinks. This makes her feel even more socially awkward over time, which intensifies her social apprehension. What's particularly interesting about Amelia is how socially adept she is. Her humor is off the charts, and as a marketing professional she is keenly aware of how to interact with others. Amelia's anxiety is not based in reality! The main issue is her perception that anxiety is a problem.

Jim is stuck in a similar cycle. He's an athletic man in his forties who works as an EMT, but he is prone to panic attacks. When panic strikes, Jim's heart palpitates and his throat closes up, and although these are not dangerous symptoms, the minute he feels them he thinks, *Oh no, I'm having a heart attack!* or *Oh no, I'm going to end up with super-high levels of anxiety and I'm not going to be able to tolerate it!* That apprehension triggers adrenaline to release into his bloodstream, which makes the symptoms cascade further: his heart rate surges, his throat tightens even more, and his muscles get so tense that it can be physically painful. Jim's breathing rate also increases—because his body needs more oxygen to power all these changes—and his adrenaline increases even more as he mounts his fight-or-flight response. Yet all of this occurs without any reason to fight or flee. In reality, there is no danger at all. Rather, Jim is responding to his internal negative perception of how he feels. *Jim's perception of anxiety is his malady.* He views panic as a problem that he must ward off lest it have negative consequences. However, his fear of fear *in and of itself* is the critical factor that maintains and exacerbates his anxiety over time.

For some, anxiety has an insidious way of expanding into more than one kind of manifestation. Janice, an aspiring actress who works as a secretary, is deathly afraid of flying. But she's not afraid just of the plane crashing. In one of our sessions, she tells me that her primary concern is that her anxiety will go so high when she's on board that her *head will explode*. More accurately, she is concerned that she won't be able to handle her fear and may run screaming down the aisle. Janice has the perception that she cannot handle high anxiety, but none of this is true. In reality, anxiety often makes people act and appear calmer—the fight-or-flight response helps people to focus more on perceived threat, which makes our actions more intentional and fluid. Furthermore, anxiety takes up internal resources, which makes it more difficult to jump up and scream. In Janice's case, she admits to me that she has never lost control of herself when feeling anxious, and if anything, she tends to sit quietly while experiencing a surge of fear. Janice also acknowledges that she has never tried to handle her anxiety about flying in any organized way. She doesn't truly know that her head will explode if her anxiety peaks while on board a plane. Instead, she just avoids flying altogether, such that when her cousin got married in Florida, she took a train from New York—a trip that lasted the better part of two full days, instead of a three-hour flight!

Janice came in for help only when her anxiety mushroomed to the point that she avoided not only air travel but all situations in which she might feel anxious and become trapped. She started avoiding not only planes but also subways, buses, and traveling over bridges or through tunnels—all of which are hard to avoid while living in New York City. So Janice's world is getting smaller and smaller because she is afraid of something that is not objectively dangerous—her anxiety—and without any real proof that her feelings could, in fact, harm her. She is convinced in her *mind* that they will, because she is anxious about her anxiety.

My experience in twenty years of working with clients is that people who suffer from anxiety often judge themselves and catastrophize about their anxiety. This means that they let their minds run amok imagining the worst possible outcomes of an action or event. The same phenomenon occurs in other areas of mental health. People with depression often avoid situations that make them feel stressed, out of fear that they will become more depressed. They harshly criticize themselves internally for feeling so down, which of course makes things worse. People with chronic pain project that mild to moderate discomforts will continually worsen or lead to debilitation, such as becoming immobilized for life. They also tend to become angry at their pain and view their struggles as an internal weakness. In all these cases, the fear of a negative outcome and self-criticism generates more distress and dysfunction than necessary.

If you come away with just one lasting insight from this book, I would like it to be this: *anxiety itself is* not *a problem, and nothing is wrong with you for having anxiety.* The mere experience of anxiety is normal—in fact it is a positive thing, as we shall see later in this book—and certainly anxiety is nothing to fear. Once we realize that, we never need to catastrophize about anxious feelings.

Fear of Uncertainty

You may be wondering: Why do so many of us seem to be afraid of anxiety today? After all, if anxiety isn't inherently dangerous but merely uncomfortable, why does it make us so afraid? The most compelling explanation I can find for this paradox is that our culture is obsessed with control. Today, we have predictions for everything, from financial markets, political elections, and flu epidemics to professional sports outcomes and the weather. And despite the fact that those predictions can be notoriously incorrect—often by a wide margin—we scrutinize them as the soothsayers of ancient Rome once examined the entrails of sacrificial animals.

We do this for one simple reason: our culture cannot tolerate uncertainty. We would prefer to predict the future and be completely wrong than to admit we have no clue what's going to happen! This is why many Americans helicopter-parent their children—hovering overhead to supervise all aspects of life in order to monitor failures and successes—not just through grade school and adolescence but well into adulthood.[9] There is even a new phenomenon called "lawnmower parenting" that takes this to the next level: many parents are not content enough with monitoring and need to swoop in to prevent their children from experiencing even a modicum of failure.[10] Why else would wealthy parents pay tens of thousands of dollars to a "fixer" who promises admission into an Ivy League college for their children? We don't believe in ourselves enough; we are terrified when life is uncertain, since it raises the possibility that things may not work out.

We are also obsessed with safety and security. In the context of our society's unparalleled and unprecedented affluence, we have become accustomed to a false sense of security. Our precious institutional systems across the domains of government, finances, education, health, and more have checks and balances to *ensure* stability and well-being, but the truth is we are much more vulnerable than we care to admit. As a result, when moments of threat penetrate through the veil of false security, we are thrust into panic.

Ironically, in this regard, individuals who live in the third world or war-torn countries are at an advantage. They never expect safety or security from their institutions, and when reality hits it is simply understood and accepted as a part of life. Perhaps it's for this reason that anxiety is higher in the United States than in all other nations on earth,[11] and wealthier nations are substantially worse off than the third world.[12] In fact, low-income countries (e.g., Colombia, Peru) have approximately half as much anxiety as middle-income countries (e.g., Brazil, Mexico), and middle-income countries have about half as much anxiety as high-income countries (e.g., United States, France).[13]

In the Western world, we tend to medicalize normal mood states. What were considered standard levels of stress twenty or even ten years ago are today a reason for a Xanax prescription. We expect our emotions to be totally even-keeled. We want everything to go off without a hitch. We cannot tolerate the uncertainty that our minds and moods won't cooperate. We cannot handle the discomfort or perceived danger of feeling anxious and unmoored. It's almost as if we want to be on autopilot so we can be continuously comfortable, happy, and successful, and when our comfort is disrupted, we cannot accept how we feel. Our inability to take things as they are leads our emotions to intensify, in some cases enough to set off a spiral that results in perpetually severe anxiety.

To clarify, I'm not saying that the pursuit of equanimity is a bad thing. It's fine to seek happiness and comfort, to a degree. But the more we expect *total* certainty and security and the more relentlessly we pursue it, cling to it, and are unable to feel good without it, the more debilitated our emotional states become. Given these heightened expectations and the anxiety that is triggered when they aren't met, we ironically find it harder—and sometimes impossible—to flourish.

I believe our society's approach to anxiety—our approach to life!—has made the prevalence and severity of anxiety concerns much worse than ever before. When I was developing my clinic in New York and I chose the name *Center for Anxiety*, many of my friends were puzzled. They asked me why I didn't choose a name like *Center for Anxiety Treatment*, or *Center for Anxiety Relief*. I explained that my philosophy for treating anxiety does *not* help people to become *less* anxious. I help people learn to live with anxiety and to make anxiety their friend. So *Center for Anxiety* seemed appropriate since the goal is to learn to thrive with anxiety—not to get rid of it!

Anxiety can do so many constructive things when we stop running away from it. Anxiety can enhance self-awareness of both our strengths and areas for growth. It can remind us of the need to be compassionate to ourselves—something sorely lacking in our society. Anxiety can also enhance our relationships. If we harness it appropriately, it can help us create a deeper emotional bond with other people. We can learn to be vulnerable with others by sharing our inner worlds with them and by giving them an opportunity to take care of us. And finally, anxiety can help us identify strengths we never realized we had. We can learn to accept that, as humans, our knowledge and control are limited. We can also use anxiety to identify our unique strengths and push beyond our limits.

Anxiety may be a positive sign of high intelligence. There is a burgeoning body of research to suggest that individuals with anxiety disorders have higher IQ scores than "healthy" people.[14] Furthermore, anxious individuals tend to be more attentive and likely to remember details[15] since the same neurotransmitter associated with anxiety— GABA—is also related to human memory.[16] My own clinical experience bears out that patients with high levels of anxiety also have greater capacity for awareness of self and awareness of other people's needs. As well, they are often more conscientious and have a stronger sense of being driven to do big things.

Some of the most successful people in history have had significant anxiety. For instance, Mark Twain,[17] one of the most brilliant literary minds of his era, is known to have struggled mightily with his mental health, including anxiety symptoms, particularly during the latter part of his life. In today's world of entertainment, much the same is true. Dick Cavett,[18] a leading talk show host, has undergone electroshock treatments in his fight against decades of anxiety and depression. Actor Jim Carrey[19] has acknowledged that he suffered from anxiety and depression and took Prozac for years, although he stopped because it didn't help him. Carrey also says he no longer drinks or takes drugs of any kind, choosing instead to accept who he really is. "I only act in the movies," he says. The famous comedian Howie Mandel[20] is yet another individual who has openly discussed his anxiety, which includes obsessions and compulsions about germs.

Numerous prolific pop stars also have acknowledged suffering intense anxiety, panic attacks, and clinical depression, from Selena Gomez[21] and Adele[22] to Lady Gaga[23] and Bruce Springsteen[24]—"The Boss"—who revealed that he suffered two emotional breakdowns and should have been hospitalized for one of them. Many people are amazed to learn that these performers, who project so much energy onstage, also suffer from anxiety and depression.

The renowned psychologist Professor David H. Barlow, who has had a profound impact on my own work, has a deep appreciation for the paradoxical benefits of anxiety. In one of his most influential books, he put it this way:

> Without anxiety, little would be accomplished. The performance of athletes, entertainers, executives, artisans, and students would suffer; *creativity* would diminish; crops might not be planted. And we would all achieve that idyllic state long sought after in our fast-paced society of whiling away our lives under a shade tree. This would be as deadly for the species as nuclear war.[25]

Learning to Thrive with Anxiety

The insights that took shape as I walked to my office in Manhattan that day a decade ago served me especially well some years later, when I was working with a twenty-six-year-old client named Ashley. Having graduated from New York University a few years earlier, Ashley had found a well-paying job in marketing. She lived in Manhattan and was dating Kevin, a twenty-seven-year-old financier to whom she was attracted and attached. On the surface, her life appeared to be great, but as she sat in my office, I could see that despite the apparent successes, she was wound up and consumed with anxiety.

Ashley said that she occasionally experienced shortness of breath, heart palpitations, and muscle tension. She couldn't stop worrying about her job, even though she was well-positioned in her company, and she worried constantly about being able to afford rent, even though she was flush with cash and in line for a sizable annual bonus. She also worried about Kevin, not so much about their relationship but whether he might get sick. She also worried about getting sick herself or being injured in an accident. She worried about terrorist attacks.

Instead of dealing with her anxiety, Ashley tried to ignore it and push through, but this seemed to be having deleterious effects. By the time she called my office, she had started to restrict her eating during the day—not because she was concerned about her weight but because she didn't want to take breaks from work to eat, since her worries would come back to the surface. She was also becoming quite anxiously clingy with Kevin, calling him repeatedly if he did not answer the phone. This sent Kevin into a pattern of withdrawal, although he loved Ashley. As well, any time Ashley noticed symptoms like rapid breathing or palpitations, she would pick up her phone and go right to WebMD. This only fed her anxiety, since Ashley would misdiagnose herself with any number of medical ailments.

Many of my professional colleagues (though fortunately not all of them!) would view Ashley as neurotic and sick with anxiety, even though she was high-functioning. Had she come to one of them, she would have certainly emerged from a consultation with a prescription for psychiatric medication and no concrete skills to manage her feelings.

But as I talked with her, I had an overwhelming sense that she was fundamentally a healthy individual who could learn to manage her anxiety better, with or without pharmacology. She was clearly spending way too much energy trying to reduce her anxiety, which in fact fueled it. It occurred to me that if Ashley would pour that same level of energy into understanding herself, being more self-caring, and nurturing her relationships with other people (including Kevin), she could learn to blossom throughout her life—not despite her anxiety but because of it. The fact that Ashley was worried about many matters was *not* a sign that she was somehow sick but rather an indication that certain things about her had to change, and that if she changed, she could be fine—even better than fine.

In our work together, I explored with Ashley that her high anxiety indicated a need to reduce her stress level. Her mind was telling her, *Ashley, you've got to learn to relax!* Her tendency to work harder when anxious was making things much worse. I encouraged her to pay more attention to her worries and feelings. She practiced this and started to emerge from this emotionally fraught period of her life more well-balanced, successful, and happy.

Ashley and I also identified that her anxiety sometimes reflected legitimate concerns. Most of her health obsessions were superficial, but in one case she really did need to see a doctor. Her cholesterol was extremely high, and she had to get it down. Ironically, Ashley's health anxiety was making it hard for her to take care of this issue; she was too nervous to face the reality of her high cholersterol. I suggested that she see a cardiologist, who recommended cholesterol medication and consultation with a nutritionist, which helped get Ashley to a healthier state.

Ashley and I also worked to increase her self-care. I encouraged her to take a technology-free lunch break each day and to turn off her phone and stop checking email at a certain time each evening. Ashley began to eat a nutritious breakfast every day and then healthy snacks every three or four hours. She also joined a kickboxing class twice a week. Because she was highly motivated, she made it her priority to do all these things and even a few additional self-care rituals for good measure.

As a result of this work, Ashley's relationship with Kevin started to improve dramatically. She stopped being so clingy, which gave Kevin the space to start showing more affection when Ashley was anxious. More importantly, she opened up to Kevin about how anxious she was feeling. Instead of taking her anxiety out on him by showing insecurity, she shared with Kevin her fears about him getting sick. Initially, Ashley was very anxious about appearing vulnerable because she feared it might turn Kevin off, but when she opened up to him about her real feelings, he was deeply moved. He felt loved and cared for, and in turn made her feel loved and cared for, and they became closer—which secured their attachment and helped Ashley to relax a lot more.

Finally, I recommended that Ashley meet her fears head-on and learn to accept the limits of her control. I framed this in spiritual terms, encouraging Ashley to consider that human beings are—in the greater context of the universe—very small and limited in our scope of agency. I suggested that Ashley keep a journal. I asked her to write down the worst things that could possibly happen to her and then read the script to herself over and over. I asked her to accept her fears, while recognizing that some of them were likely not based in reality. The key was for Ashley to learn to be comfortable with feeling *uncomfortable*. She needed to increase her capacity to handle worrisome thoughts and potentially adverse situations. I even recommended that she use her phone to make audio recordings of her worst fears and then listen to them during her morning commute. Suppressing them out of her mind—by reassuring herself with WebMD searches—would never work.

Ashley's entire life changed. She not only felt less anxious but also started to thrive. Her relationship with herself, others, and her spirituality grew by leaps and bounds, and the result was emotionally palpable in her day-to-day life. Interestingly, in Ashley's case, all of this occurred without the assistance of any medication.

While some may require more professional support along the way, I believe that what Ashley experienced is possible for anyone who suffers from anxiety. As I've noted, the presence of high levels of anxiety is often a sign of high intelligence, high energy, and a unique capacity to flourish. Attempting to block or dispose of anxiety is counterproductive, as this approach depletes your internal energy supply. Instead, you can channel that same energy into becoming comfortable with uncertainty and harness your anxiety to help you prosper. And that, in turn, will help you feel better prepared for anything that comes your way.

What to Expect from This Book

The three-part structure of this book mirrors my belief that working with your anxiety can enhance life on three distinct but interrelated levels: your connection with yourself; your connections and relationships with other people; and your connection with the spiritual dimension. I use a three-step process for *each* level: first, we need to *recognize and identify* the basic issue that our anxiety is calling attention to; then we find ways of *accepting* things as they are; and finally, we *transcend* what we first perceived as limitations, ultimately realizing these are assets and repositories of strength. That all adds up to *nine* interconnected strategies, or tools, that will teach you not only how to avoid the pitfall of seeing anxiety as a weakness but also how to turn it into one of your greatest strengths. I present one tool in each chapter, and when you get comfortable using these tools, you will be able to handle adversity to a greater degree than many think is possible. Readers who wish to learn more about any of the tools in this book are welcome to visit my website or contact me at dhrosmarin.com for additional written and video material.

Anxiety can teach us a new sense of meaning and courage and faith in ourselves. Anxiety can teach us to transcend our perceived limits and, as a result, to have a better sense of mastery over ourselves. We can also enhance our awareness of others' feelings and concerns. Part of that process is learning to rely on others whom we can trust and relinquishing our need to control people by connecting with them as they are—even if they're not perfect, even if they're not meeting our expectations. Finally, we can use anxiety to accept that sometimes things are simply out of our control. Once we do this, it ironically becomes easier to push forward to achieve our innermost hopes and dreams.

You should use each of the nine tools in this book as long as you find it beneficial. If one or more don't work for you, let them go for the time being. You may or may not wish to return to those later in life. In the meantime, focus on the chapters you find most effective as you proceed. For that reason, I recommend recording your responses to the questions and other elements of each tool in a journal, either the conventional paper kind or an electronic version.

Please bear in mind that a book like this is not intended as medical advice since I cannot possibly cover every eventuality involved with everyone's individual anxieties. When people come in for professional treatment, they receive more detailed strategies tailored to their specific needs. In some cases, you may find it helpful to take up specific issues and insights that arise while reading this book and discuss them with your therapist, or to seek therapy if you're not presently in treatment.

In the last three chapters of the book, I elucidate how anxiety can enhance our sense of spirituality. My graduate school mentor, Dr. Kenneth I. Pargament, defined spirituality as "the search for the sacred."[26] He meant that any way of searching for sanctified aspects of life—those that transcend the material world—is inherently spiritual, whether or not it is "religious" in nature. Anxiety can be a catalyst for our spiritual growth. For example, anxiety can remind us of our human limitations, thus helping us be grateful and humble. Further, by accepting the limits of our control, we can learn to maintain equanimity even in times of challenge and struggle. Most of all, anxiety can help us maintain hope and faith in ourselves as we drive with fortitude toward fulfilling our life goals and dreams. Many people may find this process to have religious themes, but not everyone does. You don't need to be a person of a specific faith in order to grow spiritually from working with anxiety.

Along these lines, faith is a powerful human force, but it involves so much more than simply believing in a set of specific doctrines. Faith is also about remaining steadfast to what we value when under stress. It's about recognizing our capacity for greatness—having faith in ourselves—and establishing our purpose and mission on earth. Faith is also about having the freedom to live a valued life, despite anxiety. This entails learning to accept that we cannot control many aspects of life, including how we feel, at times.

Here is a spiritual parable that I believe describes the situation we are all in with regard to anxiety: A traveler is walking along a path through the woods when suddenly a fearsome-looking animal jumps out and seems like it's about to attack. When the traveler tries to run away or get around the animal, it moves to block the trail and grows more ferocious. Whichever way the traveler moves, the animal cuts off their progress, and the intensity of its growls increases. The traveler eventually realizes that the animal only *appears* to be dangerous. In reality, it doesn't intend to fight or cause harm—it actually wants the traveler to become its owner and friend. The traveler starts to pay attention to the animal, engaging with it and even giving it food, and the animal becomes happy and content. They continue through the woods together. The animal protects the traveler from dangers along the way and helps to navigate and traverse the terrain.

Then, one day, the animal starts growling at the traveler. Initially alarmed, the traveler realizes that the animal is trying to send a message. The traveler moves forward, and the animal growls loudly! The traveler moves backward, and the animal gets even more angry. Attempting to move left and right elicits the same response. The traveler realizes there is only one option: going down into the ground. The traveler uses a shovel and starts to dig into the earth, and the animal calms down. The traveler continues to dig and dig and eventually uncovers a buried treasure of gold.

When anxiety strikes, we tend to get annoyed. Why doesn't the anxiety beast get out of our way? We look for distractions or a way out of the quandary: Is there a drink I can have or recreational drug I can take to make it all go away (at least for the moment)? Can I busy myself with work or by obsessively reading and posting on social media? These strategies tend to just make anxiety worse. However, if we harness the power of anxiety, we can thrive in ways we never thought were possible.

The message of the parable is clear: we should not sidestep anxiety or back up and deny that it is there, but rather stop and evaluate the situation. What is our anxiety trying to tell us? The answer is that we need to dig down deep into ourselves, although doing so makes us uncomfortable. We need to experience anxiety in order to transcend it. And although it may not seem to be the case at first glance, what lies inside, what our anxiety is pointing us toward, is a set of precious gifts. In this case, the gold isn't material wealth but a deepened sense of connection—with ourselves, with others, and with our spirituality. Ironically, and paradoxically, we can thrive with anxiety.

PART 1

ENHANCING CONNECTION WITH OURSELVES

CHAPTER 1

KNOWING OURSELVES

Anxiety Can Teach Us About Our Strengths and Areas for Growth

*A*nxiety: the word itself fills many of us with loathing and dread. And that's a shame, because anxiety can enrich our lives and help us adapt creatively to an ever-changing world. One critical way that we can thrive with anxiety—which is the topic of chapter 1—is that this source of agitation *can teach us a great deal about our strengths and areas for growth*. Stress and anxiety (which are similar but different, as we shall see) can help us recognize when we are running low on resources, thus serving as a helpful warning that allows us to rebalance before things get worse. Those who recalibrate in times of stress end up living healthier, stronger, more connected lives. Moreover, anxiety is an indication that we have a reservoir of inner strength to face adversity in the world, and it can thereby help us to lead and succeed. Conversely, too little anxiety may be a catalyst to struggle and failure.

Anxiety or Stress?

Jenn is the mother of three young children and also holds down a full-time job as a paralegal at a family law firm. Her husband also works full-time, and his job requires frequent travel away from home, which makes caring for their kids challenging at times. Nonetheless, Jenn told me that everything was going well for her, despite her busy schedule. "My kids are healthy and I like spending time with them," she said at our first session. "My husband is wonderful. I like my job helping lower-income people get legal support and deal with complex family situations. It feels like meaningful, important work."

Then Jenn took a deep breath and a troubled look crept over her face. "But I'm having all this . . . *anxiety*," she said. "I'm feeling a lot of panic, including difficulty catching my breath and heart palpitations. I'm even having mood swings. Sometimes I get really angry and irritated and then I get afraid I can't control myself, which makes me feel really anxious about *everything*." She paused, but I sensed that she had more to say so I simply nodded.

"On top of that," she went on, "I'm having really uncomfortable physical sensations of anxiety. I feel a lot of muscle tension. My neck is particularly painful, although I also feel tension in my shoulders and my back. When I wake up in the morning, I have this dread that I'm not going to be able to make it through the day. And I often feel uncomfortable for an hour or more before bedtime because I'm thinking about everything that I have to do the next day. I'm feeling so overwhelmed and anxious and I don't understand why."

After waiting for her to finish, I smiled and said, "Jenn, I have good news for you and bad news for you."

"Please," she said, "can I have the good news first?"

"The good news is that you're *not* anxious," I said.

"What?" she said with an incredulous look. "What do you mean I'm not anxious?"

"What you're describing," I said, "is not really anxiety. The bad news is that what you're describing is stress. You're so stressed out that you've become a bundle of nerves."

"Well, what's the difference between anxiety and stress?"

"That's a great question," I said, and I proceeded to explain by describing anxiety.

As we'll see later in this chapter, when people have a fear reaction that is disproportionate to the actual level of threat, that's anxiety.

"Great," she said. "So what's stress?"

"When people have an excess of life demands over and above the resources they have to meet those demands, that creates stress," I responded.

Balancing Demands and Resources

We all have a limited number of resources in various domains, such as time, money, emotional strength, and social capital of friendships. All of these facilitate our ability to respond to the demands of life events. When the demands placed on us outstrip those resources, we experience stress. In a simple analogy: If you are ten minutes away from an appointment that starts in five minutes, you will feel stress for (at least) five minutes. Similarly, if you have monthly financial demands that exceed your income and savings, you'll experience prolonged levels of stress to the extent that you are short on cash.

Oftentimes demands and resources are less tangible than time or money. For example, emotional demands can pile up and exceed our emotional abilities, resulting in significant stress. If you have to deal with a complicated family situation—say, a difficult parent or a child with an eating disorder—that can make it virtually impossible to handle other life stressors. In fact, for some people, even having a minor personal altercation at work can be a catastrophic stressor that throws them for an emotional loop for several days.

If you're not tuned in to your stress level—the extent to which your life demands exceed your resources—you may feel completely depleted and not even realize what is happening. When this happens, stress can beget more stress very quickly. Indeed, stress can have real-world consequences, affecting our moods, physical sensations, productivity, decision-making, and ultimately our happiness and well-being.

When I explained all of this to Jenn, she still looked a bit baffled. "But I'm having heart palpitations," she said. "Isn't that a sign of a panic attack?"

I explained that yes, her symptoms were similar to panic, but they were not coming from anxiety. I pointed out to Jenn that her elevated heart rate and constricted breathing were *not* being caused by something she didn't need to fear, which meant she wasn't anxious. Instead, Jenn was genuinely overwhelmed by not having the resources to handle the stressors in her life.

"Does your 'panic' go up and down based on how afraid you are?" I asked Jenn. "For example, do you have concerns that you may suddenly have a heart attack and die when you have panic-like sensations, even though you have no known medical problems?"

Jenn acknowledged that, no, she didn't worry about things like that. I then asked whether her "panicky" sensations rose or fell depending on how many demands were being made on her and how few resources she had.

"Yes!" she said. "That's exactly what's going on. Like the other day, I was at work when my son's school called and said he was running a fever and could I come and pick him up. Well, we were short-staffed at work, and I was in the middle of helping a family that had just been evicted find a place to stay. My husband was traveling out of state on business, so I started calling friends I trusted to pick up my son, but I couldn't reach anyone. After the third fruitless call, I started hyperventilating!"

Jenn paused to take a deep breath, almost as if she was afraid that she'd start hyperventilating right there in my office. "In fact, that was the day I called you," she said. "I was starting to feel panic, and that's when I started searching the web for anxiety clinics."

"I'm glad you called and came in," I said, "if only so I can clarify that you are *not* suffering from an anxiety disorder. You are overstressed, which is giving you a moderate level of anxiety-like feelings. But there's a difference between that and panic disorder or another form of anxiety. In truth, it's not bad news to learn that you're stressed, since it is fairly easy to deal with."

I went on to explain to Jenn that the way stress makes us feel overwhelmed follows an almost mathematical formula: the amount of demand being placed on your system (for example, having challenges at work, dealing with a sick child at school, emotional strain), minus the amount of resources you have to draw on (for example, time, family, friends, equanimity), equals the level of stress you will encounter at any given moment.

I also explained that stress has a devious way of multiplying itself unless we remain aware of it and make concrete efforts to manage it. When people feel stressed out by change-of-life events, such as getting married, getting divorced, having a child, losing a loved one, work changes such as a promotion or getting laid off, or being diagnosed with a medical condition, they tend to focus on everything *but* managing their feelings. In this sense, our natural tendency is to push the feelings of stress away, because thinking about them makes us feel overwhelmed. However, as a result of this, we become *less* adept at managing our demands, and our stress increases over time. In addition, life-change events often occur together—being laid off from work tends to come with financial changes, for example. This can make it more difficult to get sufficient sleep, which can cause edginess and lead to altercations, which can greatly deplete our emotional resources.

Most people who experience stress say that their symptoms happened "out of the blue." In reality though, stress is rarely out of the blue. It usually builds gradually. Our demands start to increase, and our resources become depleted over time, until we feel so uncomfortable that we cannot avoid recognizing our stress. Therefore, being aware of stress at low levels to prevent it from mounting is the best medicine, since this enables us to balance our resources and demands and make sure the latter never greatly exceeds the former.

There Are Only Two Solutions to Stress

Getting back to Jenn, I explained to her that when it comes to stress management, there are two and only two potential solutions. One: you can increase your resources. Or two: you can reduce the demands you are facing. Ideally, you should do both. However, as I informed Jenn, this is mostly good news since increasing resources and decreasing demands is a surefire way to reduce stress. In Jenn's case, this meant that once she found more balance, she could be confident that her "panic" would go away.

And so I told Jenn flat out, "I don't think you need anything else. For example, if you increase your sleep, bolster your child care supports, and perhaps reduce your hours or learn how to say no at work a bit more, I think you will feel a world of difference."

Jenn looked stunned. It hadn't occurred to her that the solutions could be so simple and basic.

"I'm glad that you started to feel uncomfortable," I added.

"Why is that?"

"To use an automobile analogy, it's like driving a car that's leaking oil. The more oil you lose, the more likely your engine will seize up and require a very expensive repair job—or go totally kaput. But if you notice the problem early enough, it might require only a minor repair to get the leak fixed. Stress is only a problem when we don't deal with it. That's when it can get a lot worse. People who are chronically stressed and don't act to reduce their stress levels are more likely to develop depression and other mental health concerns—including actual anxiety disorders. Any of those may lead to physical health issues, difficulties in relationships, and other life problems. So I'm really glad that you started to feel uncomfortable because that's what brought you into my office."

"What you're saying," Jenn interjected as the traces of a smile crossed her face for the first time, "is that it's a good thing that I'm experiencing this anxiety—or what I *thought* was anxiety! I didn't realize the blessing of feeling panicky. Now I feel like I have the beginning of a plan going forward. If I hadn't started to feel so stressed and uncomfortable, I don't think I would have come in. I would have just sucked it up and soldiered on."

Stress Is the Canary in the Coal Mine

In many cases, the anxiety-like symptoms that come from high stress are the canary in the coal mine—they are a first indication that something is wrong. In fact, feeling uncomfortable due to stress can save your life.

Cardiac heart disease is the number one killer in America,[1] but it often goes undetected. Having high blood pressure can be fatal over time,[2] but that's also often unnoticeable. Similarly, many types of cancer are treatable and nonfatal but only when detected and treated early, before they can develop and spread.[3] In the same vein, when people have anxiety-like symptoms due to stress, their bodies are alerting them to the fact that something needs to change. If we attend to the discomfort—if we remain aware of it and deal with it by bolstering resources and decreasing demands—we can turn our lives around and get back on track. The key is to keep our attention focused on whatever is causing our feelings, instead of just "sucking it up," as Jenn put it, and ignoring or suppressing those feelings.

By contrast, those who ignore stress typically get into trouble. First, there are often physical health consequences of long-term stress, which can include cardiac disease,[4] high blood pressure,[5] cancer,[6] autoimmune diseases,[7] metabolic syndromes,[8] postoperative medical complications,[9] and general all-cause mortality.[10] More immediately though, many people turn to maladaptive solutions when suffering from stress.

In milder forms, many who are stressed are unable to tear themselves away from the internet and social media. Ranting at people or political situations on endless Twitter threads can give us the illusion that we're attending to important matters, when in fact the *real* goal of such behaviors is to distract ourselves from uncomfortable feelings. In more severe situations, some people may overeat and become obese, or become addicted to alcohol or substances.

For these reasons, I sometimes wish that my patients would be *more* anxious, because anxiety-like symptoms can increase motivation to get help sooner, before other mental or physical health problems develop. In these regards, the discomfort from anxiety is often a catalyst to knowing ourselves and recognizing that something is out of balance, giving us a chance to rectify the situation before the imbalance gets worse.

Many are under the misimpression that focusing on the causes of stress will only make matters worse. And yet, *just the opposite is true*. If we can summon the courage to deal with what's really bothering us, we can then take concrete steps to deal with it. As stated above, there are two and only two strategies to reducing stress: (1) increase your resources and (2) reduce your demands. Let's look at some concrete steps to take.

Increase Your Resources

Sleep

If I have one piece of advice to offer individuals struggling with stress (or anxiety, or depression, or pretty much *any* mental health concern), it's to increase and improve sleep. By a fair margin, sleep is the *most* important factor predicting better physical and mental health.[11] In fact, being chronically sleep deprived—which has been a societal norm ever since Thomas Edison's invention of the lightbulb—is one of the key factors why anxiety is so highly prevalent today.[12] This is particularly the case among adolescents and young adults, who are more likely to use electronic devices into the wee hours of the night.[13]

How much sleep is enough? According to the US Centers for Disease Control (CDC), the average adult younger than sixty years of age needs *seven or more* hours of sleep per night. Adolescents tend to need *eight or more hours*, and older adults need *seven to eight hours*.[14] Getting less than this amount of sleep is tantamount to asking for a mental health problem! Conversely, if you are feeling stressed or anxious, try following these guidelines to get enough sleep for just two weeks and see how much of a difference it makes.

Why does sleep help reduce stress and anxiety? There are direct physiological reasons, including that sleep helps our brains and bodies to rest and rejuvenate and rebuild after facing the stressors of each day, which adds to our resources in a significant way. Another explanation though, which we will discuss more in part 3, is that sleep helps us to accept that not everything is within our control. By going to bed—and stopping work for up to a full third of each twenty-four-hour day—we acknowledge that we can only do so much. This cognitive perspective is an extremely helpful resource that we can draw upon in facing day-to-day stressors. Once we accept that we are only human and there are natural limits to what we can do, we tend to take on less and give ourselves more of a break.

Exercise

The American Heart Association recommends that all adults get at least 150 minutes of moderate to vigorous exercise over a week.[15] That means we need to break a sweat for an average of thirty minutes a day, for five days each week. The American Psychiatric Association surprisingly does not have any specific guidelines about physical exercise, and perhaps for this reason it is relatively uncommon for mental health practitioners to recommend exercise for those who are struggling with anxiety or other conditions.[16] However, the existing data is very clear that thirty minutes of exercise five times per week is a *minimum* for maintaining adequate mental health.[17]

Why does exercise help reduce stress and anxiety? Similar to sleep, exercise has many direct physiological effects. These include releasing endorphins as well as building aerobic capacity and physical strength. All of these bolster our resources to deal with the demands of life. Another aspect of exercise, which we will discuss more in chapter 3, is that it helps us to accept discomfort and persist through challenges. While many people love exercising, the physical experience of exertion is inherently unpleasant at some level. By habituating to the discomfort of exercise and rising above it, we teach ourselves to weather the vicissitudes of life, and this perspective is a critical resource to deal with day-to-day stress.

Social Interaction

A third important strategy to managing stress is to maintain close relationships. We will discuss this more in part 2, but at a basic level here are a few key recommendations. First, I recommend to *all* my patients never to go more than forty-eight hours without having a face-to-face conversation with someone they care about. To clarify, I don't mean just talking about the weather but rather conversing in a meaningful way about what's on your mind and what's on their mind. Having intimate conversations forges stronger emotional bonds, and doing this at least every other day is a basic human need. Another aspect of human interaction is physical touch and affection. This is obviously easier for couples who are partnered or married, but it's no less of a need for any human being regardless of their relationship status. It's not a coincidence that our mental health as a society has dropped off a cliff simultaneously as we've prioritized productivity and success over human relationships!

Decrease Your Demands

Reducing demands is generally harder than increasing our resources. Nevertheless, there are a few things that we can do.

Time Off from Technology

Electronic devices are no longer just for work. They are veritable appendages that we rely on day and night as clocks, for travel, for shopping, for news or weather, and, of course, for communication. Aside from these tasks, many have developed the need to check in on social media not only daily but often hourly (or even more frequently) and not just one platform but several. Current research suggests that the average American checks their phone ninety-six times per day, which is approximately ten to twelve times each waking hour.[18] When standing in lines, on escalators or elevators, we cannot resist scanning and responding to messages, as if our friends and professional contacts expect to have a response instantaneously. The insidious stress caused by these incessant demands is hard to quantify or even describe. At no time is the stress of technology greater, though, than at bedtime. Instead of sleeping—which we need as a critical resource to deal with stress—we are stuck on our devices.

I must admit: at times, I have fallen into patterns of overusing technology myself. It's almost impossible not to! But I have a cultural advantage that has kept me (somewhat) sane. Arianna Huffington, the founder of the enormously successful news platform HuffPost, used technology so relentlessly that one night in 2014, she fainted from exhaustion, falling face-first onto her own kitchen floor. She needed comprehensive reconstructive surgery to repair her shattered cheekbone and the bones around her eye. Huffington subsequently rethought her life and wrote a fascinating piece praising the age-old traditional Jewish custom of refraining from productive work—including technology—for one day each week on the *sabbath*.[19] As Huffington put it, "Our decision-making is impaired when we don't give ourselves enough time to disconnect and recharge."

In this regard, I am blessed as a sabbath observer—each week from Friday night to Saturday night, I shut off my phone and computer, spend time with my family, and refocus on my spiritual values. (Of course, genuine emergencies can sometimes interrupt my observance.) My professional colleagues sometimes ask me how I can afford to do this with all my professional commitments. Quite frankly, I have the opposite perspective: I don't understand how busy professionals keep going all week in the current day and age without a significant break.

To be clear, I do not recommend that all people keep a weekly sabbath. But I strongly recommend that all people schedule some breaks from screen use. I tell all my patients to turn off their devices at a minimum for a half hour before bedtime, plus for another thirty minutes during each day (such as when exercising or during meals), and to take one protracted break of an evening off from technology once each week (for example, two to three hours while going out with a partner or friends). One more recommendation about technology: please don't sleep next to your phone! Keep it at least ten feet from your bed, ideally in another room altogether. This simple practice can reduce sleep latency (the time it takes to fall asleep), nighttime awakenings, and other sleep problems.[20]

Say No!

The television host Larry King wrote in one of his books that he often created conflicts in his schedule because he could never *say no* to anyone who invited him to be on their show. One time, he agreed to appear in three different cities on the same day at around the same time. As the day approached, he grew increasingly stressed and uncomfortable, but he ignored the feelings and told himself that he would figure it out; however, he couldn't devise a way out of the quandary, and his body suffered the consequences—he had a heart attack and almost died.[21] Many of us fall into a similar, if less dramatic, mental and emotional trap, but the results are essentially the same. Being unable to *say no* creates unnecessary pressure in our lives that can have significant consequences.

In a paradoxical way, however, we do tend to *say no* to time off from work, even when we are entitled. Among the workers of the developed nations of the world, not only are US workers given relatively few vacation days when compared to other countries, but they also leave a fair amount of what they *are* given on the table.[22] According to *Harvard Business Review*, since 1996, the number of vacation days taken by American workers has declined from about twenty-one days to sixteen days as of 2016,[23] and it continues to decline. Furthermore, the majority of employees who do take vacation bring their work along, even though this practice is known to undermine key benefits of taking time off.[24] Conversely, research shows that workers who take more time off are likely to be more successful at their jobs and have a greater likelihood of receiving raises or bonuses.[25]

Accept Your Limitations

Beyond *saying no* to others, we need to *say no* to ourselves at times by not taking on more obligations than we are reasonably capable of fulfilling. To our great detriment, our society tends to value productivity more than relationships. We value accomplishing and being productive—in particular, financially—more than connecting with others and creating loving relationships. We will discuss how anxiety can help *enrich* our interpersonal relationships in part 2, but none of those strategies are possible to implement if we're too busy or too stressed out to prioritize human connection. To make things more complex, family, civic, community, and volunteer causes can often be sources of stress and strain if we are overfocused on what we need to *do* as opposed to the goal of connecting with others.

The psychology behind this phenomenon of overworking is fairly basic: it's hard for us, as human beings, to accept our limitations and ultimate lack of control. This will be addressed in part 3, but suffice to say for now that we need to be keenly aware that we have limited resources as well as demands that we cannot avoid. Only you know how many projects you can handle at once and how many hours you can work in a given week or month before running yourself into the ground. Pushing *just* beyond those limits is fine—in order to expand our horizons and increase our strength. But pushing too far beyond our existing limits is never a good idea.

The Blessing of Anxiety

If you follow these guidelines—ones I share with almost all my patients—you will reduce your stress levels and live a more relaxed, healthier life. Of course, it's unrealistic to eliminate stress altogether. The realities of life are such that things sometimes will get overwhelming. That is generally okay—experiencing a depletion of resources and/or excessive demands *once in a while* can increase our tolerance for stress, help us identify ways to be more efficient, and even lead us to identify new resources we didn't realize we had all along. Furthermore, if suffering from stress leads us to implement even a few of the strategies I've discussed so far, we will have turned our stresses into a great blessing—one that teaches us about our strengths and areas for further growth.

But what about anxiety? Is anxiety also a potential blessing? In order to address this question, we first need to define and describe anxiety, and contrast it with fear. When my clients ask me "What is anxiety?" I tell them that *anxiety* is the experience of fear without an actual material threat being present. Therefore, anxiety is caused by a neural misfire of the fear circuit. Put another way, *anxiety involves the experience of fear in response to the misperception that things are dangerous, when, in fact, they are not.* Allow me to explain.

When you encounter an immediate threat to your safety—such as a proverbial saber-toothed tiger (although today it would more likely be a speeding Mack truck bearing down on you)—your brain registers the threat and activates a fear circuit. This, in turn, triggers the adrenal glands to secrete adrenaline (also known as epinephrine) into the bloodstream. This potent hormonal compound instantly creates a cascade of physiological changes within the body, all of which are intended to help us stay safe from the perceived threat. The changes—also known as the "fight-or-flight response"—include the following:

- the pupils dilate to expand your field of vision and increase your perception,
- the digestive system slows in order to divert energy to muscles and vital systems,
- blood gets diverted from your extremities into the torso to help your organs function optimally,
- muscle fibers tense up to prepare you to act with greater strength,
- the heart rate increases to circulate more oxygenated blood to the muscles (which enables them to respond stronger and faster), and
- the breathing rate increases to supply the increased need for oxygen.

All these facets of the fear response—which are involuntary and occur automatically—help you to notice danger and respond to it by springing into action. And so *fear is a good thing*—a very good thing! People who don't have enough fear tend not to survive. In fact, shortly after birth, neonates are tested to see if they have something called the Moro reflex, more commonly known as a "startle response." In some hospitals a small horn is used to emit a loud sound near the baby's ear, and in others the baby's neck and head will be lifted a few inches off the table and then dropped down suddenly, to see whether the startle response is present. Neonates who don't exhibit a Moro reflex are immediately referred for a consultation with a pediatric neurologist because a lack of this critical defensive response tends to be a sign of early injury, infection, or disease, such as cerebral palsy.

Each week, hundreds of people come for treatment at Center for Anxiety offices complaining about physical symptoms of anxiety. They report having heart palpitations, shallow breathing or difficulty catching their breath, muscle tension, stomach upset, numbness and tingling in their extremities, or dizziness or blurred vision. All these symptoms occur because they are by-products of the normal fear response.

- Chest palpitations occur because the heart is pumping more to circulate oxygenated blood.
- The sensations of difficult breathing or needing to catch one's breath occur because the body is trying to breathe more oxygen, and the lung muscles need to work harder to make this happen.
- Muscle tension occurs because the body is mobilizing muscles— especially in the neck and back—to prepare oneself to fend off a threat.
- Stomach upset is an interesting one—this occurs because the body stops digesting food in order to divert its energies to keeping safe and sound.

- Numbness and tingling in the hands and feet occurs since blood is diverted to the torso in order to conserve energy and minimize blood loss in case one is (successfully) attacked.
- As for dizziness and blurred vision, these occur because of pupil dilation—as a protective measure, the eyes allow in more light and increase their field of vision even though this results in lower accuracy of sight.

Regarding dizziness, if you think about this, it makes a lot of sense. After all, if a Mack truck is barreling toward you, it doesn't matter if you can read the license plate (accuracy of vision), but you *definitely* need to know if it's to your right or left (field of vision).

The best-case scenario for a human being is that we have a robust fear response. Throughout life, if we experience genuinely life-threatening situations, the fear response helps keep us safe. Even if we never need to use it, fear is a critical tool to maintain our physical well-being and increase the chances of our survival. It is our body's way of optimizing our safety when we are in danger. Fear is a gift from God. Keep it and be grateful!

However, fear is not the same as anxiety. In contrast with fear, anxiety involves the experience of a fight-or-flight response *without* the presence of an actual reason to be afraid. When the adrenal glands are triggered by the brain in the absence of a real threat—when our minds misperceive that things are dangerous even though, in fact, they are not—we are experiencing anxiety, not fear. If you are having the set of physiological and psychological experiences I just described, but *without* that truck careening toward you—that's *anxiety*. I must emphasize that while fear does occur within our culture, most often what we experience today in the Western developed world is anxiety—because even when resources are tight or lacking, we generally are physically safe or at least not at imminent risk for death.

It's worth noting that in some cases, it can be challenging to draw a clear line between fear and anxiety. For example, *health anxiety* involves excessive concern about matters that could, under certain circumstances, be dangerous. To make matters worse, this can sometimes shift over time. For example, during the pandemic it was initially suspected that COVID-19 could be transmitted through touch, and it was not an uncommon practice to disinfect surfaces (or even fruits and vegetables!). However, over time it became apparent that contagion of the virus was primarily if not exclusively facilitated by airborne particles exchanged during close contact with infected individuals (for example, during unmasked conversations).

In all cases, however, fear involves a healthy emotional response that mobilizes us to take reasonable precautions given the information one has in hand about what is necessary for protection. Anxiety, by contrast, involves anything over-and-above what is reasonable to avoid a real and tangible threat.

So how is anxiety a blessing? By its very definition, anxiety is unnecessary and based on an error. What good can come out of a mistake?

False Positives Versus False Negatives

Too much anxiety can be very uncomfortable and even debilitating. Yet being overanxious is much better than misperceiving that things are *not* dangerous when they actually are. In this regard, anxiety is a strength because it means our built-in warning system is working. It may be inconvenient to have a hypersensitive smoke alarm that goes off too readily, but this is far preferable to having one that doesn't alert you until the whole house has caught fire. If I had a choice, I'd much prefer to be anxious and overly reactive than super low on neuroticism and not responsive enough to potential threat.

Put differently, anxiety is essentially a "false positive" fear response. In the medical world, a false positive is an error in which a test result incorrectly indicates the presence of a condition, such as a disease, when it is not present. Conversely, a "false negative" test result incorrectly indicates the absence of a condition when it is actually present. If we are talking about a serious condition such as cancer or heart disease, it should be clear that, while a false positive can cause a certain amount of needless distress until it is corrected, a false negative is much worse because it is downright dangerous to think you're okay when you are not. If you don't have lung cancer and receive a false positive result, it will be a few tense weeks until the misdiagnosis is confirmed to be incorrect, but you won't die from lung cancer. But if you receive a false negative test result assuring you that you do not have lung cancer, the condition will continue to develop undetected until it's too late.

When it comes to anxiety, the presence of physiological symptoms, such as accelerated breathing or heart palpitations, might make you think you're having a heart attack. After you race to the nearest emergency room, you may be relieved to find out you're only having a panic attack. Clearly, that's a better outcome than not realizing that you're having a heart attack until you keel over and die! The latter is not fiction. According to Harvard Health Publishing, about half of heart attacks are mistaken for less serious conditions.[26] Known as "silent heart attacks," symptoms of myocardial infarctions can be so mild and brief that they are often confused with indigestion.

Yes, it would be better to be 100 percent accurate all the time and never have false positive or negative results. And yes, going to the emergency room unnecessarily isn't pleasant. However, of these two options—mistaking a panic attack for a heart attack or mistaking a heart attack for heartburn—which would you prefer?

Superhuman Strength

We've learned that anxiety involves the same response as fear, albeit without a real danger. It follows that anxiety—just like fear—involves a mobilization of superhuman strength. One of the first "panic disordered" patients that I ever treated was a man in his thirties named John. He said he often had extremely strong panic attacks when he was driving. These attacks were so virulent that he was afraid he was going to crash his car, so he severely restricted his driving.

At our first session, John related an attack he had recently had while traveling on a multilane highway at sixty-five to seventy miles per hour. It was during the winter in Canada, with lots of snow on the highway and more piled up on the shoulder. He was riding in the left-most lane, and he started to feel panicky. *I have to get off the highway!* he thought, because there was too much snow on the left shoulder and he was afraid of crashing. The right shoulder had been plowed and looked clear, but to get there he'd have to maneuver across three lanes—each filled with traffic—at a relatively high speed. Swiveling his head from one side mirror to the other, John worked his way across each of the three lanes in what seemed to him like an eternity, but in reality was just a few seconds. Finally reaching the right lane, he pulled onto the shoulder and stopped his car. He was still breathing heavily and his heart was racing, but he was at least able to open his window and breathe in some fresh air.

Because this was one of the first cases of panic disorder I'd ever encountered, I went to my supervisor to explain John's situation and ask how I should handle it. My supervisor told me it's common that people with panic disorder are afraid to drive. "But," he said, "let me ask you a couple of questions. When you got your driver's license, did they ask you if you wear corrective lenses?"

"Sure," I said.

"And did they ask if you have any neurological conditions, such as epilepsy or Parkinson's?"

I recalled that they had.

"Okay," he said. "Did they ask if you have panic disorder?"

"No, I'm pretty sure they didn't ask me that."

"They didn't," he said with confidence. "I know because there isn't a Department of Motor Vehicles in the world that asks about panic disorder. Do you know why?"

"No," I responded, curious where this was going.

"It's because panic isn't dangerous for drivers," he responded. "And I'll prove it to you. I've been running this anxiety clinic for ten years, and we have seen more than seventy-five hundred patients; take a guess how many panic patients I've seen in that time who have crashed their cars."

I didn't know, but I was beginning to catch his drift. "Zero?" I asked.

"That's right," he said. "Zero. In fact, people are *better* at driving their cars when they are panicking. With your fight-or-flight system kicked into gear, you're able to drive with what amounts to superhuman strength. And your patient had that very experience with the same result: he wove in and out of sixty-plus miles per hour traffic in the snow and did just fine!"

I came to realize that when John was having a panic attack strong enough to trigger the fight-or-flight response, the adrenaline that seeped into his bloodstream did not make him more erratic; in fact, *it made him a better driver*. Once I explained to John this truth about panic, he was able to calm down. This was because John's perception that his panic was dangerous was ironically making him more anxious.

Notably, according to the *National Law Review*, the most common cause of auto accidents is driver inattention[27]—whether caused by distractions (such as sending text messages), being overtired, or intoxication. When you're having a panic attack, however, none of those concerns are material because you are at peak alertness, even if it doesn't feel that way. If I had the choice to be in a car with someone who is panicking or not, hands down I'd prefer option A.

Relatedly, athletes commonly report getting the jitters and even feeling nauseous before performances. Glenn Hall was arguably the best goalie ever to play for the Chicago Blackhawks hockey team—he was known to fans as "Mr. Goalie." And vomiting was famously a vital part of his pregame ritual. Remarking on his entire nineteen-year NHL career, he said, "I did it before almost every game because I played better when I did and I was hyper." Interestingly, Hall knew that anxiety wasn't anything to be afraid of, and in fact indicated that he had the strength to be competitive. "It was pretty natural. I worked myself into it. I reminded myself I was representing my family and it would be unforgivable to not play at a certain standard."[28]

Several of my patients who perform in public, such as actors and musicians, have told me that if they don't have butterflies or a certain level of stage fright before they go on, they might have a subpar performance. As one of them put it, "I'd much prefer to be anxious than sluggish on the stage."

Anxiety and Leadership

These common forms of preperformance jitters also have their counterpart for those in leadership roles. A certain level of anxiety can prime people for leadership, since being at the helm of a group of people requires anticipating how things might go wrong and taking into account various outcomes, both good and bad. As a leader, one needs to weigh the odds of a certain approach being successful or not, enumerate the possibilities of each result, and develop strategies for potential situations. Whether it's a creative, business, or scientific project, you have to be prepared for not only what could go right but also what could go wrong for you and for other people involved.

Being able to anticipate when and how things may go wrong, and taking into account various possibilities and outcomes, are both critical when running an organization or leading people in any situation, from law enforcement to planning a benefit concert. No one likes a leader who is unreliable, drops the ball, and doesn't see problems ahead of time. To these ends, anxiety can help leaders to be more cautious in their decision-making, enhance problem-solving, and be less likely to make rash decisions without thinking about consequences in advance.

Anxiety also motivates us to react to many challenging situations faster, stronger, and with more drive. Sometimes this causes problems, of course, but I've found in my clinical practice that anxious people generally have a lot of passion and energy and a ton of benefits to offer the world, once they learn how to harness their angst in a productive way. Just like fear, anxiety can shorten our response time, improve our performance, and even increase our perception and cognition.

To be clear: too much anxiety *can* cloud your judgment and be counterproductive. But at low or even medium levels, anxiety can increase your sense of responsibility, your responsiveness and awareness, your anticipation of issues, and your ability to generate a plan B. That level of awareness can ultimately save stress, money, and time. Of course, if your anxiety leads you to overthink things by also devising a plan C or plan D (and certainly plans E and F!), that is generally counterproductive. However, if your options are having too little anxiety or too much, I would prefer to have too much any day. Again, it's better to see things as dangerous when they're not than not to see things as dangerous when they are.

You may be wondering, *If anxiety is such a good thing, why does it make us feel so uncomfortable?* Think of it this way: You're sitting in your driveway, getting ready to leave for the store or work, and you notice your engine is racing. Most engines idle at about six hundred to eight hundred revolutions per minute but may rev even higher while warming up, which is normal. But if the engine is still revving high while idling, even after it's warmed up, you could have a problem. An engine that idles high wastes fuel, causes extra wear on your motor, and can even lead to unsafe starts. It doesn't mean that your car is shot, just that you need to get your engine adjusted. In a similar way, anxiety is not an indication that you are broken; it means that things are going well, but you are "running too hot," and you need to make some adjustments.

Again, though, it's better to have a car that runs too hot than not at all.

The Risks of Too Little Anxiety

The best way I can explain the distinction between too much anxiety and too little is by comparing the cases of two patients I was seeing at around the same time, who came from such similar backgrounds that they could have almost been brothers. Indeed, their first names even began with the same letter, which helped to link them in my mind. These two young men in their early twenties both came from upper-middle-class families in New York suburbs, were both enrolled in local liberal arts colleges, and were considering degrees in law. However, that was where the similarities ended. Diagnostically, they were polar opposites.

Adam was struggling with what is often called *failure to launch*. He was typical of many young men and women in their early twenties from comfortable backgrounds, who don't feel much pressure to get their act together and are underperforming. As a result, they are plagued with sadness and self-doubt about their inability to move forward.

Adam initially came across as self-confident, even nonchalant, but his grades weren't especially good, despite his desire to pursue a law career. He also hadn't yet begun studying for the Law School Admission Test (LSAT) that would determine whether he could get into a reputable law school. He was smoking weed on a regular basis, often slept in, and had recently dropped a course that he perceived as too demanding. Adam acted as if there was no problem, and when I queried him, he announced that things would "just work out." He had come to see me only because his parents were concerned, and he felt they were overreacting.

Adam acted as though he was set for life—even though he didn't actually have that much family money. We met a few times, but he never seemed motivated to change his approach. To get Adam moving, he needed to be uncomfortable, but he always felt comfortable, and eventually he stopped coming. The next time I heard from him, nearly a year later, he had bombed the LSAT, was on the cusp of not finishing his degree, and had zero prospects of gainful employment. His parents were at their wits' end, and his use of drugs had gotten completely out of hand. But he remained sanguine about the future. As a result, there was really nothing I could do. I even said to him, "I wish you were more anxious!"

Artie, by contrast, was a bundle of nerves. Although his grade point average was impressive and he was spending his days and nights prepping for the LSAT, he was feeling extremely panicked. He spent so much time studying that his social life was minimal, and he didn't seem to be having the kind of fun college experience that you might expect of someone with his financial resources. He wore a suit and tie to our first session because he wanted to make a good impression—as opposed to Adam, who had shown up twenty minutes late with a torn Phish T-shirt and smelled like he hadn't showered in a few days.

Clinically, Artie was *much* easier to work with than Adam. He didn't perceive his family's money as a reason to take it easy; rather he felt excessively impelled to ensure his future success. He didn't rest on his laurels enough—he was overly stressed and tense, at the expense of his well-being. However, looking back at the larger picture, my basic impression of Artie was that he was in a good place overall and essentially just needed to learn to relax. I asked him to take down his stress level a little by taking time off from studying and going to parties to hang out with people more on weekends. At one session, I even raised my voice a bit and said, "Artie, you need to chill out!" I even encouraged him to start listening to Phish and go to a show. I secretly hoped he might run into Adam there and that maybe some of Artie's anxiety and drive would rub off on him. Alas, that never happened. Furthermore, unlike Adam, Artie listened to me, and once he was able to relax, it didn't kill his motivation and drive or get in the way of his productivity—on the contrary, he was able to work even harder and more effectively.

. . . .

TOOL #1: IS IT STRESS OR ANXIETY (OR BOTH)?

If we acknowledge our anxiety and learn how to work with it instead of denying or fighting it, our anxiety will end up helping us. But first, we must develop the ability to distinguish anxiety from stress. This requires taking some time to focus on what's going on within ourselves.

STEP 1

In order to use this tool, first choose a time when you are free from distractions for at least five to ten minutes, preferably alone. Sit in a comfortable chair or at a desk. And turn off your phone!

STEP 2

Now look back at the most recent times when you have felt intensely "anxious" (stress, fear, or anxiety)—if you are currently feeling anxious, then focus on the present moment—and inquire of yourself whether you are experiencing significant stress. For example:

- Do you feel that you don't have enough time in the day to get things done that you need to do?
- Do you feel overwhelmed by work, school, or other responsibilities?
- Are you short on time, money, or other precious resources?

- Are you or someone you love experiencing a health concern that is weighing on you emotionally?
- Do your anxiety-like sensations become more intense when your demands exceed your resources?

If you answered yes to one or more of these questions, you are feeling at least some degree of significant stress.

Bear in mind that you can simultaneously feel both stress and anxiety, so the fact that you are feeling stress does not automatically rule out that you may also be feeling anxious. But it's important to recognize each feeling separately so that you do not confuse basic stress with anxiety.

STEP 3

If you are experiencing stress, you have *only* two possible solutions: (1) increase your resources, or (2) decrease your demands (or both).

Increase your resources with the following:

- Improve your sleep quality and quantity. Try to get at least seven to nine hours of sleep per night for the next two weeks.
- Get moving! Physical exercise is critical to maintaining strength. Try to get thirty minutes of vigorous cardiovascular exercise at least five times per week over the next two weeks.
- Get connected by speaking about your feelings with a friend (or a therapist) regularly over the next two weeks.

Decrease your demands with these strategies:

- Take a tech break: every day for thirty minutes, plus a longer break each week, plus no screen time a half hour before bedtime each night. This alone will change your life!

- Say no to others when you are overstressed.
- Accept your limitations by recognizing that you are human, and that's okay.

STEP 4

Now look back again at times when you have felt "anxious" (stress, fear, or anxiety), and inquire of yourself whether you are experiencing significant anxiety. Remember that anxiety involves a fear response when there is nothing truly dangerous to be afraid of. For example:

- Do you have concerns that you may suddenly die when you have panic-like sensations, even though you have no medical symptoms?
- Are you overly concerned by what others think about you, even if they haven't said anything critical?
- Are you more worried than you need to be about everyday events, such as your family's well-being, health, and finances?
- Are you excessively concerned about getting sick?
- Do you feel fearful about coming into contact with spiders, dogs, snakes, or other common creatures?

If you answered yes to one or more of these questions, then congratulations, you have anxiety! Again, be aware that you can simultaneously feel both stress and anxiety.

STEP 5

This book is chock-full of strategies to deal with anxiety, but in this first tool we are focusing on just one: recognizing the blessing of fear and anxiety. Take a few minutes to contemplate and recognize that, just because you're anxious, this doesn't mean that something is wrong with you! On the contrary, anxiety is an indication that your fear response—which is critical to human survival—is intact. Yes, you may need to learn to chill out and take things down a notch, but you're better off having too much anxiety than too little.

Think about how your anxiety

- helps you to be aware when things may go wrong,
- helps you to perform and accomplish things, and
- primes you for leadership roles.

. . . .

CHAPTER 2

ACCEPTING OURSELVES

Anxiety Can Lead to More Self-Compassion

In order to understand the nature of anxiety and why it can be an asset rather than a liability, we need to identify, as nearly as possible, how and why anxiety gets out of control. As I explained in chapter 1, many people confuse *stress*, which involves a depletion of resources (for example, finances, health, relationships, time), with *anxiety*, which involves a misfire of the fight-or-flight system. Either of these can beget more anxiety and lead to a cycle in which we lose control of our emotions. Sometimes stress can trigger a process of anxiety unfolding, and other times anxiety compounds upon itself and becomes worse. In still other cases, something as simple as indigestion or a breathing issue can lead to significant anxiety. If the air quality is low one day, and you're having a little trouble breathing, or there's a temperature change in the heating, ventilation, or air-conditioning (HVAC) system in your office and all of a sudden it gets too hot by a few degrees, that could also be the initial trigger that leads to anxiety. In all these cases, we need to understand *how* and *why* we get anxious. This chapter will slow the process down step-by-step to provide an explanation of what I call the "anxiety spiral," and with that in hand we can start to reverse the cycle and begin to thrive with anxiety.

The Anxiety Spiral

Let's start with a crucial question, namely, What do you think about *yourself* when you experience anxiety? Many of my patients are not even aware that the moment they start to experience the physical cascade of the fight-or-flight response, they begin to think the *worst* about their anxiety. But once we're able to drill down to the bottom of things, virtually every patient I have met will share that their first response to the firing of their fight-or-flight system is a catastrophic response to anxiety. *The feelings themselves become something that they fear.* Even worse, they often judge, blame, criticize, or otherwise negatively evaluate themselves for having what they perceive as a weakness.

Sometimes they think the worst. *I must be dying!* they will think, or *I'm going crazy and cannot handle this*, even though they've experienced the same symptoms in the past without such results. Naturally, these catastrophic thoughts make their anxiety worse.

At that point, their self-evaluation typically takes a downturn. *What's wrong with me?* they think. *Why me?* they ask. *I don't see anyone else reacting like this*, they say, as they compare themselves to other people. *I am the weakling in the room*, they say to themselves as self-criticism starts to bubble up.

There is a *small* drop of validity to these perceptions. As I explained in chapter 1, anxiety involves a misfire of the fight-or-flight system. It is a kind of false positive—an unnecessary and unpleasant fear-like experience in the absence of a real threat. Put differently: the fight-or-flight system is a marvel of psychophysiological engineering, and when we get anxious, we are essentially misusing it by interpreting the world as more dangerous than it is.

However, anxiety is nothing to fear in and of itself. My office has serviced over ten thousand patients and we have never had a patient die from anxiety! No one has even been hurt from their anxiety symptoms or "gone crazy" from the acute experience of anxiety. Yes, people can develop behavioral problems in the context of anxiety, including alcohol or substance misuse, self-injury, and suicidality. And yes, chronic stress and anxiety can increase risk for a number of health problems, as we discussed in chapter 1. But let's be very clear that anxiety itself is not dangerous. Moreover, if you want your anxiety to decrease, the last thing you want is to flood your system with more adrenaline. So reacting with catastrophic or self-judgmental thoughts to the fear response only makes it worse.

In reality, anxiety is nothing to criticize yourself about. It makes no sense at all to judge yourself for experiencing anxiety. As fallible humans, from time to time we are going to misinterpret situations and accidentally trigger our magnificent fight-or-flight response. At these times, we will experience not just fear but anxiety. I would go as far as to say that if a person doesn't experience misfires of their fight-or-flight system today, something is probably wrong! They are probably not aware or alert enough of real potential dangers.

At a recent get-together, one of my friends casually spoke about his experience shopping at Costco. "I always get some brain fog and start to feel tense and edgy after a few minutes of being in a big-box store," he said. I was surprised because he is a well-adjusted individual with a particularly calm demeanor; why would Costco make him feel anxious? Just then, he shared his secret and said, "But I think to myself that this is a normal experience. Who doesn't feel uncomfortable at Costco? And that settles me down. After a few minutes in the store, I'm good to go." Reflecting on the anecdote, I realized that this is *exactly* why my friend is so calm! He gets triggered by anxiety just as much as anyone else. But his anxiety doesn't magnify because he uses self-talk to express validation and self-compassion. This prevents him from catastrophizing and feeling shame, and as a result he's even able to enjoy the experience after working through the initial triggers.

Anxiety doesn't just happen inexplicably and suddenly, although it may feel that way. Instead, it represents a subtle series of interlinked steps. I call this process the "anxiety spiral" because, although the initial experiences of stress, fear, or even low levels of anxiety are to be expected and don't necessarily lead us into trouble, what happens next is potentially a gargantuan problem. The way that we internally react to the experience of stress, fear, or anxiety is what leads to substantially more anxiety (the anxiety spiral). However, if we follow the guidelines in this chapter, the initial discomfort will simply subside over time, without any resulting drama or significant concern. In the latter case, we can start to thrive with anxiety.

Once you respond in a negative way to stress, anxiety, or fear, the very experience of these feelings becomes something that makes you afraid, upset, concerned, and anxious. Catastrophizing about anxiety triggers a release of additional adrenaline into your bloodstream, compounding the cascade of physical symptoms. Worse than catastrophizing, though, many people think that something is wrong with them for having anxiety, and *that's* where things can get really problematic. Because the next time they experience anxious feelings, they're not only going to have to deal with the anxiety, which in itself is stressful, but they will also have to deal with their own self-judgment, which makes a bad situation worse.

According to Dr. Aaron Beck, the father of cognitive therapy, a particular situation in and of itself never leads to a negative emotion.[1] Situations don't directly cause our feelings. Rather, there is a stop along the way called *cognition*, which involves our thoughts. With any situation, I must *interpret* it a certain way in order for a particular emotion to develop; it's always a two-step process.

Let's say you are backing out of your driveway, and you hit something metallic-sounding. You slam on the brakes and your first reaction is one of *fear*: "Oh my God, I hope I didn't hit someone!" Then you get out and you see a child's bicycle and you say, "I'm such an idiot! Why didn't I see that?" You immediately start to feel *sad*. But then, you see that your bumper is dented, and you escalate to *anger* at whomever left the bike in your driveway. "That neighbor's kid is always leaving his bike everywhere!" Or, if you see no damage to car or bike, you might take a deep breath of relief and end up feeling *grateful* that you didn't hurt anyone and there was no damage.

Each of these is a different emotional experience: the first one is fear; the second is self-judgment, which may quickly lead to depression; the third is anger; and the fourth is gratitude. They're all legitimate emotional experiences in the context of the action, and the critical factor that determines which one we experience is *what we are thinking about the situation*.

COGNITIVE MODEL

Situations don't cause our feelings. There is always a stop along the way called cognition. It's always a two-step process.

Situation	**Thought**	**Emotion**
something happens	the situation is interpreted	a feeling occurs as a result of the thought

Along these lines, if something happens to trigger physical sensations associated with the fight-or-flight response, but your thinking mind realizes that there is nothing to fear, *you will not develop significant anxiety.* Conversely, if we interpret the initial experience of anxiety as something dangerous or a weakness of some sort, that interpretation increases the experience of anxiety. Once that occurs, we enter the anxiety spiral, which involves rapid and often unconscious iterations of anxiety sensations and negative thinking. The more anxious we feel, the more we interpret our anxiety with worry, disappointment, concern, and the like. And the more concerned we get, the more our anxiety symptoms spike in the moment.

People will often report that their anxiety is completely unpredictable, but in reality that is seldom the case. In fact, I would say it's *never* the case—the course of anxiety is reliably predictable. When you slow down the process, you can recognize a clear cycle of development between the initial experience of distress, your negative interpretation of that distress, and subsequent worsening of anxiety symptoms.

Catastrophic Thinking, Self-Judgment, and the Anxiety Spiral

Julian, a man in his late twenties, came to see me complaining of panic disorder. His symptoms had started innocently enough. He had a little bit of difficulty breathing because he lived in Los Angeles and the air quality was especially bad for a period of time. However, Julian's mother had had significant chronic obstructive pulmonary disease (COPD), and as he was growing up, he had watched her struggle to catch her breath every day. He also recalled her chronic bronchitis and constant doctor visits. So when Julian had trouble breathing one day, it triggered a full-blown panic attack. Instead of attributing his breathing troubles to air pollution, he went down the anxiety spiral. His first thought was, *Oh my God, I'm gonna die! I'm gonna end up being like Mom with COPD for my whole life.* Immediately, and subconsciously, Julian plunged from some troubled breathing, to negative memories, to complete and utter panic. That panic, in turn, constricted his breathing even further, and his interpretation of it grew correspondingly darker.

Julian developed severe health anxiety. He went to every COPD expert in Southern California. He underwent all sorts of tests and procedures and began spending hours on the computer scrolling through WebMD. Each time, he detected a new symptom and became more obsessed. Whenever he felt his breathing constrict, he would immediately jump to terrifying conclusions, and his heart palpitations increased. From there, he started to notice phlegm in his throat, which he interpreted as coming from his lungs, and his anxiety would ratchet up another notch. Of course, none of the medical doctors was able to tell him what was going on because they didn't see any signs of COPD. He even had a PPD (purified protein derivative) skin test, which is used to diagnose silent, or latent, tuberculosis infection. Eventually he gave up on Western medicine and went to a naturopath, who recommended nutritional supplements and tinctures, from echinacea to CBD oil. Finally, several years later, during his annual physical, his general practitioner figured out what was going on.

"I've got news for you," his physician said. "This isn't a breathing problem. I think you have developed an anxiety problem. You need to see a mental health professional."

At that point Julian called my clinic and decided to come to New York for two weeks to work intensively with me and my staff. It took us only a few minutes with him to determine that he was indeed very anxious! So we taught him about the anxiety spiral and how he had gotten caught in it. He was a quick study, and after just two sessions things started to click. He realized, intellectually, that his lungs were fine and that he actually had an anxiety problem. But on the third day, he was a no-show. One of my staff members went to the place where Julian was staying to check on him—and he answered the door still in his pajamas. Julian said he was so upset at himself that he literally couldn't get out of bed.

"I just wasted three years of my life," he said of obsessing about his supposed pulmonary problem. "I feel like such a loser."

We convinced Julian to come back to the office and explained that he had been suffering with this issue for three years, and it was obviously going to take more than just a couple of days to treat him. We also provided him with a lot of information regarding how common anxiety disorders are. After making sure he was stable, we asked him to come in the next day to continue treatment, and he agreed to do so. When he arrived, we focused on self-compassion and avoiding self-judgment.

To begin with, we recommended the three areas for building up resources that I discussed in chapter 1 as ways to cope with stress: getting more sleep, increasing exercise, and making sure to engage socially with his friends. Those critical strategies provided Julian with the firm base that we all need (whether or not we feel stressed-out and anxious).

Beyond that, we emphasized how critical it was for Julian *not* to get sucked into the next steps of the anxiety spiral: misinterpreting breathing discomfort as a catastrophic indication of a chronic lung disease, beating himself up for having anxiety in the first place, and criticizing himself for "wasting" three years by chasing his tail. We pointed out that, first, in the context of a normal lifespan, three years isn't all that long—especially if, at the end of it, you have placed yourself on a more enriching path. And Julian was only in his twenties! Along these lines, we framed for Julian that if he could get on a good path at his relatively young age, he would be more resilient and stronger to face future life stressors and mental-health concerns. Indeed, so many patients with anxiety who tackle the problem end up living stronger lives than they would have if they never experienced anxiety in the first place.

More than anything, though, Julian needed to learn to be compassionate toward himself. We alerted him to the dangers of failing to take any constructive action. "If you keep putting yourself down," we reminded him, "then anxiety will be the least of your worries. You could wind up becoming clinically depressed." Relatedly, for people who are anxious, a little self-care goes a long way. It's important to take the cue from anxiety, to be attentive to your physical and psychological needs and practice self-compassion and care. Instead of pushing yourself harder in order to avoid thinking about anxiety, as many of us tend to do, practice self-compassion. After all, if your dog was panting and puffing during a walk, wouldn't you let it rest and have some water? Treat yourself with at least as much compassion as you would your dog!

The Stages of the Anxiety Spiral

People often say that an anxiety attack came over them "out of the blue," but when you slow down the process it typically follows a predictable pathway. Catastrophic thinking and self-judgment are the strongest forces in perpetuating and exacerbating anxiety over time. When we feel anxious, we tend to interpret our feelings as an indication that we are somehow weak.

To summarize, here is how the anxiety spiral develops:

- **Trigger.** Stress, fear, or even a random event initiates the spiral process by triggering the sympathetic nervous system and its fight-or-flight response. We saw with Jenn in chapter 1 how stress can be a trigger even when we aren't aware of it. For Julian, the trigger was an especially poor air quality day that caused difficulty breathing. For others, it could be symptoms in the aftermath of anger or sex. The trigger is much less significant than how we respond to it.
- **Catastrophic thinking.** As our tension mounts, our minds kick into gear and we think the worst about our anxiety. We may think that our anxiety is endangering our lives (remember John driving on the snow-covered highway in Canada?). We may even view our

anxiety symptoms as something dangerous, as Julian did. These thoughts increase the secretion of adrenaline into our system, which makes our anxiety worse.

- **Self-judgment.** As we feel an increase in physiological responses, we tend to judge ourselves harshly for experiencing anxiety. This can happen subconsciously, below the threshold of our awareness. We judge ourselves to be weak, feeble, and incapable. We may imagine that others can *see* what we are *feeling* (even though they generally cannot), and we feel embarrassed because of how we feel.

- **Full spiral.** Our negative interpretations of the initial anxiety-like experience increase our physical symptoms to the point that our fight-or-flight response continues to be triggered. We experience the full force of physiological reactions, which provide more kindling for the fire of self-judgment to burn, and the increased apprehension caused by our negative interpretations sends our anxiety symptoms even higher.

Cutting to the Heart of Your Anxiety

Some years ago, a patient named Samantha called me from Europe for help with anxiety symptoms that, at times, led her to make impulsive decisions. She immediately jumped to self-deprecation when feeling anxious, and the most frequent thoughtless impulse she had when that occurred was to get involved with another person romantically. The excitement of her romantic escapades allayed her anxiety for a while, but as soon as the anxiety went away, Samantha almost always realized that the romantic attraction wasn't really love, and she beat herself up mentally even more. She then made matters worse by texting her closest girlfriends to report her actions and berating herself for repeating her self-destructive behavior. Her friends were as supportive as they could be, but the frequency and intensity of Samantha's destructive cycles were more than they could handle, and they were losing patience with her. Samantha was avoiding her anxiety through social interactions—romantically and with her friends—and it wasn't working. In fact, these patterns were making her anxiety much worse.

We had been working together for some months, and Samantha had come to realize that acting out with men—and subsequently venting to her friends—had become go-to ways of dealing with any anxious feelings of inadequacy that came up. (She was not even aware of these patterns before starting therapy.) She realized she was telling herself that if she couldn't succeed emotionally, she could at least succeed romantically. Of course, this plan never worked, and her cycles left her feeling deeply shameful. Following this therapeutic realization, she initially became stronger. She committed to working on herself and gaining strength through acceptance of her anxiety, instead of resorting to problematic relationships.

However, like all people, Samantha hit a rough patch and struggled to maintain consistency. In Samantha's case, it was barely a few weeks before she slipped. One thing led to the next, and she acted out on her well-practiced reflexive reactions to have another fling when feeling anxious. She then, predictably, texted her friends, who scolded her, and Samantha started to fall into a state of self-loathing and despair. At that point, though, she chose a different path: she reached out to me for help. I reinforced that important step forward, and I reminded Samantha that she'd been in this state before, and that the antidote to the negative self-talk and behavior was to recognize the anxiety spiral and practice self-acceptance and self-compassion.

Samantha decided to spend a day practicing self-care; she took herself to lunch, ran a couple of errands, and got off social media, where she had been obsessively posting about things that didn't really matter to her as a way of burying her true concerns with her behavior. The next day, when I asked her if she was still feeling bad about her "mess-up," she replied, "I thought about it and realized *I'm glad I messed up*. This all happened so that I would have an opportunity to accept myself. The next time I feel anxious about a possible slip-up at work, I'll do something nice for myself instead of pursuing some kind of romantic diversion." She also called her girlfriend to apologize for venting to her, explained the insight she'd had, and asked for her friend to please remind her in the future to take care of herself if she slipped back into self-blame.

A Positive Spiral

The anxiety spiral starts with benign symptoms and is followed by catastrophizing, self-blame, and self-criticism, which makes anxiety worse. However, there is an alternative: once we experience anxiety symptoms, we can instead choose to accept them and be kind to ourselves. If we do this, not only will we feel less anxious but we will develop a closer relationship with ourselves and start to thrive as individuals.

I would say this latter approach is a "positive spiral." We are not born destined to be anxious. We can break free from the anxiety spiral. And when we do, anxiety can enhance our lives. To be clear: we may not have a choice about whether we experience initial symptoms of fear or small surges of anxiety once in a while. But we can *definitely* choose whether to catastrophize and blame ourselves (leading to the anxiety spiral) or accept and be kind to ourselves, which effectively turns anxiety into a strength that can help us to thrive.

When people enter the positive spiral, they feel powerful because of anxiety instead of defeated by it. They *take the initial cues of anxiety and turn them into strengths*. They don't allow anxiety to get the better of them. From working with hundreds of patients, I've found that the main barrier to entering this positive spiral is that it just needs to click that you *can* overcome it and don't need to be the kind of person who is stuck or whose path is obstructed by anxiety. You have the power of choice to rise above anxiety and not get sucked into the spiral, and once you choose the alternative path and practice it, things get so much easier.

This is what the positive spiral looks like:

- **Trigger.** The physical sensations here are the very same as with the anxiety spiral, because you cannot control the initial experience of stress, fear, or whatever event triggers or initiates your fight-or-flight system. But in order to enter the positive spiral, you must recognize that the moment your fight-or-flight system is activated by adrenaline, your "rest-and-digest" system is *also* set into motion by acetylcholine (as will be explained in the next section).

- **Accept your anxiety.** Instead of catastrophizing, accept that you are feeling anxious and recognize that your anxious feelings will eventually abate. Remember that acute anxiety is *not* dangerous and *cannot* make you "go crazy"; it's simply a discomfort and nothing to worry about. Furthermore, don't fight the discomfort, because fighting it just makes things worse. Instead, try to let anxiety wash over you and simply try to notice how it feels without trying to make it go away, until it naturally ebbs on its own.

- **Self-compassion.** Instead of judging yourself for feeling anxious, accept yourself and practice self-compassion. Remind yourself that it is natural for your adrenaline to be triggered from time to time, and that it's good to know your fight-or-flight system is working. *None of this means that you are broken, weak, or inferior to anyone else.* Along these lines, be kind to yourself and give yourself what you need when you feel anxious. Support yourself with compassion as you accept and tolerate the discomfort of anxiety.

- **Reduction of anxiety.** When you accept your anxiety and practice self-compassion, it's only a matter of time until your anxiety subsides. Often it's just a matter of minutes, though it can take longer depending on the nature and intensity of the initial trigger and the extent to which you practice acceptance and self-compassion. Over time, you can develop a stronger, more connected relationship with yourself—one that allows you to thrive more than if you had never been anxious in the first place!

The Rest-and-Digest System

Sir Isaac Newton notably stated that for every action there is an equal and opposite reaction. While Newton was referring to the world of physical forces—and he codified this statement into his third law of motion—the same can be said for anxiety. We learned in chapter 1 that the fight-or-flight system is a natural and healthy response involving the release of adrenaline into our bloodstream, which keeps us safe in times of danger. When the fight-or-flight system is triggered by the perception of threat, the physical sensations associated with anxiety are generated as a by-product. As long as the fight-or-flight response is not continually triggered, anxiety symptoms will subside on their own as adrenaline levels wane.

Fortunately, human beings are built with a *second* system to directly counteract the effects of our fight-or-flight response. This is known as the rest-and-digest system, and it is primarily set into motion by the neurotransmitter acetylcholine.[2] In this regard, acetylcholine and adrenaline are opposites; adrenaline has an immediate inhibitory effect on acetylcholine and temporarily suppresses its effects throughout the body in the moments following adrenal secretion. However, shortly after adrenaline is released into the bloodstream, production of acetylcholine *increases* and its levels *rise* within the nervous system over a subsequent period of 30 to 120 minutes.[3] While this may seem paradoxical, it is not; the rest-and-digest system is automatically triggered following the fight-or-flight system's surge in order to help the body settle down.

These two effects—*fight-or-flight* and *rest-and-digest*—are often referred to by the names *sympathetic* (fight-or-flight) and *parasympathetic* (rest-and-digest) nervous systems. The *sympathetic* nervous system secretes adrenaline to immediately get us moving and keep us safe when we feel threatened. The *parasympathetic* nervous system synthesizes acetylcholine, which helps to gradually cool down our systems in the minutes and hours following the experience of a perceived threat.

When the rest-and-digest system is activated, the body experiences a number of important physiological changes. If you compare these effects to those of the fight-or-flight system in chapter 1, you will see that they are exactly converse:

- The pupils constrict to reduce your field of vision and increase detail perception.
- The digestive system reactivates.
- Blood vessels dilate, resuming normal blood flow to your extremities.
- Muscle fibers relax.
- The heart rate slows to its normal rate when the body is at rest.
- The breathing rate also slows down to a normal rate.

You may be asking why the fight-or-flight response happens right away, yet rest-and-digest takes time to have effects on the body. Physiologically, the reason is that adrenaline is both a neurotransmitter and a hormone, so it acts on the brain but also goes directly into our bloodstream, where it is deployed throughout the body quickly with immediate effects. By contrast, acetylcholine is a neurotransmitter but *not* a hormone, so in order to trigger physiological changes, it needs to work its way throughout the nervous system via neuromuscular junctions without entering the bloodstream. But there is another, even more important reason why the rest-and-digest system is slower-acting than fight-or-flight: if the parasympathetic nervous system were just as fast-acting as the sympathetic nervous system, people would never have a fight-or-flight response at all, since its effects would immediately be counteracted. If this were the case, our fight-or-flight systems could never protect us during times of threat, when we need to muster a response without any delay.

Sympathetic (Fight-or-Flight) and Parasympathetic (Rest-and-Digest) Responses, and Anxiety

When we are triggered by a perceived threat, the sympathetic (fight-or-flight) response releases adrenaline, and we experience symptoms of anxiety. Shortly thereafter, the parasympathetic (rest-and-digest) response releases acytelcholine, which will gradually bring us back to a calm state.

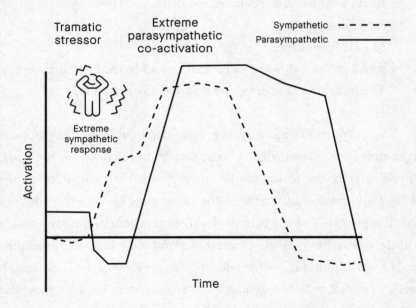

Peter Payne, Peter Levine, and Mardi Crane-Godreau, "Corrigendum: Somatic Experiencing: Using Interoception and Proprioception as Core Elements of Trauma Therapy," *Frontiers In Psychology* 6 (2015), 93, 10.3389/fpsyg.2015.00093. This image has been recreated and modified under the Creative Commons 4.0 International license, https://creativecommons.org/licenses/by/4.0/.

This information (*psychoeducation*, as it's called in therapy) has huge implications for how people should think about their anxiety. The first step to activate the positive spiral involves recognizing that in the moments that follow our experience of anxiety, our bodies have *already* begun to generate neurochemical compounds to counteract the effects of the fight-or-flight system and spawn a rest-and-digest response. If you don't continually trigger the fight-or-flight system, the sympathetic response *will* dissipate, and the parasympathetic response *will* take over and slow things down. You *will* relax over time. If you simply let it run its course, adrenaline will stop flowing and acetylcholine will do its job to calm you down.

If you are experiencing high levels of anxiety, simply thinking about this will decrease your tension and apprehension. How can I be so confident this will work? Because if you recognize that anxiety is a natural response, that it is not dangerous, and that your body has a natural rest-and-digest response, what is there to be catastrophically afraid of?

Think about it: Why don't panic attacks go on forever? You *must* have a built-in system to deal with this and stop the body's engine from overheating! You just have to wait for that system to kick in.

Accept Your Anxiety

Recognizing that our bodies are built to experience, withstand, and naturally decrease our levels of anxiety is a critical first step to entering the positive spiral. But the next step is even more critical. One of the most important keys to dealing with anxiety—upending and reversing the anxiety spiral—is simply to *accept your anxiety*, as opposed to suppressing it.

Acceptance of anxiety involves allowing anxiety to wash over you, without fighting or trying to decrease it in any way. By contrast, suppression involves efforts to curtail, stop, or even hide the experience of anxiety.

Suppression of anxiety can include pushing away distressing thoughts, feelings, and sensations; distracting yourself by focusing on anything else aside from what makes you feel anxious; and avoiding situations in which you think you may experience anxiety symptoms. Suppression is a common response to anxiety. After all, anxiety is uncomfortable, so it makes sense that people try to avoid feeling anxious. However, suppression tends to make anxiety worse.

In a landmark experimental study at Boston University's Center for Anxiety and Related Disorders,[4] researchers examined what happens when individuals with anxiety disorders accept or suppress their negative emotions. They showed anxious individuals a brief but extremely distressing video involving brutally violent footage, while asking about their levels of anxiety and measuring their physiological reactivity (heart rate) before, during, and after the experiment.

Before watching the video, participants were randomly assigned to one of two conditions. In the first condition, participants were instructed to *accept* their emotions: "Struggling against natural emotions can intensify and prolong your distress. Allow yourself to accept your emotions without trying to get rid of them." In the second condition, participants were told to *suppress* their feelings: "You should not have to put up with more discomfort and distress than is necessary. Try to reduce your negative emotions by controlling them."

Can you guess what happened? Both groups reported equal levels of distress from watching the video clip, since it was genuinely horrific. However, participants in the acceptance group displayed less anxiety after watching the film than those in the suppression group. Furthermore, suppression participants experienced an *increase* in heart rate while watching the video, whereas the acceptance participants experienced a *decrease* in heart rate relative to their baseline before watching the same video. In other words, despite the fact that both groups were equally stressed by the clip, suppression was associated with greater anxiety and greater physiological reactivity. By contrast, *those who practiced acceptance were objectively less physiologically stressed than they were before they experienced anxiety in the first place.*

This is just one example of hundreds of research studies that have shown the power of acceptance in coping with anxiety. One of the most up-and-coming clinical psychotherapeutic approaches for dealing with anxiety and other concerns today is acceptance and commitment therapy, also known by the acronym ACT.[5] At the core of this wonderful treatment approach is the notion that by accepting our feelings, as opposed to fighting them, life immediately becomes easier. A famous ACT metaphor (among therapists) crystalizes this concept:

Imagine that you fall into a large hole in the ground. You cannot climb out and there are no escape routes. You feel trapped and distressed. However, you search the hole and find a tool bag that contains a shovel. You immediately reach into the bag, pull out the shovel, and start digging. You dig faster and faster, frantically trying to dig yourself out of the hole. After several minutes, you are tired, sweaty, covered in dirt, and deeper into the hole than you were before you started digging. You take a break but quickly grow tired and distressed by your predicament, so you pick up the shovel and start digging again. You increase your rate and intensity of digging. But this only leaves you more tired, sweaty, dirty, and farther into the hole. Eventually, you realize that the shovel is just making things worse and there is only one option: accept that you're stuck in a hole and make the most of it. Once you do that, you no longer feel trapped and distressed, and over time you even start to like being in the hole, since you have plenty of time to sit and think.

The paradox and irony of acceptance is that once we stop fighting against negative emotions, they reduce and often go away entirely. When it comes to anxiety, the physiology behind this is clear: when we fight against our anxiety, our fight-or-flight systems are retriggered, and this perpetuates and exacerbates our anxious feelings. Conversely, when we stop trying to change our anxiety—when we just let go and allow ourselves to be anxious—the adrenaline fades, and we allow acetylcholine to bathe our neural systems, leaving us to enjoy the wonderful effects of the rest-and-digest response.

A Personal Experience of Accepting Anxiety

I've given over two hundred talks in the last decade, speaking to crowds as large as five hundred people and ranging from high-stress academic sessions at Harvard Medical School, Dartmouth, and Columbia University, to informal addresses with small gatherings at community organizations. A few years ago, I was invited to speak to a group of high school girls aged fourteen to seventeen years. I must admit that I did not prepare for the talk as I should have. Given the audience, I didn't take things as seriously as I might have at a scholarly conference. Given my nonchalance, when I was introduced and I got up to speak, I was surprised to find myself feeling a cold sweat. As I walked to the podium, my hands were clammy, and my mouth was dry. I even felt myself shaking a little bit, and as I started to speak I heard a small quaver in my voice. I looked out at a sea of open, smiling teenaged faces and I said to myself, *Oh my God, you're afraid of speaking to high schoolers! Really? This is the easiest audience you've ever had!*

It completely took me by surprise, but fortunately I knew what to do. I overcame my instinctual reaction to panic and judge myself, and instead I could hear myself say in my mind: *Okay, time to practice what you preach. Just accept it and let it ride. Don't fight it.*

I noticed that there was a glass of water in front of me, and I deliberately chose *not* to drink it! I knew that pausing my speech to gulp, or looking away, or adjusting my tie, or any other distractions with which I could have preoccupied myself, would just make it worse. So I kept talking—I kept reading my prepared remarks and smiling until the anxiety faded on its own. The entire ordeal took, *maybe*, two minutes tops. After I felt relaxed, I took a drink to positively reinforce my body for what it had accomplished.

On my way home that night, I was trying to figure out what on earth had happened. *Why is it, David*, I thought, *that you can speak at a grand rounds in front of your academic colleagues—even a circle of neurologists, who as a group are breathtakingly brilliant—without any problems? But you became anxious speaking to high schoolers?* I realized that I'm not only more prepared but also a bit amped up before I give a talk to eminent scholars, and so if I feel a little bit uncomfortable I interpret it immediately as just nerves, which I would expect to have. But when I felt uncomfortable in front of that group of teenagers, I wasn't expecting to be at all nervous, and *that's* what freaked me out. The reason my anxiety increased so rapidly is that I subconsciously started to catastrophize about my anxiety itself. The way I got out of the cycle was by using a conscious mental process to interrupt the process, and in less than a minute the nervous reaction went away.

The humbling truth is that, although I counsel countless patients on how to see anxiety as an asset, I'm totally capable of having a surprise surge of anxiety myself! The only thing that saved me is that I didn't overreact or criticize myself. I somehow remembered to follow my own advice.

Accept Yourself

As important as it is to accept anxiety, it's even more valuable to accept yourself as you are and not beat yourself up for having anxiety. Let's be real: no one is perfect. Everyone has something they need to change and improve. What's the point of life if you don't have something to work on? In fact, people who think they are perfect are in serious trouble! Either they aren't aware of their problems, or they *are* aware but they don't want to admit or deal with them. I'm not sure which is worse. I will tell you, though, that the hardest cases I have ever seen are the wealthiest, most successful, and best-looking people. When your life is "perfect," you're at serious risk for emotional and behavioral health concerns because, when you inevitably realize that you're *not* perfect, it's hard to accept. At that point, the only direction is down.

The Perfect Family

Madison seemed to have it all. She was still a teenager when I first saw her as a patient, and she had come from an exceptionally wealthy family who owned a lavish multifloor apartment overlooking Central Park. Her parents were on the boards of several New York and New England institutions—they were a family to be reckoned with. Madison was classically good-looking, and each of her siblings was more attractive and accomplished than the next. You might say her family was as close as we have to American royalty. She was also the most acutely suicidal patient I had ever met.

Madison had such deep self-loathing that she could not accept even a modicum of a compliment or positive remark without trying to deflect it. The sad secret behind Madison's low self-esteem is that she had been sexually abused by a sibling for many years, and she considered herself irreparably damaged and a disgrace to her family. It didn't help that when she finally worked up the courage to tell her parents about what had happened, they told her not to tell anyone because it would bring shame to the family's reputation. On top of her pain, she now had to suppress her trauma and her anger at the person who had abused her. As a result of being told to bury her feelings, her negative emotions dramatically increased; she could not control having daily flashbacks of her abuse, which terrified her, gave her jitters, and led to a hypervigilance response. Worst of all, though, she came to the point that she hated herself for not being able to control how she felt.

Madison's self-judgment progressively increased over time. When her hypervigilance made it hard for her to sleep well, she criticized herself for not being able to sleep. Then, when she felt crazy during the day from chronic sleep deprivation, she would berate herself more and even resort to self-injury at times. Occasionally, while sitting at her desk in high school, her body would suddenly and involuntarily contort and her limbs would start twitching because of her emotion dysregulation, sleep deprivation, and internalized anger, and she detested her body because of this. The pressure to appear normal when she was feeling emotionally and physically on edge only fueled her anxiety further.

Given her family background, Madison had super-high expectations of herself; she felt she should be able to handle anything, but the only way she had to manage all her symptoms was by suppressing her emotions. It was only a matter of time before she just couldn't do it anymore and she became acutely suicidal. Her parents found her asleep on the bathroom floor after she had ingested two bottles of pills that should have been lethal. After being intubated for two weeks, she was brought to the hospital, where I began to work with her. At that point, her parents had no choice but to acknowledge—publicly—that something was wrong. Still, Madison had (and still has) a *long* road ahead to accept herself.

Self-Compassion

We have identified that the positive spiral involves thinking differently about anxiety—recognizing that it is not dangerous and that as human beings we have internal resources and physiological mechanisms to manage our anxious feelings. We have also discussed that accepting, as opposed to suppressing, anxiety is the best approach, and furthermore that accepting ourselves and our limitations and struggles is critical to healthy emotional development. To be clear: Considering the ideas in this chapter to think about anxiety, and yourself, differently is important. But without behavioral change, you are unlikely to correct negative attitudes toward yourself and adopt a more positive framework. To make a change, we need to *apply* self-compassion on a regular, even daily, basis.

Self-compassion involves *being kind* to yourself, even if you don't think you deserve it. This requires showing understanding and accepting ourselves specifically when we suffer, fail, or feel inadequate. *Beyond thinking and feeling less judgmental toward ourselves, it involves practicing self-kindness.* The effects of this approach on anxiety are well documented in the psychological literature. People who practice self-compassion are more resilient during times of stress, less likely to be and feel isolated, and substantially less likely to struggle with mental health concerns including depression and, of course, anxiety.[6] There is even a growing body of data to suggest that self-compassion is associated with better physical health.[7]

As I've said, one of the keys to turning your anxiety into an asset is learning to practice self-compassion. That involves increasing your self-care but also being kind to yourself rather than judging yourself as if you're the only person in the world who has difficulty with a particular issue. If you are struggling, all that means is that you're a human being. All of us struggle, often through long stretches of time. We scramble with our careers, our romantic relationships, and other aspects of life. Whatever issue you may feel stressed about now, ask yourself, *How many of the other eight billion people on this planet are likely tussling with the same problem right now?* When you think about the greater context of humanity, our concerns seem all too common, and worthy of validation and support.

The biggest challenge with self-compassion is that it requires being kind to yourself specifically when you don't feel that you deserve it. One night I was at a dinner where a colleague of mine in the mental health field gave a talk during the meal. It was going fine, but at one point he inadvertently mentioned information about a patient of his in such a way that it was clear to some of us who he was talking about. He caught himself and tried to recover in the moment, but many in the audience were already aware of what had happened. He finished his speech nonetheless, and people applauded—politely. As he sat down, though, I saw that he was crushed.

They had just served dessert, so I took my little bowl of ice cream and went over to where he was seated. I gave him a pat on the back and said, "We've all said things we've regretted at times—I know I have. You still did a fantastic job. Now let's enjoy our ice cream." He looked at me like I was crazy. But I began eating my ice cream and I nudged him a bit to indicate he should join me. Somewhat reluctantly, he did. And by the time we both finished, he had a wry smile on his face.

"I felt like I was going to choke on my ice cream," he told me a few days later, "because I didn't think I deserved it. I wanted to leave early, go home, and indulge in a bout of self-loathing, but now I'm feeling a little bit better about it all."

Many people struggle with self-compassion because they are concerned that it will lead to complacency. They argue, or fear, that giving too much leeway to ourselves when we drop the ball will reinforce "bad behavior" and lead us down the wrong path. However, the opposite is more likely to be the case. At the societal level, we readily appreciate this fact. The US government gives over fifty billion dollars in international aid to provide for economic and military needs around the globe. We also have social policies in place, like the No Child Left Behind policy that guarantees basic education to everyone, regardless of their financial resources. We do this not only because it's an American value but because it's strategic. Investing, both abroad and at home, in people when they are struggling helps to stimulate growth and increase opportunity for everyone.

However, we often don't practice compassion toward ourselves as much as we do for others. When it comes to us personally, we are quick to say, "If I didn't earn this, I don't deserve it, and so I'm not giving it to myself." When you think about it, though, if you feel bad about yourself, that's precisely the best opportunity to be compassionate. In one sense, it's the *only* opportunity to practice self-compassion. After all, if you take care and reward yourself only when you deserve kindness because of your accomplishments or successes, that's not self-compassion at all.

How Much Self-Compassion Do You Have?

There is a famous management adage: if you can't measure it, you can't change it. In that vein, it's a very good thing that the burgeoning science of self-compassion has witnessed the development of psychometric assessment tools to quantify how much (or little) self-compassion people have. The best-known tool is the Self-Compassion Scale.[8] An excerpt from the scale is below. As a rough guide, average scores for each item are around 3, so scores of 1 or 2 indicate "low" self-compassion, whereas 4 or 5 indicate "high" self-compassion.

Regardless of how self-compassionate you presently are, you can increase your self-compassion by regularly practicing exercises. Here are a few options:

Take a break when you don't deserve it. Whether you deserve a break is irrelevant. If you need a break, take one—*simply because you're human and you need it.* Doing so will help increase self-acceptance and is a step toward building a positive spiral.

Do yourself a favor. Make a list of things you need, or even just things you like, and do one thing each day—*especially* on days when you mess up or feel you don't deserve it.

Tolerate yourself with love and patience. Set aside one minute for this exercise. For the first thirty seconds, think about a time when you messed something up or said something you regret. Conjure it in your mind and think deeply about exactly what you did wrong. Then, for the

How I Typically Act Toward Myself in Difficult Times

Please read each statement carefully before answering. Indicate how often you behave in the stated manner.	Almost Always 5	4	3	2	Almost Never 1
1. I try to be understanding and patient toward those aspects of my personality I don't like.					
2. When something painful happens, I try to take a balanced view of the situation.					
3. I try to see my failings as part of the human condition.					
4. When I'm going through a very hard time, I give myself the caring and tenderness I need.					
5. When something upsets me, I try to keep my emotions in balance.					
6. When I feel inadequate in some way, I try to remind myself that feelings of inadequacy are shared by most people.					

next thirty seconds, say something kind to yourself—preferably out loud but at least in your mind. Make it encouraging and nice, speaking as you would to a friend who made the same error. Be balanced and fair, but also be kind.

Watch Your Language!

The words and phrases we choose when we are alone, either mentally or verbally, are revealing. They also make an enormous difference. Being self-compassionate doesn't mean that we cannot hold ourselves accountable. But it means we need to be kind, caring, loving, and generous, even when we struggle and fail.

In our society, we tend to curse ourselves as if we are actually evil, nasty, stupid, or all three. Even if we don't use "curse" words, our thoughts or language are often mean-spirited. If our boss or spouse or teammate used that kind of language, we would be deeply offended, probably angered, and hurt. Yet we routinely degrade ourselves with negativity.

Most people self-criticize for good reasons. They are trying to improve themselves and keep themselves honest and accountable. However, self-judgment is an ineffective tool for correcting anxiety. Indeed, self-judgment is exactly what sends us into the anxiety spiral after the initial experience of stress or fear. Judging yourself for feeling anxious is like beating someone up when they are on the floor in order to get them to stand.

Let me be clear: *negative self-talk tends to make anxiety spiral out of control.* When dealing with anxiety, we need to become more aware of the way we think about and speak to ourselves. It's critical to slow down the anxiety spiral and become more conscious of the ways in which we interpret and understand our triggers. We must avoid self-deprecation, because mean language makes us feel even worse about ourselves. Constant carping can perpetuate and exacerbate anxiety for a lifetime.

How can we hold ourselves accountable while being self-compassionate? The first thing to do is to wait a couple of days after making a mistake, to give yourself time to cool down. Don't try to criticize yourself in the heat of the moment. Set a reminder in your phone or put it on your calendar to have a conversation with yourself about what happened within the next forty-eight hours.

Next, when you're ready, have that conversation about what happened. Go for a walk for half an hour or even an hour. Give yourself the appropriate amount of time to think about what happened and to have an internal dialogue about the issue. If you were holding someone else accountable, you would allocate the time required to explain your concerns and hear their perspective. Do the same for yourself.

Finally, while out on your walk, start the conversation by sticking to the facts. Simply describe what happened. No negatives, judgmental comments, or put-downs. Nothing more than simply describing what happened.

From that point, there are several directions the conversation can go. You could try to figure out why the mistake happened in the first place. You could try to determine what needs to change in the future. But at all costs, please be kind to yourself. Your mental health depends on it.

. . . .

TOOL #2: THE POSITIVE SPIRAL

Anxiety gets out of control when we enter the anxiety spiral and the initial experience of an adrenaline surge leads to catastrophic thinking, self-judgment, and a worsening of anxiety. Conversely, we can utilize the opportunity of the initial fight-or-flight response (whether triggered by a real or perceived threat) to enter a positive spiral, which begets acceptance of our anxiety and self-compassion. When we take this approach, we harness the power of anxiety to increase our self-acceptance, thereby turning anxiety into a strength that can help us thrive. Here are some concrete steps to take when you start to feel anxious, in order to enter the positive spiral.

STEP 1

Remember that your *fight-or-flight* (sympathetic nervous system) response has an equal and opposite reaction called the *rest-and-digest* (parasympathetic nervous system) response. Over time, your anxiety will fade as adrenaline wanes and acetylcholine makes its way through the nervous system.

STEP 2

Do not fight your anxiety! Don't suppress or curtail or try to decrease it in any way. Simply accept it and *let it ride.* Let your anxiety wash over you. Allow yourself to experience anxiety without trying to change it. Simply observe the feelings, even if they are uncomfortable, and wait for them to pass. (Yes, they will eventually pass.) Turn anxiety into a strength by taking the opportunity to accept discomfort in your life.

STEP 3

Accept yourself. Don't judge yourself for feeling anxious. Anxiety is a normal response that all of us have. Furthermore, everyone who experiences anxiety has a reason why they are anxious—that could be something in the past, or a current stressor, or another factor. Don't judge yourself harshly or self-criticize. Thrive with anxiety by learning to be more accepting of who you are.

STEP 4

Practice self-compassion. Doing so does not mean you will become complacent or lazy. On the contrary, when you are struggling, give yourself a break and a hand—just like you would to a friend who's having a hard time. Remember that practicing self-compassion means being kind to yourself specifically when you do not feel like you deserve it! Take the opportunity to become a more compassionate person.

CHAPTER 3

TRANSCENDING OURSELVES

Anxiety Can Provide Opportunities to Push Beyond Our Perceived Limits and Develop Inner Strengths

S o far, we have addressed how anxiety can help us know ourselves better. Stress, for instance, is the body's way of telling us that we need to rebalance. We've also learned that anxiety can help us gain self-acceptance and self-compassion at levels we might not have achieved if we had never been anxious in the first place. We now know how to avoid getting stuck in the anxiety spiral by accepting anxiety and not falling prey to catastrophic thinking or self-criticism, and by practicing self-compassion. However, if the strategies in chapters 1 and 2 are the only ones you follow, you are unlikely to thrive with anxiety—in fact, you are likely to continue to struggle. I say this because, so far in this book, we have not yet stood up to our anxiety, and so it can still have power over us.

In many respects, dealing with anxiety is a lot like dealing with a schoolyard bully who tells you to hand over your lunch money or he'll beat you up. Until you stand up to the bully, you'll keep going hungry. But if you say, "I don't care what you do to me; I'm not giving you my money," you may have some scary encounters, but eventually the bully will look for an easier target. Likewise, when we stand up to our anxieties and face them directly—when we confront our deepest, darkest fears—we recognize that we possess profound internal reservoirs of strength to overcome our demons. When we tap these reservoirs, we transcend our anxiety, resulting in enhanced courage, self-confidence, the strength to face adversity, and the feeling of happiness that results from triumphing over our fears instead of avoiding them.

Exposure Therapy

In the early years of my training and practice, I was fortunate to spend four months as a visiting fellow at Professor David H. Barlow's Center for Anxiety and Related Disorders at Boston University. Barlow's method of treating anxiety is based on a variant of cognitive behavioral therapy called *exposure therapy*, and although I didn't spend a lot of time working with Barlow individually, the work I witnessed there was a truly formative experience for me.

I realized what a potent paradigm exposure therapy is for helping people deal with anxiety. In some cases exposure therapy may not be enough by itself to overcome all forms of anxiety, but I do think it's a necessary and valuable aspect of anxiety treatment—something we refer to in my profession as *first-line therapy*—the preferred initial treatment recommended for many forms of anxiety.

When my visiting fellowship ended, I wanted to continue to learn about exposure therapy, so I went on to study with one of Barlow's students, Professor Martin Antony, and I spent a year and a half at his Anxiety Treatment and Research Clinic in Hamilton, Ontario, Canada. Dr. Antony, who has written a number of important books on the applications of exposure therapy to various aspects and types of anxiety, became my clinical supervisor, and what I learned from him and his colleagues expanded my understanding of exposure therapy enormously.

The rationale for exposure therapy seemed self-evident to me. To overcome one's deepest anxieties, including panic attacks, specific phobias (such as fear of flying, elevators, spiders), or social situations, we need to build up our courage by facing these situations until they no longer elicit an anxiety response. In one of his many books, Dr. Antony writes:

> Experience has probably taught you that confronting feared situations causes you to feel uncomfortable, and avoiding or escaping feared situations leads to a sense of relief. However, avoiding the situations, objects, and feelings that make you anxious also almost guarantees that your fear will continue bothering you over the long term. . . . In reality, staying in a situation despite the fear it arouses usually leads to a reduction in fear. It may take longer for your fear to decrease when you stay in the situation, but the long-term benefits will be greater. By staying until your fear decreases, you will learn that you can be right in the middle of the situation and feel relatively comfortable.[1]

This captures the essence of what drew me to exposure therapy—facing our fears instead of avoiding them strengthens our ability to be comfortable with the very distress and uncertainty that we find so disconcerting about anxiety. *Exposure therapy works by gradually building up one's tolerance to facing anxiety.* Of course, you start with small steps and build up to medium and then larger steps. If you're afraid of driving, you may start by simply turning on the engine while in an empty parking lot.

Over time, you move to basic maneuvers on side streets, then main streets with low traffic, then rush hour, then an empty highway, then one that's busy, and eventually driving in traffic during bad weather.

How do we know which situations are *more* and *less* fearful for a patient? It's simple: we ask them. Specifically, patients are taught to rate their anxiety on a scale of 0 to 10, 0 being completely calm and 10 being the worst anxiety they've ever had. That way, I know if they are at a 1 to 3, their anxiety is relatively low; if it's 4 to 6, they have midrange anxiety; and 7 to 9 is high. As a general rule of thumb, exposure therapy is most effective when patients are in the 7 to 9 range during sessions. Yes, that means they are uncomfortable! But despite that momentary surge in anxiety, not one of my patients has ever regretted the experience.

I need to be clear that a guideline for clinicians providing exposure therapy is never to ask a patient to do anything that is objectively dangerous. In fact, at my clinics, our standing policy is that clinicians may never ask patients to do something the clinicians wouldn't do themselves. Notwithstanding that fact, two questions generally arise when I tell people about exposure therapy. The first is, wouldn't it be simpler to teach anxious patients how to relax via mindfulness meditation and deep breathing? And, perhaps more to the point, isn't it cruel to make someone go through all that psychic pain in the first place, like retraumatizing a victim of childhood abuse by asking them to relive it?

Cruel to Be Kind

Despite some very impressive results—four decades of research demonstrates that exposure therapy has large and enduring effects on anxiety disorders[2]—this method of treatment has not yet fully entered the mainstream of psychotherapy. One key reason was echoed in a *New York Times* article from twenty years ago about Barlow's work, entitled "The Cruelest Cure," which summed up the divide as follows: "His treatment promises to be psychotherapy's ultimate fast track, but while many clinicians praise its well-documented results, others take a dimmer view of what one clinician calls 'torture, plain and simple.'"[3]

I view that last remark as both unfair and inaccurate. Facing your fears isn't pleasant. But to me, there is no greater kindness a clinician can provide a patient than to believe in their abilities. I would even say that failing to push patients to face their fears is tantamount to infantilizing them—saying that they cannot handle things. Exposure therapy allows anxiety patients to transcend their fears by uncoupling fearful associations with certain activities and situations. The take-home message of treatment is clear: *we can confront our fears and tolerate anxious feelings.* Not only do patients who complete exposure therapy learn to project more positive outcomes, but they also become more comfortable with both anxiety and fear.[4]

The question of whether it would be simpler and kinder to teach patients how to relax when their anxieties make them feel so uncomfortable is an old debate among cognitive behavioral therapy researchers. Professor Joseph Wolpe, a primary figure in the field (who mentored Dr. Barlow), developed a way of helping patients to calm themselves through a series of muscle-relaxing techniques, which were then utilized during exposure therapy—in other words, while the patients faced their fears. However, at this point in history, numerous studies have shown that relaxation techniques—whether involving soothing imagery, calming mantras, or meditation—are not only limited in their efficacy but can actually dull the effects of exposure therapy.

In one landmark piece of research on the subject, seventy-seven patients with panic disorder were randomized to receive exposure therapy with or without relaxation. Relaxation yielded poorer outcomes.[5] Similarly, a recent review article that crunched the numbers on seventy-two studies with 4,064 anxious patients revealed that exposure therapy was the most effective clinical approach, and muscle relaxation was associated with significantly *less* treatment efficacy.[6]

Based on my own clinical experience, I believe that relaxation is counterproductive when used in the treatment of anxiety. *Most people can handle anxiety much better than they think!* But you won't realize that until you face your fears and get that message into your gut. Perhaps the best way of stating the case for exposure therapy is to explain, as simply as I can, how the brain processes and stores anxiety-provoking thoughts and events.

The Neurobiology of Exposure Therapy

What eventually convinced me of the efficacy of Barlow's process was understanding its neurobiological basis. The human brain consists of various areas, including the *prefrontal cortex*, which handles abstract thought and basic planning; and the *midbrain*, which contains the amygdala and hippocampus. The amygdala is a small almond-shaped structure that comes online when the fight-or-flight response is triggered. Next to it is the hippocampus, a pair of coiled structures whose name comes from the Greek word for "seahorse," which it closely resembles. Among other tasks, the hippocampus encodes our short-term memories into long-term memories, a crucial step in determining our mental and emotional associations.

When a disturbing emotion or event triggers your amygdala, the hippocampus joins in and deeply encodes your memory of the triggering experience. That combination is the reason many people remember exactly where they were on the morning of September 11, 2001, when the Twin Towers at the World Trade Center collapsed. The intensity of the emotions that were felt at that moment seared the details of that morning into the brain by activating the hippocampus. By contrast, most people don't remember where they were on September 10 or 12 of that year; the information of those moments wasn't programmed as deeply because their emotions were not involved. Similar processes occur when people have positive events, such as a first kiss, a major athletic win, or a significant academic accomplishment. The extent to which the amygdala and hippocampus are triggered will govern the depth to which the memories are encoded.

In this regard, phobias technically don't simply come from *bad* experiences. They come from having *strong emotions* at the time of that experience. For example, if you associate flying on an airplane with an especially terrifying flight you had or even reading about a plane crash, that indicates that you had a powerful emotional response when those thoughts—now memories—were encoded. However, you could also develop a fear of flying if you happened to read a story about a plane crash when you were in a particularly elated, euphoric, or excited state.

Interestingly, this process can even be elicited by fiction. After Steven Spielberg's blockbuster movie *Jaws* was released in 1975, there was a sudden upsurge in fear of sharks, about which the public had previously shown little interest, let alone dread. The movie "generated an unprecedented audience response of excitement and terror,"[7] writes historian Beryl Francis. "The idea of marauding sharks became entrenched in the psyche of bathers around the world, creating a fear that the media exploited." Even today, "the perception that sharks are 'stalking, killing machines' remains in the public's psyche."[8] Indeed, a study published in 2015 found that 51 percent of Americans expressed being "absolutely terrified" of sharks, and 38 percent said they are scared to swim in the ocean because of them, even though there are fewer than one hundred shark attacks recorded worldwide each year.[9]

What makes exposure therapy so powerful, as I have realized over many years of working with the process, is that we are using the very power of our fear response *against itself.* By facing one's fears head-on, the patient experiences a surge of intense emotion—their amygdala and hippocampus are brought online (so to speak). This allows the cortex to encode a new memory, one that does *not* involve the fear response. *The ability of exposure therapy to elicit a strong emotional response is precisely what makes it so effective.* This may explain why relaxation dulls the effects of exposure treatment; when we decrease the intensity of our emotional response during exposure, the amygdala and hippocampus aren't engaged as much, and the new memories of overcoming our fear aren't seared into the brain as deeply.

I should add that Professor Edna Foa, another pioneer of exposure therapy who has worked with Dr. Barlow, has identified the neurobiological progression I've been describing, which she calls "emotional processing." Foa describes this as "the process by which accurate information is incorporated into the fear structure and modifies the pathological elements in the structure."[10]

Along these lines, another rule of thumb with exposure therapy is that the emotional strength of the event will largely determine the extent to which your memory is crystallized. By purposefully activating your fear response to ramp up your emotional involvement, you are learning to inoculate yourself against future cognitive threats. *When you activate your fear response instead of running away from your fear, it becomes a catalyst for change and growth.* For that reason, I don't think of the change that results from exposure therapy as a "cure," because you're not curing a disease or malady. It's much *better* than that. You're turning it into a strength—and into a gift. I'm not necessarily saying that people who undergo exposure therapy will never fear anything again, but I *am* saying that those who face their fears are transcending their anxiety by developing it into a strength to help them cope with the threat of fear in the future. It will make you more resilient in handling fear when it does crop up.

Overcoming a Phobia in a Single Day

One patient of mine named Darlene grew up in a home that, unbeknownst to her family, harbored a nest of spiders. When she was still a child, her brother was bitten many times and became sickened. In one case, he had to go to the hospital. Witnessing that event was terrifying and embedded a profound fear of spiders in Darlene's memory. Simply speaking about this connection in a therapist's office wasn't nearly enough for her to remove the feeling of terror that sprang up at the sight of the tiniest spider. Despite her awareness of her fear, her world became smaller and smaller over time. By the time Darlene came to my office, her phobia had gotten to the point where she would shake out her bedclothes at night to be certain no spider was hiding there. She would not be able to sleep if she saw so much as a small shadow that resembled a spider (or anything close). And needless to say, she would never go out in the woods for fear that a spider might drop on her from a tree.

We began relatively early in the morning, having Darlene look at still pictures of spiders in my office. She winced and closed her eyes at first, but I encouraged her to take a good long look. Over the course of a few hours, her anxiety subsided enough that we could make it to an exhibit on spiders at the American Museum of Natural History. The exhibit was definitely an immersive experience—there were enlarged (human-sized!) pictures of spiders, webs, nests, and more. Live, exotic specimens were placed behind glass enclosures. Darlene turned white. At one point she froze completely, and at several points she felt the need to sit down and catch her breath. I could almost see her hippocampus "firing up" inside her midbrain, searing into her mind new memories that she was not truly in danger. It took three to four hours, but eventually Darlene felt relatively comfortable. She was able to walk around the exhibit, and on a few occasions I even "caught" her looking inquisitively at the spiders instead of showing a grimace.

We broke for a well-earned late lunch, and then it was time to up the ante. I introduced her to my friend Mike, the "spider wrangler" (yes, there are such professionals), who brought an assortment of live spiders—including several tarantulas—to my office. Mike explained that tarantulas seldom bite, and only do so in self-defense, such as if they are pinned down on their backs. Darlene and I agreed not to try to elicit that response, and we proceeded to view, and eventually handle, the spiders. We started with one the size of a thumbnail and worked up to a big, hairy one about six inches in diameter. The highlight of the day was at the end: Darlene posed for a picture with a hairy tarantula perched on her shoulder. In just one day, she had overcome her phobia, and now, several years later, it has still not returned.

How does exposure therapy work? Well, as Darlene will tell you, it wasn't a pretty sight. Several times during the day, she felt she would vomit—I recall that at one point I heard her make an audible gag. She also reported that her level of anxiety during the exposure treatment in my office was even higher than she had felt when her brother almost died! This is actually an important clinical factor: in order to encode a new set of thoughts of spiders into her cortex, Darlene needed to activate her amygdala and hippocampus to the same extent (or higher) than when she had encoded her original fearful memories. In this sense, the more the midbrain "heats up" through the experience of intense emotion during exposure therapy, the more readily the new memory will be scorched into your brain. As I stated earlier, this approach turns anxiety from a disorder into an asset—the more one feels anxiety during exposure therapy, the stronger its effects tend to be!

Other Fears

Specific phobias are unique in that they are highly discrete, which explains why they can be overcome so quickly. Most other anxiety and related concerns, such as social anxiety, panic disorder, obsessive-compulsive disorder, and generalized anxiety disorder, need more time to overcome. However, the same principles apply to anxiety in all its forms.

Just as exposure to the source of a phobia can effectively end your enslavement to the internal terror, applying these principles to coping with other anxieties allows you to reframe your thinking about what is generating your particular form of anxiety. In much the same way, you can become inoculated against your anxiety triggers so that your stress responses become increasingly less intense. The goal of exposure therapy is to get to the point where you tell yourself, in effect, *I don't give a damn if I feel anxious! I'm going to do this anyway. Even if my anxiety makes me feel uncomfortable, I'm not going to let my fear stop me. I'm a soldier, and I'm going to keep marching through the swamp!*

Given that anxiety has many forms, there are different ways of doing exposure therapy. Here are the four primary types:

Exposure Type	Examples of Treatment Methods
In-Vivo (Real-Life) Exposure	accompanying a patient on a plane; bringing a spider or snake into a session
Imaginal Exposure	thinking about a distressing situation with lots of detail; recounting a traumatic event out loud
Interoceptive Exposure	intentionally constricting one's breathing; running in place; increasing the temperature of the room
Virtual Reality Exposure	using digital devices (see below)

Which of these is most appropriate for a given patient depends on the nature of their specific anxiety or phobia. In some cases, several types of exposure may be useful in combination.

One limitation to in-vivo exposure is that some of the suggested actions may be impractical or downright dangerous. What if I don't have the resources to take several plane trips and pay for my therapist to come with me? What if I live in the country, far from any tall buildings? And of course, we cannot put war veterans back into combat situations to face their demons.

This is where the development of virtual reality (VR) has proven to be a godsend. In recent years, virtual reality exposure therapy (VRET) has grown in acceptance by the scientific community. At the same time, VR gear has become readily available and relatively inexpensive. Today there are several VRET kits that come preprogrammed with clinical scenarios to deal with post-traumatic stress disorder from combat experience, as well as other challenging situations.

Years ago at Dr. Antony's clinic, I used this approach with patients for flying phobias. Using a total-immersion headset that allowed a 360-degree view and even the ability to look out through windows, patients felt that they were on a jetliner. We also used large subwoofers that credibly reproduced the loud roaring sounds of jet plane engines and the feelings of turbulence. Using a computer with a monitor, I was able to program all sorts of scary situations—the appearance of lightning, the sound of a thunderclap—all while communicating with the patient through a headset. This field is much more accepted now, but back at that time (2012) Dr. Antony wrote:

> VR for social anxiety is not widely available as a self-help treatment. However, centers around the world offer VR treatments administered by experienced VR therapists. . . . As VR becomes more widely available, we expect to see innovations in the use of this technology for treating social anxiety and other anxiety-related problems.[11]

Avoidance: The Strategy That Never Works

The opposite of exposure (facing one's fears) is avoidance, which is akin to the "flight" aspect of the fight-or-flight response. Avoidance takes many shapes. I have learned in my clinical practice that humans are astonishingly creative at avoiding uncomfortable feelings, especially when those feelings hide fears that we have chosen not to deal with because they don't fit with our preferred self-image. And anxiety is particularly uncomfortable. There are literally thousands of ways to avoid our anxieties, many of which we are unaware of.

The Cognitive Behavioral Model of Anxiety

The main problem with avoidance in all its forms is that it maintains the link between our thinking and our anxieties. As we learned from Dr. Aaron Beck in chapter 2, our feelings are caused by a two-step process: something happens, and then we *think* about what happened. The second step (not the first!) determines how we feel.

How do you change the way you *think*? Well, one particularly effective way is to change how you act. *The way we behave changes the way we think, which in turn influences how we feel.* That may seem counterintuitive; people often assume that the way they think or feel affects their actions. But the reverse is also true. When you do something positive, it's likely to affect the way you feel about things in a positive sense, and you are more likely to repeat that positive action. *In short, your emotions follow your behaviors.*

Sometimes the actions that change how you feel can be relatively minor. In one classic social psychology study, for instance, two groups of subjects watched cartoons and rated how funny they found them. The control group just watched the cartoons, while the second group were told to hold a pen in their teeth, making their face involuntarily take the form of a smile throughout the cartoons. This group found the same cartoons funnier than the control group, simply because their face was effectively smiling.[12]

To translate this into everyday life, if you go into an office meeting and you look down at the floor because you fear making eye contact, you'll be less likely to be called on to share your opinions. This might make you feel less anxious in the moment, but if you continue to practice this form of avoidance, you will *always* feel anxious because you'll never learn to be brave at work. Avoidant actions maintain the link between fear and anxiety. Conversely, if you sit upright and look people in the eye to exude a sense of confidence externally—even if you feel small inside— you *will* change your thinking and be more likely to have opportunities for professional growth, which will increase your confidence further.

COGNITIVE-BEHAVIORAL MODEL

The cognitive model (chapter 1) was later expanded to include behavior and renamed the cognitive-behavioral model. It teaches us that the way we behave shapes our thoughts, which in turn influences how we feel. Along these lines, when we act afraid, we are more likely to have anxious thoughts and experience anxiety.

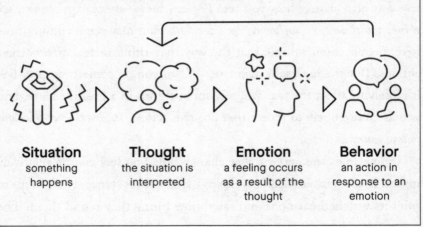

Situation
something happens

Thought
the situation is interpreted

Emotion
a feeling occurs as a result of the thought

Behavior
an action in response to an emotion

What's the Big Deal?

You might ask, *What if I avoid certain things that make me anxious just because I don't like them? Is this really such a big deal?*

The problem with avoidance is that if you continually "flee" from that which makes you uncomfortable or anxious, you will never get the data you need to change your thinking, and so your anxious emotions will always remain stuck around that situation. Remember John, the anxious driver from chapter 1? Once I explained to him that even a severe panic attack made him a sharper, safer driver, he decided to push himself and drive. It was challenging at first, but over time he got better and overcame his fears.

Similarly, when people with social anxiety and shyness decide to speak up, wear bold clothing, and make small talk, they typically relish learning that, almost always, no one else notices their anxiety. In fact, people with social anxiety tend to command more respect from others once they overcome some of their anxiety—since they speak less, their words are valued more. But avoiding situations reinforces the underlying fears and doesn't allow these concepts to penetrate.

We need to understand that in most cases, thinking about anxiety-related subjects and experiences is not accurate, so our anxiety is misplaced. The vast majority of things that evoke anxiety are probably never going to materialize. People who suffer from fear of flying say they are afraid they might die in a plane crash. And yet, the annual risk of being killed in a plane crash for the average American is about *one in eleven million*, whereas the annual risk of being killed in a motor vehicle crash is only about one in five thousand.[13] So if you have fear of flying, it isn't because you looked at a mortality table. Avoidance reinforces these false anxiety beliefs and makes them a part of your personality. By contrast, facing our fears and venturing beyond our comfort zones enables us to reprogram our thoughts and, ultimately, overcome our fears.

I can't say often enough that the main drawback of avoidance is that *it maintains the link between your thinking and your fear.* And unless you face your fear, you won't get to realize that the consequences you are afraid of are *highly unlikely to occur.* It's not enough to just understand this intellectually though. In order to generate the power needed to break that link, the process has to penetrate the heart of your mind via your gut, which requires facing your anxiety head-on.

Avoidance takes on three major forms: behavioral, cognitive, and pharmacological. Let's discuss all three.

Behavioral Avoidance

Behavioral avoidance encompasses overt, observable actions we use to prevent anxiety from occurring or to stop it as soon as it rears its discomfiting head. If you have a fear of public speaking, for instance, you might drop a class when you discover that you would have to give a speech in that class. In Darlene's case, as we saw, she avoided not only direct contact with spiders but situations where she *might* encounter an arachnid.

People who are triggered by financial anxiety may avoid balancing their checkbooks, reading their credit card statements, or even paying bills. Many people with panic disorder avoid certain places or activities, which can include exercising or even having sex, because those actions can raise our blood pressure and that can create panic-like sensations. Someone who has social anxiety may avoid raising their hand in class, asking someone out on a date, or even having their picture taken for social media because it might call attention to them. They may not go shopping for clothes because they don't want to ask the salesclerk for help. Likewise, people who have obsessive-compulsive disorder (OCD) are often afraid of contamination, so they may stop using public transportation where they are likely to come into close contact with others, or they may even stop touching their own phones. And if they do end up using public transportation, they may decontaminate themselves afterward. (One of my patients would strip down to his boxers at his doorstep each time after venturing outdoors.)

All of these avoidances are maladaptive because, along with perpetuating the initial anxiety, *they actually make things worse.* Paradoxically, the more someone avoids social situations, the more likely they are to find themselves out of touch with changing customs and, so, less able to navigate social waters. The more a person avoids dealing with their finances, the more likely life will compel them to pay even *more* attention to finances when their credit card is declined or the electricity is shut off. If you fear going to the dentist because you are extremely uncomfortable with dental procedures, you may end up needing even more uncomfortable procedures—instead of getting a tooth filled, you suddenly learn that you need a root canal!

Mark was a thirty-year-old programmer for a new internet company who was afraid to speak up at work, and as a result he was underappreciated. This was particularly painful to Mark because he often had great ideas for how to improve the business, but he never broached them in meetings. He was aware that other people in his office said stupid things all the time and made ill-advised suggestions that didn't work out. In frustration, Mark shared his ideas with a few coworkers he was comfortable chatting with alone, and then was doubly dismayed when they ended up voicing these ideas at meetings and getting credit—and promotions—for Mark's ideas. He got upset and depressed and realized he needed to address the situation in therapy. When he came in for treatment, he was shaking in his boots because he knew he had to make decisions about how to deal with his fear.

As we worked together, Mark slowly started to assert himself more in his office. Instead of confiding in a friend, he went to his supervisor with one of his new ideas. Although he found it difficult to work up the courage, he was gratified when his supervisor clapped him on the back and told him he had a really sound idea. That scenario repeated itself several times over a period of a few months, and Mark saw that he had already come a long way.

Relinquishing Control

A longtime friend of mine had an excessive fear of heights, so he asked my professional opinion. I told him that the best way to conquer his fear was to face it. I suggested that he go to the top of the tallest building he could legally gain access to and look over the edge of the roof. "You're crazy," he said. "There's no way I'm gonna do that! I could lose control of my bladder or bowels. I don't know what's gonna happen. I might even jump!"

I knew he wouldn't jump because he wanted very much to live. I also thought it was highly unlikely that he would soil himself, since he hadn't done this since he was a young child. "There's only one reliable method, and that is to let go of this fear," I insisted. "Stop fighting it, let go, and let it wash over you. Accept that you're not in control of your feelings all the time, and that's okay. Let yourself panic and march on."

My friend rejected my advice outright.

About a year later, however, I received an email from him saying that while on vacation in the Bay Area, he felt drawn to the Golden Gate Bridge. As he got there, he recalled our discussion and, without thinking much about it, he decided to traverse the entire length of the bridge on foot, looking over the railing as he did so. He said he was shaking the whole time. All the objections he had raised threatened to come over him: losing control of his bowel and bladder functions, the fear that he might impulsively throw himself into the bay. He said that it was the most terrifying thing he'd ever done, even though none of those things actually happened. But by the end of walking the bridge, he felt so happy because he had stood up to his anxiety. "I'm really glad that I was anxious, because now I learned that I *can* overcome my own anxiety," he said. *"I don't have to be in control!"*

Transcending Anxiety with Exposure Therapy

Rebecca, a twenty-two-year-old woman with OCD, was obsessed with the fear that she would have a brain aneurysm and die unexpectedly. Although Rebecca had no proof that she actually *had* an aneurysm, she was preoccupied with this fear. She obsessively tried to keep her stress level low because she believed that even a modicum of anxiety would cause her blood pressure to spike and her aneurysm to explode, and she would die. Over time, her avoidances grew more and more, to the point that she stopped dating because she was afraid that men would think she was crazy if she shared her fear. She even stopped leaving her house except to go to the school where she worked. One day, she was reading a magazine article about a person who had an aneurysm and died. After she read that, she couldn't even go to work for a few days. That's when she decided to come in for treatment.

We began by encouraging Rebecca to practice self-compassion in many of the ways described in chapter 2. I also had her see a neurologist and get an MRI; if we learned one thing about her brain, it was that she did *not* have an aneurysm. She was in perfect neural health, except for her obsessions. With that level of medical clearance, I told Rebecca that we would next be reading stories and watching videos about people who died from aneurysms. Her response was simple: "Hell, no! There is no way I'm doing that!"

"The decision is yours," I said. "But then I think you're going to be plagued by this fear and obsession for the rest of your life." Rebecca still preferred to try the other strategies for a couple more weeks, but when her anxiety didn't go away, she decided to give the exposure treatment a try.

We started by having her create a hierarchy of the graduated levels of her most feared outcomes, beginning with her fear of the very word *aneurysm*, to getting excited and having her blood pressure spike (which she feared would trigger an aneurysm that would require surgery), all the way up to her worst fear: being alone without her phone or ID, without her parents' knowing, and taking the "risk" that she might die with her body ending up unmarked in the city morgue.

Once we had assembled her hierarchy, we started slowly. First, we had her say the word *aneurysm*, but at first she could barely get it out of her mouth without freaking out. Over thirty minutes, we worked up to her saying it repeatedly, with a fair amount of anxiety but still at a level she could manage. She practiced accepting and tolerating her anxiety *without beating herself up*—simply experiencing anxiety and letting that be okay. From there, she progressed nicely.

Within a few weeks, we were having detailed discussions about aneurysms and even looked at illustrated medical pictures of aneurysms. Next, we were reading stories about people who died from aneurysms, including young people, which shook up Rebecca quite a bit because of her own age. At several points she started shaking and looking away from the screen, but I asked her to keep watching with me.

The following week, we took it up another notch and watched videos of brain surgery to correct an aneurysm. Rebecca said that was the most difficult thing she had ever done, yet within ninety minutes she was able to calm down and keep watching without letting her anxiety get the better of her. At that point, we targeted other aspects of her avoidance. For her "graduating" session, we asked Rebecca to check into a hotel room without using a credit card, leaving her phone at home, and jogging in place for ten minutes—all with no way for her family to know if she had had an aneurysm and died.

By the time we ran through the entire hierarchy of fears, not only had Rebecca become less anxious and less debilitated by her anxiety, but *she ended up stronger and more capable and confident than she had ever been.* I leveled with her that anyone can have an aneurysm at any time, although it was unlikely for her since she had been checked out much more thoroughly than most people would normally be. "We all have to live with some level of uncertainty," I told her. "All we can do is accept it and get on with our lives."

Rebecca took her newfound comfort with anxiety into her dating life, which improved markedly. We stayed in touch by email over the next year or two, by which time she had met someone and gotten married. After the wedding, we lost touch, but three years later I received an email saying she was having a flare-up of her anxiety and would like to talk again.

"I've got good news and bad news," Rebecca said by phone. "I'm pregnant. But the bad news is that they saw something in the ultrasounds of the baby's brain." It wasn't an aneurysm, but it did mean that after the birth the doctors would have to perform some sort of surgery to correct the baby's condition.

"You don't sound nearly as anxious as I would be if I were in that situation," I said. "I would say you're not even anxious—you're afraid, and that's to be expected."

"I'm drawing on everything you taught me," Rebecca said. "I'm recognizing I have to face uncertainty."

"You're doing great!" I said. "In fact, I think you may have a thing or two to teach *me* about anxiety!"

When the baby was delivered, the doctors did perform a critical surgery; the baby survived and was doing well when we last spoke. Most of all, though, I was blown away by how well Rebecca had handled the whole situation. Both of us realized that had she not acknowledged having crippling anxiety in the first place, and had she not learned how to manage it by facing her fears, she would never have handled this new life hurdle as well as she did.

Cognitive Avoidance: Checking Out

The best way I can describe cognitive avoidance is that it means being *physically present but mentally absent*. In essence, it's a shell game that you play with yourself by hiding your own feelings from your conscious mind, the way a con artist uses misdirection to hide a pea by moving three shells around.

I met with Anne, a woman in her thirties who had a fear of heights—specifically of taking elevators in tall buildings. Anne had accepted a position as an accountant at a large firm in New York City. She was thrilled because this was her dream job, but the only problem was that the office was on the forty-fifth floor. She called my office in a panic, saying that she needed to get over her fear of elevators in just one week. I explained that she would have to face her fear and that we would start by using exposure therapy. We went together to the Marriott Marquis in Manhattan, just off Times Square, which has a huge atrium with glass elevators that let you see just how high up you are—a potential nightmare for anyone with a fear of heights. We got on an elevator and I suggested that she look down through the glass as we ascended.

Anne didn't seem to be anxious at all after going up a few times, which puzzled me. Then I noticed a glassy look in her eyes, so I asked her what she was thinking about. "I'm thinking about anything at all *other* than the elevators. I'm in my head, completely somewhere else."

"As long as you're doing that," I said, "you're not going to get over your avoidance."

Anne was using her mind to try to trick her body. When people do that, exposure won't work because they are engaging the prefrontal cortex and its abstract thinking capacity, which does not allow the amygdala and hippocampus to "fire up" so that new memories can be encoded. In effect, by using cognitive avoidance, one is not achieving escape velocity because there isn't enough power being generated to lift you off from the old, anxiety-ridden memory. We may think that we're protecting ourselves, but cognitive avoidance prevents us from being able to change.

To some extent, we all engage in cognitive avoidance at times without being aware of it. We may have uncomfortable moments in a social situation and immediately look down at our phones instead of engaging with fellow humans. We may blast away our negative emotions through binge-watching Netflix since this occupies our mind with less aversive things. It's an easy escape to be physically present but mentally absent by thinking about a meal we just had, an outfit we'd like to buy, or a ballgame we were watching last night instead of what's really bothering us.

Levels of Dissociation

Sometimes the mind gets so good at avoiding upsetting thoughts that it takes us out of reality. (I'm not talking about a psychotic state, such as schizophrenia, which is not an anxiety disorder and which has more complex causes.) When emotions are intense and we get really good at distracting ourselves from them, we may develop what's called *dissociation*. When we dissociate, we are not mentally present. This often happens in the aftermath of having been in combat or a car crash or having experienced abuse in childhood. This state consists of blunting emotion so that we feel detached from ourselves. It's the brain's way of helping us to calm down in the short term, but if it lasts more than thirty days, then it's important to get professional help.

In more intense forms, dissociation can lead to *derealization*. This is hard for me to describe because, fortunately, I have never experienced this state, but my patients have said it is a dreamlike, disturbingly eerie feeling that the people and things around them are not real.

The next level of dissociation is called *depersonalization*, during which a person momentarily forgets who they are. They lose a sense of personal identity and feel like they are observing their body from outside it. In extreme situations, people may even have a breakdown in memory and forget their own pasts altogether. Again, this is hard to describe in words, but certain movies, like Alfred Hitchcock's *Vertigo*, have succeeded at visually portraying this kind of fugue state of disorientation, often triggered by intense stress.

The good news is that in most cases, varying levels of disorientation can be overcome. Should you encounter any of these conditions, it's important to figure out what is triggering the state, which is usually extreme anxiety or a memory of trauma.

A client I worked with named Mateo had been serving in Afghanistan when he came under fire while driving an armored vehicle. An explosion on the road just in front of him caused him to swerve reflexively to one side to prevent him and his fellow troops from being killed. Unfortunately, the only path available was occupied by a young Afghan child, whom he ran over and killed.

Mateo was far more traumatized by running over the child than by his own brush with death. But as he related his story in my office, he seemed to be zoning out. He clearly did not want to relive this event, which he had largely blocked from conscious memory. During treatment, he was able for the first time to recapture a memory of the boy's mother crying out in grief and anger at Mateo. But he also needed to come to terms with his own grief and pain. We eventually had a series of virtual reality sessions programmed to re-create that kind of scenario so that Mateo could be exposed to the situation again and again, until it lost its power to terrorize his mind.

Worry As Avoidance

Not all forms of cognitive avoidance are as extreme as dissociation. In fact, the most common anxiety condition—generalized anxiety disorder (GAD)—typically centers around the original description I gave earlier: being *physically present but mentally absent.*

Professor Thomas Borkovec, a psychologist at Penn State, believes that worry (the central symptom of GAD) is not a feeling or a thought but rather a *behavior*.[14] Specifically, Borkovec says, worry is the mind's way of avoiding facing the real extent of our fears. When people worry incessantly, they typically repeat the same low-level concerns in their mind over and over again. They may think, *What if I have cancer?* or *What if I run out of money?* and those worries clink around in their head throughout the day.

However, when you speak with worrywarts, it's uncanny that they never answer their what-if questions; that is, they typically *avoid* truly thinking about what it would be like to have cancer. They won't truthfully think about what it would be like to need to consult with oncologists and undergo chemotherapy or surgery, and the impact it may have on their family to live with a deadly disease. Those who worry excessively about money don't actually go through mental exercises of thinking what it would be like to declare bankruptcy. Instead, they keep their anxiety at a low level by asking and perseverating constantly on superficial what-if questions. Worrywarts use worry to avoid having a truly overpowering and uncomfortable emotional response, and as a result, the worry *reinforces* the anxiety instead of alleviating it.

Given what we've learned already, it's obvious why worry tends to persist for so long. The amygdala and hippocampus never come online when we are worrying at low levels, so worrywarts never reset their experiences with new information. In reality, the sources of worry are generally not as likely to occur as previously thought. However, by not going into the concrete details about health or financial anxiety, individuals with GAD are left in a perpetual gray zone: they are slightly anxious and use cognitive avoidance as a thought-suppression technique to quash higher levels of anxiety.

Borkovec's counterintuitive theory has dramatically advanced clinical treatments of GAD. Exposure therapy is now used to treat people with obsessive worry by *having them detail specific high-level concerns more intensely than they have ever thought about before.* To achieve escape velocity from generalized anxiety, we need to turn on our emotional rocket boosters and engage the amygdala-hippocampus connection.

Borkovec developed a process of setting aside a thirty-minute worry period. In clinical practice, the worry period is scheduled for the same time and in the same place every day. During the worry period, patients with GAD are encouraged to have more intense and detailed worries than they've ever had. To do this, they create their own script in first person, present tense, to make it feel more immediate. In the case of financial worries, a script might look something like this:

I'm standing at the cash register with a pile of groceries in my cart. My credit card is declined by the card reader. I put in another card, and that is also declined. Then I enter my bank debit card and that is declined too. The clerk says they will hold my groceries behind the counter while I go in search of cash or call my bank. The people in line behind me are groaning and starting to move to another register. I call my bank and am told that my overdraft protection won't cover the shortfall because I don't have the funds. I am mortified and feel like a failure.

After patients write their script (usually with the help of a therapist), they are encouraged to say it out loud, or they can record it on their phone and play it back, over and over again during the worry period. Whenever patients feel tempted to worry throughout the day, they are urged to tell themselves that they will deal with their concerns during the worry period. This helps them to *stop* worrying superficially, which is an avoidance, and only engage in the process of exposure, which helps them approach and ultimately overcome their anxiety. Over a period of a few weeks, GAD patients who implement this approach generally come to a state of acceptance and start to feel better.

Pharmacological Avoidance

Just as we may try to bypass negative emotions by avoiding situations that make us feel anxious, or by avoiding thinking about such situations, we can also numb ourselves through the use of alcohol and drugs—recreational and prescription—to distract the mind as a way to avoid confronting our fears. This is possibly the most dangerous form of avoidance, given the potential for addiction. Yet addiction is only one red flag I associate with this maladaptive coping strategy. In my view, the larger danger is that relying on alcohol and drugs can prevent us from facing our fears, which in turn increases the likelihood that our anxiety will spiral in the destructive ways I described in chapter 2.

We can't overlook that the primary purpose of using prescription or recreational drugs is to avoid negative emotions. Taking psychiatric meds *reactively* (per required need) whenever you feel an onrush of fight-or-flight symptoms tends to give anxiety a lot of power over you in the long run. If you are using substances, whether prescribed or not, you'll never need to transcend your anxiety. And then your anxiety will always be in control of you, to some extent.

Does that mean we should never take prescription medications? Of course, the answer to that is a firm no. However, identifying who is a good candidate for medication and to what extent, when, and which medications to use are *very* complex clinical questions.

We've all learned a lot from the opioid crisis, physicians and patients alike. People with intense physical pain take painkillers because they (believe they) cannot transcend the pain on their own. However, it's now abundantly clear that by taking opioids such as OxyContin when pain is initially high, people lose their tolerance to the drug and stay on similar or higher doses even when their pain decreases. This, in turn, decreases their tolerance for pain, and in many cases the painkillers take control of their lives. Responsible doctors now understand that opioid painkillers should be a last resort, and even then they should be used sparingly— giving patients an opportunity to face and increase their tolerance to "breakthrough" pain, which involves sudden, brief flare-ups of pain from chronic conditions like arthritis or cancer.

The sudden flare-up of an attack of intense anxiety or panic is a kind of psychological equivalent to breakthrough pain. If someone has a sudden eruption of panic or anxiety, and they immediately resort to a pharmacological intervention to tamp down their distress, it's important that they learn—at least partially—to face and manage their anxiety. Bringing anxiety into a manageable range using chemical means, by taking medications precisely as prescribed by a responsible clinician, is not only a good thing but also a form of self-care. More than half of my patients take prescribed medications, and many benefit from them. However, the responsible pharmacologists that I collaborate with all recognize the importance of not snuffing out 100 percent of a patient's anxiety by using medications, because this leaves them more susceptible to anxiety in the long run.

The federal government now recognizes that one particular class of anxiety drugs—benzodiazepines (for example, Xanax, Valium, Klonopin, and Ativan)—has significant risks, and that many people want to get off them. Early in 2022, an arm of the National Institutes of Health (NIH) announced to researchers that they were soliciting grant applications "to facilitate the deprescribing of benzodiazepines for individuals who wish to cease use of this medication or for individuals for whom harm of benzodiazepine use may outweigh benefits." The NIH is using the immense power of its grant purse by issuing funding specifically for research to develop ways to have physicians and therapists help certain patients stop using this class of drugs.[15]

Proactive Vs. Reactive Pharmacology

The most widely utilized prescription for psychiatric conditions is Xanax (alprazolam), which belongs to the class of drugs known as benzodiazepines (benzos, for short). In 2018, it was prescribed an astonishing twenty-one million times in the United States alone.[16] Xanax has a half-life as short as six hours, which means it goes in and out of the human system relatively quickly. Along these lines, Xanax is often prescribed "per required need" (PRN), which means that patients are instructed to take the pills when they feel an onset of anxiety, in order to stop feelings of distress before they get intense.

If I had to pick my *least* favorite way of dealing with anxiety, it would be prescribing a benzodiazepine on a PRN basis. The main message of this prescription is that people cannot tolerate high anxiety, and the mechanism provides an escape hatch so the patient never learns how much distress they can tolerate—certainly they don't habituate to the distress or overcome it.

In his excellent and alarming book *Anatomy of an Epidemic: Magic Bullets, Psychiatric Drugs, and the Astonishing Rise of Mental Illness in America*, investigative journalist Robert Whitaker has a full chapter dedicated to the topic of benzos, and Xanax is front and center.[17] His conclusion is very simple: *incidence and severity of anxiety disorders has grown by leaps and bounds since benzos have become mainstream.* Providing a fast-acting, reactive relief from anxiety perpetuates our fear of fear, and the anxiety spiral grows over time.

Not all medications are created equal, however. Many times, anti-depressant drugs such as Celexa or Zoloft (both in the category of selective serotonin reuptake inhibitors, or SSRIs) are used for anxiety. Unlike PRNs, such drugs are almost always taken daily at a prede-termined time (morning or evening) and typically do not have any clinical effect for at least four to six weeks after starting the regimen. In such cases, patients *must* tolerate their anxiety for a period of time before achieving a therapeutic effect. Furthermore, these types of medications will not extinguish anxiety if taken acutely or in larger quantities. SSRIs, then, are a decent pharmacological option, espe-cially for individuals who don't have the financial resources to engage in psychotherapy, or individuals who are too distressed to get out of the house into a therapy room.

Here are a few key recommendations to follow to make sure one is using medications responsibly, in a way that doesn't conflict with the principles and advice that I've been recommending in this book:

1. **Maintain medical oversight.** Has a responsible physician approved of your medication use? If you think it may be necessary to increase or decrease your dosage, never do so without consult-ing with your prescriber.

2. **Use caution when taking nonprescription medications.** Self-medicating is always a tricky business. Many people feel there's no harm in having a few drinks or using marijuana to relax—and there may not be on occasion—but you should follow guidelines similar to using prescription meds. What would your doctor say about your level of use? If there would be a medical objection, it's important to rein things in.

3. **Don't rely on medication alone.** Most important, are you also seeking guidance from a therapist? If you can't afford psychotherapy and your health insurance doesn't cover it, support groups can provide a place to process how you feel with the comradery of others. Either way, the goal of medication should not be to get rid of your anxiety but to take it down to a manageable level so that you can learn to use it to thrive.

Benzos on the Job

Mario, an emergency medical technician (EMT) with his local fire department, was in his midfifties. Although Mario enjoyed his work, he found the job stressful, so much so that he had occasional dizzy spells and constricted breathing as a result of panic attacks. One of his friends at the firehouse confided in Mario that taking a small dose of Klonopin (a benzodiazepine) helped him relax during stressful times, and he offered to share his meds with Mario, who began taking a 0.5 mg pill whenever he felt anxious. But over time, he was taking them three, even four, times a day.

Soon, Mario found that he relied on the pills to get to sleep after hectic twelve-hour shifts. He also noticed that he was feeling more anxious over time, whenever he wasn't taking Klonopin. He started using the pills when he was in social situations because he noticed that his hand was twitching—a problem he had never had before. Mario decided to come in for treatment and we had a conversation about tolerating anxiety.

Mario said that while he could tolerate everybody *else* being stressed out around him, he couldn't tolerate his own level of anxiety.

I asked, "What if you could learn to tolerate your own anxiety?"

Mario looked puzzled and asked me, "What do you mean?"

"You're avoiding your anxiety through your use of meds," I said. I explained that he could use the kinds of exercises I've described in this book to be able to tolerate his anxiety better. I also put him in touch with a psychiatrist, covered by his health insurance, to help him understand which medication, and how much, he should be using given his current level of tolerance.

Mario's psychiatrist identified that he was too "stuck" on Klonopin to switch completely to a different class of medication. So he prescribed Valium (another benzodiazepine), without a PRN. Mario took one dose each night before bed, another when he woke up each day, and one more at three o'clock to get through the afternoon. Over the course of about a month, the afternoon dose was eliminated, and eventually his morning dose was cut in half.

Alongside these changes, Mario worked with one of my clinicians on exposure therapy. He identified situations that made him feel uncomfortable and ways to increase his tolerance of dizziness, and he got to work! For instance, Mario sat in a swivel chair and turned around ten or fifteen times until he felt *very* dizzy. We also had him breathe through a narrow coffee straw to simulate the feeling of constricted breathing. He felt super uncomfortable doing these exercises, but they were not dangerous. Over time, he was able to work up the straw-breathing from ten seconds to twenty seconds and finally up to a minute and two minutes.

Two months later, Mario looked like a new person. He was down to just a half dose of Valium at nighttime to help get to sleep, and his tolerance for anxiety had increased by leaps and bounds. He still had some work to do, but he was on the right track, truly transcending his anxiety instead of letting it rule over his life.

. . . .

TOOL #3: FACING UP TO ANXIETY

Anxiety is scary, but—as long as we stand up to it and don't let it rule our lives—it's not more powerful than we are. Facing anxiety requires activating strength and courage that we have inside. Further, when we confront our anxiety head-on, we use it for good by searing into our minds that we have deep internal reservoirs of strength. The most concrete step we can take to actualizing this is simple: *start facing your anxieties!*

Consider just one anxiety that you could start to face at this point in your life. Ask yourself: *What am I avoiding because of anxiety? Are there any situations I steer clear of* (behavioral avoidance*)? Do I stop myself from thinking about certain things* (cognitive avoidance)? Here are some common fears and various forms of avoidance that people tend to engage in.

Anxiety	Avoidance
Spiders	Going camping
Flying	Planes, airports, videos of flying
Shyness	Speaking up in class, meeting new people, parties
Panic (for example, heart palpitations)	Exercising, having sex
Post-traumatic stress disorder (for example, accidents)	Driving, stories or videos of accidents, war films
OCD (for example, contamination fears)	Public toilets, shaking hands
Agoraphobia	Leaving home, situations where you might panic

Medical or dental	Visits to doctors or dentists
Public speaking	Office meetings, conferences, seminars
Financial	Balancing checkbook, credit card statements

- Pick one anxiety from the list (or another if it's more relevant) and identify how you avoid it.
- Now, visualize yourself facing your anxiety by eliminating, or decreasing, the avoidance. Take a moment to envision what it would be like to transcend your anxiety to some degree.
- Then, when you're ready, take a step forward. Face your fear. Allow yourself to feel anxious! And relish the difficult but wonderful process of resetting your thinking and transcending your anxiety.

· ·

PART 2

ENHANCING CONNECTION WITH OTHERS

CHAPTER 4

KNOWING OTHERS

Anxiety Can Help Us Be Attuned to Others' Emotions

In part 1 (chapters 1–3), we focused on how anxiety can enrich our relationship with ourselves by enhancing our self-knowledge and self-compassion and providing opportunities to transcend our perceived limits. In part 2 (chapters 4–6), I will shift gears and describe how anxiety can foster greater closeness and connection with other people.

The basis of all relationships (with ourselves, with others, and with spirituality) is knowledge and awareness. To this end, chapter 4 focuses on illustrating how *anxiety can help us thrive by improving our awareness and responsiveness to others' emotional tendencies and states*. Emotional awareness may seem like an intuitive, subconscious, and uncontrollable process—something we are either born with or not. But psychological science has revealed that being aware of others' feelings, as well as understanding and managing them, involves clear skills that almost anyone can learn. Such skills—which are critical for forging and maintaining close relationships with others—can be *greatly* enhanced by our own experience of anxiety. This chapter will show you how.

Learning from Our Own Anxiety

Curt had first come to see me when he was nineteen years old because his parents were concerned that he wasn't doing as well in college as they expected. I found Curt to be surprisingly well-adjusted and personable. Yes, he was more interested in socializing with friends than applying himself to the advanced business courses his family wanted him to take in preparation for a role in his family's real estate business. But he was happy and not unsuccessful in any significant way. In effect, the main issue I felt that Curt needed help with was how to cope with his family's excessive and unhealthy expectations.

After a few sessions, Curt's parents lost interest in paying for therapy since they disagreed with my assessment that he was doing very well. I next heard from Curt when he was in his midthirties. By that point he was financially independent and could afford therapy on his own. But he was still feeling pressure from his family to be more aggressive and productive with his work within the family business.

The crux of the problem seemed to be that while Curt's brothers were routinely making lucrative deals, he wasn't quite as driven to be as productive as they were, since he wasn't as good at playing "hardball" during negotiations, nor was he majorly successful at closing deals. At the same time, Curt had a highly valuable, albeit somewhat intangible, skill: he was able to keep the family unified and on an even keel. Curt was the one who smoothed things over when tensions and tempers started to get out of hand—in some cases threatening to destroy the entire business. He was also the primary reason why the lower-level employees were happy. While his brothers routinely ruffled feathers by focusing almost entirely on the bottom line and business growth, Curt genuinely understood what each employee needed in order to stay on staff. He was, in essence, the head of human resources, although that was not his job description or title. Curt was also much more connected to his own family. His marriage was wonderful, his kids adored him, and he was loved by virtually everyone he encountered. He was a generous, kind, and sensitive human being.

What was Curt's secret? As an anxious child who had struggled in school and suffered his share of teasing, Curt had learned at an early age to empathize with others who grapple with fitting in. Curt's sense of being a disappointment to his parents as a teen, and now as an adult, was also *a source of thriving* for him. He viscerally understood how critical it is for children—*all children of any age*—to be the apple of their parents' eyes. Curt also knew full well that all people have their strengths and weaknesses, and that academic or business success isn't the be-all and end-all of a happy life. This broad perspective on success enabled Curt to see the good in people, which helped him create rich interpersonal connections. More than anything, though, Curt was adept at channeling his inner pain and emotional struggle to be a source of recognizing and attending to others' challenges.

Curt rightfully felt unappreciated by his family because his parents and siblings compared him to the singular standard of monetary success. This was a major topic in our therapy sessions. I encouraged Curt to recognize that he was successful at what he *truly* cared about in life: relating to other people and finding ways to boost their spirits. Of course, it remained painful for Curt that his parents and siblings didn't appreciate his great capacity for empathy and interpersonal connection. But over time, he felt a weight being lifted from him and felt gratitude for his gift of being sensitive to others.

Curt also recognized that his strengths are erroneously viewed by many people as a weakness. In today's culture, we tend to prioritize productivity over relationships. We're obsessed with being successful! We respond immediately to work-related messages, sacrifice romance for career opportunities, and chase money at the expense of connection. These are not just bad habits; they have become societal values. We therefore underestimate, and often even forget, the great importance in simply sitting and discerning how other people are feeling: delving into their emotional experiences, seeing their physical sensations and actions and emotions, in order that we may connect with them on an emotional plane.

The Myth of Compassion Collapse

Many people believe that those who have suffered adversity become hardened and less open to others, but psychological science suggests otherwise. A 2019 study from Northeastern University[1] supports the opposite conclusion—namely, that most people who have faced significant adversity do *not* experience "compassion collapse," which involves shutting down when continually confronted with the suffering of others.[2] On the contrary: people with a history of adversity or trauma, the study suggests, generally feel *more* compassion for others.

In my clinical practice, the most compassionate people I've ever met have gone through significant life difficulties. I would even say those of my patients who have struggled with significant adversity are among the most thoughtful, compassionate people I know. *Having experienced anxiety, depression, or other mental health challenges can prime us to be more aware of other people's feelings.*

One of the best exemplars of this journey is Dr. Marsha Linehan, a renowned psychologist who developed dialectical behavior therapy (DBT). This treatment of borderline personality disorder (BPD) and other severe, complex mental conditions, including severe self-injury and suicidality, is remarkably effective; multiple trials across several independent research sites have concluded that its approaches are literally lifesaving for individuals with BPD.[3] Dr. Linehan's invaluable innovations in psychotherapy were born out of her own psychiatric history. At the age of seventeen, she was severely suicidal, psychiatrically hospitalized, misdiagnosed with schizophrenia, and given severely sedating medications and high-voltage electro-convulsive therapy, which was administered punitively in response to her desperate pleading for relief. Linehan despaired so profoundly in the context of her inhumane treatment that she prayed for divine help. "I was in hell," she later told a reporter. "And I made a vow: when I get out, I'm going to come back and get others out of here."[4]

Drawing on her own horrific experience, Linehan came to recognize two seemingly opposite concepts: (1) accept life as it is, not as it is supposed to be; and (2) change is necessary for growth and happiness. The "dialect" between these two concepts is the fundamental principle behind DBT. I find Linehan's story so inspiring in part because this is the very same principle that drives my own work: once we accept our anxiety and stop fighting, it ironically becomes easier, not harder, to change, since we are better able to regulate our emotions and connect to others (and to the spiritual). The main point here, however, is that Dr. Linehan likely would not have developed her unique form of therapy if she hadn't grappled herself with acute distress.

People with intense anxiety often learn valuable interpersonal skills because of—not in spite of—their anxiety. Significantly, many of my patients have gone on to become mental health professionals after coming to terms with their emotions. *It is infinitely easier to relate to others when you have experienced distress yourself.*

Anxiety Can Enhance Our Awareness of Others' Feelings

How does anxiety help us to know and understand others' distress? One primary way is that our own suffering can heighten our compassion for others. I've seen this especially in the work I've done with patients who have social anxiety disorder. A hypervigilant attitude can get in the way of happiness and also makes it harder to connect with others, since we are likely to overthink and to filter out too much of who we are during social interactions. However, people with social anxiety tend to be *extraordinarily* aware of others' thoughts and feelings, because the core of the disorder is an excessive fear of others' negative evaluations and afflictive emotions.[5] By contrast, those whom we might call the "life of the party" are often oblivious to other people's feelings. In some ways, the heightened social-emotional awareness of those with social anxiety is a gift.

For one of my patients, it was particularly clear that the same social anxiety that was his greatest weakness was also a great strength *when channeled correctly*—one that helped him be more aware of and responsive to the people in his life. Alan was feeling stuck in his job because he had been passed over for promotion several times. As we explored his situation, it came out that Alan was shy and excessively attuned to how others respond to him. As a result, he was understated and overly modest, out of concern for what others were thinking and feeling. I pointed out to Alan that this apparent weakness was also a strength. Alan's thirty-five-year marriage was strong because he's an extremely considerate person. He was attuned to his wife's needs, emotions, perceptions, vocal intonations, and facial expressions. For this reason, in his wife's eyes, and many women's eyes, he is an ideal husband. Of course, in our work together Alan needed to employ the strategies we learned in part 1, particularly chapter 3 ("Transcending Ourselves")—but when it comes to understanding others, his anxiety was a tremendous gift.

Many of today's relationships are tenuous at best. People are more prone than ever to get divorced, to end a relationship of any length over minor disagreements, to drop their friends, to "unfriend" or "unfollow" them on social media, or to "ghost" them—disappearing with no notice or explanation. Such behaviors typically occur in the absence of compassion, social-emotional awareness, and empathy for others' feelings. This is a shame. *If only we could recognize that the high levels of anxiety many of us feel today can be a catalyst to connection.* Anxiety can help us be more aware of others' complexities and struggles. Anxiety can help us pay attention to other people's feelings and experiences. When we use our own distress as a barometer to gauge and understand the feelings of others, we can enhance our connections and love. This is especially true in romantic relationships; a certain amount of anxiety can be especially attractive. This was the case with Alan, who used his experiences to pay attention to his wife's emotional states and nonverbal cues, instead of being oblivious and focusing only on his own wants and needs.

The Value of People-Watching

The main purpose of this chapter is to show how observing and acknowledging your own anxiety can make you more sensitive to the emotions of others. We are learning that our capacity for interpersonal emotional engagement is potentially *enhanced* by anxiety in counterintuitive ways. To emphasize this point, I would like to delineate how this can inform an approach to manage our own levels of anxiety.

Years ago, I learned from my religious mentors a surprising and simple concept: *you can reduce your anxiety by getting outside of yourself, noticing the needs of others, and then responding to them.* This principle has long been acknowledged in many spiritual traditions, including my own. Eastern religions teach us that being more compassionate toward others helps us to feel better about ourselves. Feelings of loneliness and alienation largely derive from trying so hard to satisfy our own egos that we effectively separate ourselves from everyone else. Perhaps for these reasons, many religious communities have some form of outreach for helping others with medical needs, food, and clothing. This may be based on spiritual principles, but it is also understood that attending to the needs of others is a potent way of coping with our own anxieties and dissatisfactions.

The scientific community hasn't studied this relationship in much depth, but when it has, the results have been impressive. Even just *witnessing* kind and caring activities performed by others promotes positive emotions and reduced stress.[6] In a social-clinical psychology experiment of my own a few years ago, I asked about a dozen of my patients who had especially intense anxiety to gather in my New York City office, where I explained my plan. We would go outside with no other objective than to observe the people on the streets of Manhattan. We would "people watch" for one hour, with the intent of identifying others' emotions and trying to surmise what they might need.

It was during an evening hour and there were hundreds of folks streaming around the streets: hot dog vendors and construction workers; mothers and fathers with children in tow while shopping; people walking in and out of medical offices, hotels, and public transportation. They were of all ages, of diverse racial and ethnic identities, and of all social classes, from people driving around in limousines to people experiencing homelessness. Our goal was *not* to interact with people or even provide for their needs in a substantive way, but simply to observe what we could about these strangers' feelings and what might make their lives better.

After observing others for an hour, we reassembled in my office and spent the next hour discussing our experiences. There was a palpable sense of excitement in the room. People were so happy to have spent a full hour getting outside their own anxiety-filled heads and to have given their full attention to noticing other people's needs. Interestingly, *I found our group of anxiety patients to be particularly adept at identifying the needs of others.* They had noticed the slightest details, like the grimace on the hot dog vendor's face because it was cold and he seemed to have not sold many hot dogs, or a child smiling gleefully because she was holding her mother's hand. They didn't just notice *a homeless guy*; they saw that he was shoeless on one foot and had a hole in the left arm of his jacket. I pointed out that the more detailed we are in our awareness of other people, the more we are tuned in to their experiences. I also pointed out that having one's own anxiety is a potential catalyst to noticing the struggles—and happiness—of others.

The following week, we took things up a notch. Besides observing people, I asked my patients to interact with them by providing for their perceived needs in *any* way they felt drawn to do. If someone was coming out of a store with a package in their arms, one of us opened the door for them. When a patient noticed someone who looked like they were down on their luck, she made an effort to catch their eye and give a big smile. One member of the group even bought a hot dog, not because they were hungry but just to lift a vendor's spirits. These acts may not seem like a big deal, but when we regathered in my office, the excitement and happiness were even more palpable than the previous week. My patients realized that their own anxiety could enhance their connection with others—using their emotional challenges as a yardstick by which they could measure, understand, and attend to other people's feelings. Where otherwise they would have just walked by these total strangers, now they were able to develop a relationship with them, however brief.

A friend of mine who lived in downtown Manhattan for many years once told me about his own experience of coming face-to-face with houseless men who were often aggressively panhandling. Sometimes he would give them some change, which made him feel good for a minute. Other times he would rush past and rationalize his guilt by saying that they would probably only use the money to buy liquor or drugs. Then one day, frustrated by these limited options, he stopped to actually speak with a panhandler. Instead of handing over some cash, he looked him in the face and asked, "How are you doing this morning?"

The man was astonished, and his whole demeanor changed. "You're the first person who talked to me all week!" he exclaimed. "I'm not doing so great, but thanks for asking."

They were in front of a diner, so after a brief chat, my friend invited him to share a burger and fries. As they ate, they had a conversation during which the man discussed the dangers of living at a shelter, and he said that the hardest part of begging on the street was the feeling of utter isolation.

My friend shared with me that *his own feelings of loneliness at that time in his life made it easier for him to initiate that conversation.* He also shared that from that one experience, he would never look at people experiencing homelessness the same way again. As for my anxious patients, it's been many years (over a decade) since we participated in that social-clinical experiment, and to this day, I still get emails from time to time that those two hours were some of the most memorable and impactful we ever spent together.

Attachment Theory

The interactions I've been describing may seem superficial. Brief encounters with strangers or sitting down to a meal with a stranger won't solve the world's major social or economic problems. But understanding the mechanisms behind interpersonal relationships has inestimable potential—for ourselves and the world. Once again, we need to start paying more attention to what's going on.

Today it may seem surprising that it was not until the middle of the twentieth century that psychologists identified how foundational the relationship of young children to their primary caregivers is for mental health. The British psychologist John Bowlby was the first to develop *attachment theory*, which described the critical importance of "lasting psychological connectedness between human beings."[7] His theory began to take shape in the 1930s, when Bowlby was treating emotionally disturbed children in a London clinic, and he concluded that early infant separations from their mothers often led to ongoing inabilities to maintain effective relationships and cope with difficulties and stresses. Over the next twenty years, Bowlby continued to study and write about the importance of human attachment.[8]

At the time, the standard of medical care in the United Kingdom was remarkably insensitive by today's norms. Children who received even transient medical care were dropped at the hospital and left there for a week or more. *Parents were not allowed into the hospital and were instructed to pick up their children after treatments were completed.* Medical "care" was sterile, impersonal, and neither warm nor caring. Hospitals were more concerned with minimizing the spread of disease than providing children with any degree of the caring touch they needed. Bowlby observed that the children who received medical treatment fared poorly, not because of a lack of medical advancement but merely because they were lacking continuous personal interaction, responsive attention, and emotional connection.

Cloth Mothers

Bowlby's work had a momentous impact on the world of psychology. Attachment theory motivated the American psychologist Harry Harlow to carry out a series of classic studies on primate mothers and infants. Harlow investigated the mother-infant bond by separating young rhesus monkeys from their mothers shortly after birth. Some of the babies were given to a surrogate "mother" who dispensed milk but was made entirely from wire. Other babies were given to a cloth mother who did not dispense milk. Harlow found that monkeys raised by wire mothers had terrible negative outcomes, including severe psychological disturbances and even death.[9] In subsequent experiments, Harlow found something even more fascinating: when rhesus monkey babies were given the choice of a cloth mother (who did not provide milk) or a wire mother (who did provide milk), *they would choose the cloth mother and cling to "her" for comfort.*[10] Together, these studies produced groundbreaking empirical evidence for the seminal importance of the parent-child attachment relationship and the value of maternal touch in infant development.[11]

Attachment in Adulthood

Over the past two decades, reams of research have emerged suggesting that attachment needs persist throughout adult life.[12] This research is so strong that it has a basis in neurobiology.[13] Development of synaptic structures within key regions of the cerebral cortex implicated in long-term memory depend on our connection with others. The neuropeptide oxytocin, which is known to ease anxiety and depression, is produced and released by the hypothalamus in response to feelings of "love." And the neurotransmitter-hormone dopamine, which regulates motivation and pleasure, is also intrinsically tied to our relationships. In sum, human beings are social animals who are programmed for connection and intimacy.

For these reasons, developing and maintaining close emotional relationships with others isn't just good for our emotional well-being; our physical health depends on it.[14] It is now abundantly clear in the literature that attachment is a key predictor of physical health, including lower levels of inflammation, cortisol, and cardiometabolic risk across the lifespan. Individuals who have a secure attachment with a close relationship partner on whom they can rely for support have better ways of managing their negative emotions, and this regulation serves as a stress-buffer that minimizes "wear and tear" on the body.[15] This is especially the case for individuals with chronic diseases, such as asthma or other pulmonary conditions, Crohn's or ulcerative colitis, arthritis, and other inflammatory rheumatoid diseases. *Love is a form of medicine.*

One of my patients, a successful man in his midsixties who struggles with obesity and diabetes, is a veritable case study in this area. Over the course of three years, he was medically hospitalized on five occasions for high blood pressure, neuropathy, kidney dysfunction, and vascular complications that affected his eyesight and ability to walk. Notably, each of his hospitalizations was preceded by a significant altercation with his wife. Furthermore, upon resolution of their marital disputes (in therapy and otherwise), his medical concerns largely abated to the point that he was able to function day-to-day outside of a hospital setting.

I've said before that our relationships with others can be enhanced by anxiety. When we draw from our own distress to recognize others' feelings and empathize with them, it enhances our interpersonal connections. As a result, our emotional and physical health stand to benefit by leaps and bounds.

Learning to Be Emotionally Aware of Others

Over the past decade, a novel clinical approach has emerged, known as *mentalization based treatment* (MBT).[16] This form of psychotherapy was created in the United Kingdom by psychiatrist Dr. Anthony Bateman and psychologist Dr. Peter Fonagy. At the core of MBT is the concept of *mentalization*, which is the process of being attentive to the mental states of others with whom we are interacting. MBT teaches patients to "mentalize"—to become more aware of others' thoughts and feelings—as a way to cultivate their social-emotional capacity for empathy, which ultimately leads to more secure attachment with others and better relationships. Multiple randomized controlled trials of MBT have found that the simple act of learning to be conscious and mindful of others' thoughts and emotions has significant clinical effects, even for patients with complex and severe symptoms.[17]

If you were fortunate enough to have parents and caregivers who mentalized with you as you were growing up—feeding, changing, and comforting you, but also *helping you get through sadness and frustration by paying close attention to your shifting emotional states*—consider yourself blessed. Regardless, the mentalization literature suggests that becoming more emotionally aware of others is a skill anyone can learn.

A starting point is to be aware of Stephen Covey's "90/10 principle."[18] This simple but profound idea essentially states that up to 90 percent of human emotional experiences are based on what happened in the past, and only 10 percent is based on what's happening here and now. That concept is something people with anxiety can readily understand. As we saw in chapter 2, what's happening in the moment is only the trigger, and the way you *think* about it is what effectively shapes your emotional state. It follows that the way a person feels is *rarely* fully derived from their current circumstance. If you have anxiety yourself, you'll be more likely to *get it* that someone can walk into an airport on a perfectly calm, sunny day and still feel terrified at the thought of getting onto an airplane.

How Emotionally Aware Are You?

Mentalization of others' emotional states requires emotional awareness. Over thirty years ago, a self-report assessment of this ability called the Levels of Emotional Awareness Scale (LEAS) was developed. The scale reliably measures four levels of emotional awareness, and evidence suggests that this awareness helps us to self-regulate our emotions, navigate complex social situations, and enjoy relationships more fully.[19] While the scale is normally used by clinicians and researchers to evaluate patients and research subjects, we don't need to go into that much depth here. You can simply apply the four basic levels in ways that I'll show you. The levels of emotional awareness in progression are as follows:

1. **Awareness of others' physical sensations.** This involves being and remaining attuned to others' feelings of pain, pleasure, warmth, cold, energy, fatigue, aches, and the like. While not all

physical sensations represent emotions, all emotions have some associated physical sensations. Thus, being aware of the physical manifestations of emotions is a first step in emotional attunement.

2. **Awareness of others' action tendencies (behaviors).** This requires cultivating awareness of the expressive or instrumental behaviors associated with various emotional states. For example, as we discussed in chapter 3, anxiety and fear involve urges to flee, avoid, and escape. Sadness is often associated with hiding, social distancing, withdrawal, and oversleeping. Anger tends to be associated with a propensity to fight or attack. Regarding positive emotions, happiness, joy, and contentment are represented by smiling, heightened engagement, and energy.

3. **Awareness of others' (single) emotions.** At this critical step in the process of building emotional awareness, we transition from being aware of physical manifestations (sensations and behaviors) to perceiving the underlying emotions that they represent. As described above, this necessitates using some balance of close observation and intuition. More important, in practice it requires drawing from our own emotional experiences to understand the feelings that others are having at any particular moment.

4. **Awareness of others' complex (blends of) emotions.** This is similar to level three, except it involves recognizing that *emotions are often messy, nonlinear, nonlogical, and even contradictory or conflicting.* For example, you may simultaneously feel both anxious and excited when facing situations that make you nervous—anxious because of the apprehension, while excited because you are in the process of overcoming your anxiety. It's even possible to feel both sad and happy at the same time. For example, one may be mourning a sorrowful loss, while feeling internally happy about the fact that one's emotions seem appropriate given the circumstances.

Learning to Mentalize

Mentalization was developed as a tool for psychotherapy patients in distress, yet all human beings can benefit from learning to mentalize, regardless of where they may fall on the clinical spectrum (whether they are *flourishing, languishing, distressed,* or *severely distressed*).

In concert with the four levels of emotional awareness, the first step in the mentalization process is to become more aware of others' physical sensations. We are often so anxious to *get to the point* of a conversation that we don't take a moment to assess the physical or emotional well-being of the person we're talking to. When you initiate a discussion with someone, do you notice whether they look tired or cold or are sweating from the heat? Can you sense when they may be feeling physical discomfort or pain? If you see them swallowing a little bit extra, do you recognize that this may indicate they're thirsty? Simply noticing these aspects of others is a step toward mentalizing.

The second thing to focus on is others' behavior. Do you observe their facial expressions and body language? Are you aware when they seem distracted, fidgety, or overly focused on their phone? It has been said that as much as 90 percent of human communication is nonverbal.[20] Regardless of whether that is true, you can learn vast quantities about people's preferences, wants, needs, and feelings by observing what they do. Behavioral observation is so critical in clinical practice that most therapists are trained to record their patients' actions systematically in every psychotherapy note. Factors can include physical appearance, including grooming; ease of establishing and maintaining rapport; speed, pitch, quality, volume, and rhythm of speech; level of sustained attention and amount of redirection needed; mannerisms, habits, movements, posture, and much more. To mentalize, you need not formally assess for these aspects of human behavior, but it does require being aware of them to some degree.

The third and fourth major aspects of mentalization involve identifying people's (simple and complex) emotions. This can include *primary emotions*[21] that occur directly and spontaneously as the result of some sort of external cue. For instance, you may notice when someone feels joy in response to good tidings or events, sadness in times of loss, fear when they are threatened, disgust in response to something repugnant, or surprise when something happens out of the blue. Or it can include *secondary emotions*, which involve feelings that we have in response to our feelings—such as anger,[22] which is often an outgrowth of fear, or shame that may occur in the wake of anxiety or sadness. To make matters more complicated, emotions often fluctuate widely and can even contradict one another: a person can feel happiness one moment in response to getting into the top college of their choice, and then feel guilt, shame, or sadness a few seconds later after learning that their best friend didn't get in.

In this regard, mentalization is both an art and a science. It's also a skill that we tend to overlook. Yet it's invaluable for communicating, whether in social settings or even in business. *This is precisely why your own experience of anxiety can be such a blessing—it can enhance your ability to notice and understand other people's mental states.*

A Double-Edged Sword

We have learned that if you learn to harness the power of your anxiety to probe the lives of others, you will find that your own fears tend to diminish. We can thrive with anxiety by learning to use our own struggles to deepen our understanding of others' struggles. This will help us avoid catastrophizing, keep us from feeling shame, and help us experience a heightened sense of being connected with others and the world.

However, I must inject a strong note of caution here. If you focus *too* intently on others' anxieties and how they disturb you, you can wind up glossing over your own issues or blaming others for your distress. This is especially true of the relationship of parents to young children who are perceived as overly anxious.

Anxious Children—and Parents

A woman in her midthirties named Samantha came to see me about some problems she was having with her nine-year-old son. She had written out a long, detailed list of exactly what he had done and when he had done it, pretty much every day for the last thirty days. She had recorded when he went to sleep and when he woke up; what he had for breakfast and what he ate for lunch; whether he went to school or came up with excuses to stay home and play his older brother's video games; how much he used the phone she had given him as a security measure. On one hand, she was acutely aware of her child and she was trying to help him. But on the other hand, she wasn't at all focused on her relationship with herself.

I had seen Samantha previously for her own anxiety. At that time, I had suggested that she apply the strategies that I explored in chapter 1. She had done so for some time, but *fell off the wagon* and was now struggling. As a result, she was an anxious mess herself. Along these lines, Samantha was *far* more intent on documenting her son's misbehaviors than helping reduce his stress levels. As a result, Samantha was infecting her son with her own anxiety, and the more anxious he became, the harder he was to manage, which stressed Samantha even further. It was clear to me that Samantha needed to take a giant step back and realize that, in psychological terms, she was avoiding dealing with her own anxiety by focusing on her son.

I have never met an anxious child who did not have at least one anxious parent. And when parents don't deal with their own anxiety, they often point to their child's behavior. The Chinese sage Confucius wrote, "When you see a good man, think of emulating him. When you see a bad man, examine your own heart."[23] That's one way of saying that instead of focusing on the perceived faults of others, we should first look for the presence of those same faults within ourselves.

When I conveyed this to Samantha and encouragd her to refocus on her own anxiety, she initially seemed surprised. But since we had a good rapport, she laughed and acknowledged that she "might be a bit tense" when I pointed out her eyes were continually darting down to look at the phone in her lap. Samantha and I worked for a few months on her own anxiety—*without discussing her child*. The result? Not only did her own stress become less problematic but her child's anxiety also dramatically improved, without his receiving any therapy at all.

How did this happen? Once Samantha was calmer, she was able to look beyond her son's irritating and stress-inducing behaviors, and she paid more attention to his feelings. Instead of focusing on the hardships of her parenting experience, she saw and appreciated her son's anxiety. This induced compassion—instead of resentment—toward her son, and she spontaneously began helping him get to bed earlier, to improve his diet (no caffeinated drinks, less sugar), and to have more physical and social activity. Most of all, she focused more attention on communicating with him, which meant spending less time on her own phone when they were together.

In effect, Samantha had been projecting her anxiety onto her child, and both of them were faring poorly. *Projection* has been recognized in psychology for some time as a common defense mechanism by which we attribute thoughts and feelings that we cannot acknowledge as our own onto someone else. In my experience, when a person is projecting their unacknowledged feelings onto a family member or romantic partner, it's hard for them to recognize the pattern. In Samantha's case, she struggled to recognize her anxiety because she was focusing so much on her son. Conversely, when she acknowledged and dealt with her own anxiety using the strategies we discussed in part 1, she was able to thrive by empathizing and seeing her son's feelings. This created greater closeness and bonding for Samantha and her son, and both of them benefited from less anxiety as a result.

Avoid Blocking or Ignoring Your Anxiety

Anxiety can enhance our knowledge of others' emotions to the extent that we follow the guidelines in chapters 1–3. If you choose to block or ignore your anxiety, *reactively* medicate it away in the moment, fear it, catastrophize about it, judge yourself for it, or otherwise allow yourself to be trapped in the anxiety spiral, you will be cutting yourself off from a great tool to connect with others.

Shandra, a high school administrator in her forties, had a major anxiety problem. She came from a family in which both her father and younger sister had serious anxiety that they were all terrified to deal with, so much so that everyone in the family was in complete denial. Their modus operandi was not to acknowledge that there was a problem at all. As a result, when students at Shandra's school had anxiety or other mental health problems, she *always* dropped the ball. Shandra didn't even *see* the kids' mental health struggles—all she saw was that they were a burden. She judged them and was freaked out by their erratic behaviors because they subconsciously reminded her of her own (and her family's) struggles.

As you can imagine, at Shandra's school, mental health problems escalated exponentially for both the students and their parents. Shandra's staff were all too aware of the problem, and they detested her for this. They saw how she failed to support them when issues arose, and her approach invariably caused more harm than good. Rather then raise the issue with her directly, though, they covered up their feelings since they weren't empowered to express themselves. They even feared her retribution.

As a result, stress and anxiety were so high among the staff that they were quitting—which left Shandra even more stressed and anxious, and made the situation worse every day. I've had countless patients from her school, and the only advice I could give them was to avoid or work around Shandra until she quits. If I had to put Shandra's condition in one brief phrase, I would say she completely lacks *emotional attunement*.

Emotional Attunement

Who are your closest friends? Who are the family members you want to spend time with? Who were your favorite teachers growing up? If you are blessed to have a mentor, what are their qualities when it comes to perceiving your feelings?

All the people you feel most drawn to likely *value your emotions, understand how you feel, and respond appropriately to those emotions on a (relatively) consistent basis*. It's also likely that they have their own set of life experiences that they use as a barometer to understand your emotional landscape and attend to your needs. Put simply: the closest relationships we have are generally with individuals who are *emotionally attuned*.[24] *Attunement* means being "receptive or aware," but etymologically the word is a concatenation of the words *at* and *tune*. And so the deeper meaning of the word is to be "in harmony" or to "bring into harmony."[25] Indeed, there is something inherently harmonious when we feel understood and cared for emotionally by others.

The psychological science on attachment theory has clarified that if you want to be counted among your friends' and family's most trusted allies, you need to master your own ability to not only understand but *empathize and respond to* their feeling states.[26] This is easier said than done since, as stated earlier, emotions are subtle and, by definition, not always rational. Emotions are also immaterial and require some degree of intuition and inference. People often say that women are more intuitive than men, as if that is based on some sort of genetic or psychophysical predisposition. That may even be true to some extent,[27] but this is probably because women in Western society generally spend more time and devote more attention to reading the emotional states of other people, including one another. If we all spent more time being "tuned in" to others' feelings, our intuitive insights would increase across the board. Along these lines, emotional attunement can be learned and even measured, as we shall see.

Attunement is similar to mentalization but takes things one step further: *instead of just being attentive to others' mental states, attunement involves responding to those states in a way that shows that they have resonated internally.* Emotional attunement is a more sophisticated process that includes emotional awareness, empathy, and responsiveness.

Breaking down emotional attunement reveals a number of different processes. *First*, we need to recognize that others' emotions are important and worth paying attention to. *Second*, we need to spend time focusing on, observing, thinking about, and figuring out others' emotions (that is, what's going on under the surface of their behavior). This requires that we avoid becoming distracted from others' feelings. *Third*, we must use our observations of others' feelings to have explicit conversations about their emotions. We need to give others a chance to describe their feelings and to help them when they struggle to do so. These first three elements are similar to mentalizing.

Fourth, attunement requires *responding* to others' emotions. If a friend or coworker is sad, we can make an effort to find out what's troubling them and then respond appropriately. If someone seems anxious, we can help them calm down, perhaps by talking about it. And if they are angry, we need to find out why and address the point they are upset about (while being mindful of our own emotional well-being).

All these processes—particularly emotional responsiveness—require continuous practice and focus, and a high level of relational commitment. Just as we ordinarily spend copious amounts of time researching the best places to live, the cars that fit most comfortably within our budgets, or our next career moves, being emotionally attuned requires time, dedication, and effort. Especially in our current ethos of pursuing productivity and success as primary goals in life, most people need significant practice to become emotionally responsive as a coworker, friend, spouse, or partner.

The starting point for cultivating emotional attunement is our relationship with ourselves. When we recognize that our own emotions are important and worthwhile, when we spend time figuring out our feelings and making them explicit by speaking about them, and when we take the time to respond and manage and regulate our emotional states, we become much more adept at managing others' emotions as well. Our ability to be aware of and successfully manage our own feelings plays a key role in striving for harmonious relationships and intimate interactions with our loved ones.

Building Attunement

Like mentalizing, building emotional attunement has elements of both art and science. Let's see what it looks like by describing how it worked with a couple whose relationship had hit a wall.

Jason and his wife, Cassia, were having trouble managing their busy work lives while raising two young children. Cassia was particularly stressed—to the point that she felt she did not have time to come to therapy sessions. As such, I worked with Jason separately and recommended that he apply the four levels of emotional awareness to his interactions with Cassia.

I began by asking whether he had noticed his wife's physical sensations. "What do you mean?" he said. "She's not doing enough around the house, and she also hasn't been much help taking care of the kids."

"Sure," I said, "but have you noticed anything unusual about her appearance recently?"

"She had too much makeup on the other day," he said.

That was more of a value judgment than an observation, I explained. "What about any deviations from her usual routine?"

"Oh," Jason said. "She has been sleeping through her alarm in the morning, which has been making her late for work. And when the kids start acting up, she escapes to the bedroom to binge-watch TV." He went on to say that Cassia was also declining Jason's invitations to go out to dinner or to socialize with friends. At this point, Jason asked me, "Do I actually have to do something about these observations?"

"No," I said. "Not yet. The goal at this point is just to notice that she is doing certain things and that her actions are driven by her emotions. Of course, it's fine if you want to help her. But the key for now is simply to notice Cassia's feelings and to share with her that you noticed—not in a judgmental way but in a kind, supportive way, to say that you see she's struggling and that you get it. *The key is to get out of your head and into hers.*"

Throughout the process, Jason was able to draw on his own anxieties to help him recognize Cassia's. For instance, he started to notice that she looked particularly tense when she got home from work. He observed her clenching her jaw—which he recognized because he does that also. He also perceived that she was withdrawn, but more specifically that she obsessively checked her email when she came home from work—because he has a tendency to be obsessive about work himself. Importantly, as he started recognizing and understanding some of his wife's behaviors, he felt a lot better since he realized that he's not the only one doing these things, and they are normal responses to stress.

Jason and I worked for months on observing Cassia's physical sensations, behaviors, and her simple emotions, and eventually, her complex emotions. At one point in our work together, Jason welled up with tears in our session while speaking about Cassia. He shared that, when he looked *behind* Cassia's eyes—behind her overt behaviors like sleeping in and social withdrawal—he perceived an intense sadness. He knew she was "depressed," but he hadn't perceived the depth of her melancholy until that moment. From there, Jason was able to see how Cassia felt utterly isolated and alone, and Jason felt sad himself—empathically sad, in a constructive way.

At that point, I realized that Jason had become more emotionally attuned, and he was ready to start speaking with Cassia about her feelings. This was a welcomed change for Cassia; she instantly felt less anxious since she was able to share her feelings and feel more supported by Jason. And so, as they started to talk openly about this for the first time, she opened up to him a little more. At one point she cried to him, "I'm a terrible wife. I'm a terrible mother. I'm terrible at my job. I'm terrible at everything! I don't know why you don't just leave me!"

Jason was overwhelmed with emotion himself during this conversation since he didn't realize that Cassia felt so bad about herself. All along, he thought she was blaming him for her stress and sadness. He took a step back from the conversation, mostly to pause and think about how to respond. During our sessions, I coached Jason to use his own emotions as a guide for how to respond to Cassia. I asked him, "How would you want Cassia to respond if you felt how she feels?"

With this prompt, Jason intuitively understood what to do. He went home and continued the conversation with Cassia. He tapped his own experience of emotional struggles and recognized how hard it must be for her to share her pain. From that place, the words rolled off his tongue: "I love you, and I will never leave you." Needless to say, this was a big turning point in Jason and Cassia's relationship. She knew that he had acknowledged and addressed her core fear and that her feelings weren't going to fall on deaf ears any longer. As a sense of relief swept over Cassia when they shared their feelings, she said emphatically, "All this time I just wanted to be seen!"

In our final sessions, I pointed out to Jason that the newly found success in his marriage was largely, if not entirely, due to his own emotional distress. He had used his experiences of sadness and anxiety to understand Cassia and make her feel comfortable enough to open up. By paying attention to his own feelings, he was able to respond appropriately and directly to Cassia's concerns. In subsequent weeks, I encouraged Jason to speak with Cassia about her family history and relationship with her parents, as this typically brings up all sorts of complex and even conflicted emotions. Cassia admitted that she felt simultaneously elated and terrified by these discussions, and Jason learned to draw from his own complex emotional experiences to connect with Cassia about these feelings as well. Like all relationships, Jason and Cassia's relationship remains a work in progress, but their marriage has been rekindled and their ship is on a much steadier course.

We Are All One

When we get out of our heads and focus on accurately seeing and responding to others' feelings, we can recognize that we are all in this together and that our suffering is shared with many others. In reality, no one lives an emotionally perfect life. This is all the more true today, in our age of anxiety. Once we realize that we are not alone in our suffering, our own anxieties become less intense. This is why accurately seeing other people's feelings is intrinsically linked to our own anxiety. The world's spiritual traditions have been saying this for millennia: in essence, we are all interconnected beings, and realizing this brings us to a form of inner peace. Significantly, this approach does not require eradicating our anxiety. On the contrary, *it involves harnessing our anxiety to better understand others and learning to thrive because of our distress, not in spite of it.*

How do we apply this profound principle in everyday life? By learning to *mentalize*, we can better recognize and understand other people's thoughts, beliefs, wishes, and emotional needs. By becoming more *emotionally attuned*, we can respond to others' feelings and resonate with them harmoniously. Both of these processes link us to others and thereby reduce our own anxiety.

I've already made the point that we should not go more than a couple of days without connecting in a meaningful way with other people. One of the best ways to foster intimate connections is what we've learned in this chapter: cultivate awareness and responsiveness to others by using our own emotions as a guide.

. . . .

TOOL #4: USING OUR EMOTIONS TO UNDERSTAND OTHERS

We can thrive with anxiety by harnessing our emotional distress to understand and respond to the pain of others. This will deepen our connection with other people and help quell the fires of our own anxiety so that we consequently reap the physical and mental benefits of having richer connections with others. If you've *ever* felt anxious before, you can use your anxiety to enhance the depth of your understanding of other people, which will help you (and them) in the long run.

Take a few minutes to make a mental inventory for someone in your life. It could be a coworker, friend, family member, intimate partner, or even a complete stranger (for the latter you may need to take some poetic and creative license to complete the exercise).

Provide at least one example of each of the following that the person may be experiencing at present. If you struggle to come up with something in one category (such as a sensation), simply quiet and focus your mind and try again. But if you get really stuck and cannot think of anything after a few minutes of focused trying, just move on to the next category.

1. **Goals:** What are some of the person's current ambitions or objectives? What are they striving to accomplish?

2. **Needs:** What do they want or require in life at this time? What would make their life easier, happier, or even just more convenient in some way?

3. **Sensations:** Do they feel pain, pleasure, warmth, cold? Do they smell or taste something? Or do they have another physical feeling?

4. **Thoughts:** What are some of the things on their mind? Try to pick thoughts that are relevant to how you think they may be feeling emotionally.

5. **Behaviors:** Which behaviors, whether subtle or overt, have they been engaging in recently? Try to identify action tendencies that are instrumentally associated with their emotional states.

6. **Feelings:** Which emotions have they been feeling lately? Which feelings underlie their physical sensations, thoughts, and behaviors? Are they primary emotions (direct responses to situations) or secondary emotions (emotional responses to their feelings)? Are they simple emotions? Do they "make sense" or seem conflictual or complex?

CHAPTER 5

ACCEPTING OTHERS

*Anxiety Can Help Us Accept
Others' Limitations*

As we learned in chapter 4, human beings are "social animals," and having emotionally close relationships with other people is critical for our mental and physical health. It follows, then, that our connections with others are not simply expendable or disposable, since *we need other people to thrive and even to survive*. On the one hand, that provides us with an opportunity: we can utilize the experience of our own anxiety to enhance our understanding of others and connect to them. But on the other hand, it creates a significant conundrum and even some risk, because no one is perfect. What should we do when we bump up against others' limitations? How can we navigate relationships with people who have significant struggles, or even major flaws, of their own? As my wife likes to say, "Life is messy!" and she is 100 percent correct! In practice, creating rich interpersonal connections requires making peace with others' limitations. Fortunately, we can draw on our own anxiety to do so, as we will see in this chapter.

Beyond Partisan Wars

In 1960, John Wayne, a movie star known for his conservative views, said of the newly elected President Kennedy, "I didn't vote for him, but he's my president, and I hope he does a good job."[1] Today this perspective sounds like insanity. In the current era, if you don't support the majority of what a political candidate stands for, or if you take exception to some (or much) of what they do or say, you cannot say *anything* positive about them at all. There is a high degree of social pressure to view politicians as all-or-nothing, good or evil, with no in-between.

The implications of this are far-reaching. Today in Washington, DC, we are faced with a near-complete stalemate. Partisan battles have locked both houses of Congress in an increasingly combative turf war. As a result, on three occasions in the past ten years, the US government has shut down because of failure to pass funding legislation—costing billions of dollars, harming businesses, and leading to the furlough of thousands of government employees from both parties. Neither side *won* anything.

To be clear, there are certain members of both parties I would never vote for. But I have friends who did vote for them—and although I disagree with their political views, we are still friends. When we put our political feelings on hold long enough to have a civil conversation, we often find that we even agree on *certain* positives about the other side. Giving someone credit for the good that they've done does *not* mean that we support all of their actions. We can *completely* disagree with people on some matters, or even view some of their perspectives as destructive, while recognizing that they are human beings with *some* strengths that are worthy of recognition and respect.

This concept goes beyond politics and partisan wars. *All of our relationships are with imperfect people.* In my clinical practice, I have seen plenty of wonderful marriages between individuals who are *vastly* different from each other. Such unions survive, and even thrive, because over time each member of the couple learns to make peace with the other's idiosyncrasies and limitations. Similarly, in my academic work, some of the best scientific collaborations I've witnessed were between individuals with opposite temperaments, abilities, and even communication styles. No one is perfect, and two people are doubly imperfect. Yet we tend to thrive in the context of close relationships. Accepting aspects of other people that we don't like, while focusing on creating something together as opposed to changing one another, is a basic human skill.

To put this in spiritual terms: the Bible says that human beings were created in the image of God.[2] There is something inherently valuable in *all* people. Granted, in some situations this is harder to recognize than others! But there is almost always something salvageable; it's rarely productive to cut people out completely.

Why Are Our Relationships So Tenuous Today?

The main reason our relationships are currently so tenuous is that we have built up an assumption that relationships should be easy. Dealing with imperfect, flawed people makes us anxious because we think that something is wrong when our relationships get rocky. In truth, *no relationship is perfect.* Why would we expect connections to be perfect? We are *all* far—very far—from perfect. We are *all* subject to biases, lack of information, problematic character traits, and selfishness, and we *all* make mistakes—serious mistakes.

Life is messy!

The background of our assumption is that we are overly focused on what we want to achieve ourselves instead of on fostering connections with others. As I said in chapter 1, our society values productivity more than our connection, and it's scary to realize that other people—who have major limitations—might make decisions that could adversely affect our achievements. This fear is not unfounded. When we enter into relationships, we *do* become more vulnerable, and it *is* scary.

Having close relationships requires connecting with imperfect people and struggling with those imperfections. *There is no such thing as a perfect marriage or friendship or business partnership or collaboration.* Hollywood and social media may portray this, but it's fake news. Put it out of your mind: perfect relationships do not exist in any context. But strong, highly functional ones do. Real relationships are challenging and require putting up with all sorts of (pardon the word) crap. When we perceive this as a fundamental flaw in our connection, rather than just a part of life, we run away and hide from connecting to others, and the personal and societal results are catastrophically bad.

Unfortunately, there isn't a simple alternative. Cutting off ties from others is typically even more destructive. In recent decades, divorce rates around the globe have soared to startling heights, and so have the costs. Consistent data highlights that children of divorced families tend to struggle with psychological and social difficulties, including heightened anxiety and difficulty forming attachments into young adulthood.[3] On a financial level, the average expense for a divorcing couple is about $15,000,[4] without adding the legal costs of contesting custody and ownership of assets, or the resulting increased cost of living associated with supporting two households instead of just one. As a result, many people—especially those on the lower end of the economic spectrum— cannot *afford* to move on with life after divorce, and they live the rest of their lives alone.

Even more disconcerting than the divorce rate is the declining marriage rate. Since 1965 there has been a consistent drop in marriages, such that nearly four in ten adults today between the ages of twenty-five and fifty-four are unpartnered,[5] and those who *do* marry will soon be in the minority.[6] Millennials in particular are characteristically unwilling to take the risk of starting a family, or even tying the knot at all since relationships are inherently hard to maintain.[7] Even dating has become unpopular in recent years.[8]

However, eschewing relationships carries significant costs, because loneliness is the number one predictor of languishing in later adulthood. In the famous Harvard Study on Adult Development, Professor Robert Waldinger found that *the quality of one's relationships at age fifty is the leading predictor of mental and physical well-being at age eighty*—more than *any other factor*, including genetics, intelligence, financial success, or even cardiovascular health![9] Generations following the baby boomers[10] tend to have an illusion that everything should be smooth sailing—but nothing could be further from the truth.

If you want to deal with only one person's imperfections, the only option is to be on your own. If you want to be in relationships, you'll have to accept that we're all fallible, including our friends, partners, and anyone else we connect to.

An Alternative Approach

Those who experience anxiety know that they are not perfect. We learned in chapter 1 that anxiety involves a *misfire* of the fight-or-flight system. It's a *false-positive* alarm that is unnecessary and unpleasant. This isn't anything to be ashamed of, but nevertheless anxiety has an important lesson for us: *we are imperfect*. We are human beings and make errors. People often respond to anxiety in maladaptive ways, such as avoidance, anger, or alcohol and substance use. All of these make things worse by hindering our ability to handle and manage our anxiety and stress. These responses are so common because human beings are complicated and don't always make good choices.

Anxiety also teaches us how to deal with imperfection. As we learned in part 1, anxiety is here for a reason. It lets us know that something is amiss, and instead of trying to quash our anxiety, we need to address whatever is causing it to manifest. When we do this, anxiety becomes a resource for thriving instead of a malady. In that same vein, *we need to accept uncomfortable aspects of relationships.* We must learn to accept that just because those we are connected to are also flawed and struggling, that doesn't mean that they can't be good confidants or companions. If we catastrophize about the imperfections or issues in our relationships, or judge others for being imperfect, we turn potentially solid connections into dysfunctional ones.

The foundation for this is what we learned in chapter 4: we need to draw from our experience of anxiety to recognize that others are struggling emotionally, too, that 90 percent of their current feelings are determined by previous life events, and that their emotions are valid given the context of their lives. When dealing with someone who struggles, ask yourself: *What sort of life experiences did they have that brought them to be so flawed? How would I fare today if I had had those life experiences?* Our own anxiety can help us to ask these questions and be sensitive to the context in which other people's issues manifest.

There is another key lesson of anxiety that can enhance our relationships. People who don't suffer from anxiety—and those who try to avoid it—might naively assume that it's possible to be in control of life. But, as we saw in part 1, our emotions sometimes do things that we don't want them to. In fact, one of the major causes of anxiety is our cultural desire to avoid uncertainty—to feel that we are in control of everything. Conversely, one of the best ways to overcome anxiety is to give up our sense of control. Here I recall a story from chapter 3 about my friend who had a crippling fear of heights. When he finally decided to traverse the entire length of the Golden Gate Bridge on foot, he was astonished—and greatly relieved—that *letting go* helped him overcome his greatest fear. As he later reported to me, "I'm really glad that I was anxious, because now I learned that I *can* overcome my own anxiety. *I don't have to be in control!*"

This is a critical lesson, since being in a relationship *does* necessitate giving up some degree of control. To so many people, the idea that we can have a successful relationship in which we can't control every aspect of it—including, especially, that we can thrive with a partner who is just as imperfect as we are—seems like a contradiction in terms. But those who have worked on their anxiety know that *control is vastly overrated.* Along these lines, as we learned in chapter 3, discomfort is a part of life. *It's okay to be uncomfortable. Good things come when we accept our discomfort—it makes us stronger and more resilient. All great relationships require some degree of discomfort.*

We all come into the world with a "package" of character traits, and we grow up in an (increasingly) imperfect world. At the risk of sounding repetitive, connecting with people means that we're living not only with our own package but also with theirs. If you want to have only one person's package to deal with, you're going to be lonely. If you want companionship, you're going to have to deal with two people's imperfections, and it's going to be messy at times.

Making Peace with Others' Idiosyncrasies

Rosemary was an investment banker in Manhattan. She was married to Sal, who had been working in the World Trade Center in downtown Manhattan on September 11, 2001. Sal survived the attack on the Twin Towers but with a significant cost: from that day forward, he suffered from chronic depression and PTSD. Initially, Rosemary was supportive of Sal, and they built a family together. But over the years she grew increasingly angry and bitter when he did not recover. As she put it to

Sal, "It's been twenty years since the attack—you almost died, but you're still alive. You've got beautiful kids and a wife who loves you. Get over it!"

Rosemary's anger only made Sal feel more depressed, and as their family grew, the burden of finances and young children drew them both in a downward emotional spiral. Sal's depression spawned further inaction on his part, and Rosemary became even more frustrated with him. She then withdrew from the relationship by excessively focusing on her banking career, which helped financially but created more depression and shame for Sal, and they drifted even further apart. To make matters worse, Rosemary would habitually question why Sal would get triggered every time they drove through a tunnel commuting into the city, and why he wasn't more aggressive in pursuing a career.

As I worked with them, I saw that in many ways Rosemary's workplace attitude was more intense than Sal's, who was a lawyer but worked for a small firm. He was *certainly* not a high-powered litigator or someone doing major mergers and acquisitions. On the other hand, Rosemary regularly rubbed elbows with high-powered (and selfish) men she worked with in her investment banking firm. Unlike for Sal, for them the calamity of 9/11 was a distant memory, and they were highly driven to make lots of money. So one day I asked Rosemary flat out why she hadn't married one of the people in her firm; someone more similar to her in terms of emotional strength and career ambition.

Rosemary initially seemed baffled by the question—she could not explain her choice. But over the course of a few sessions, we identified that Rosemary needed an emotionally sensitive man like Sal in her life. She recalled that she had dated a number of bankers in the past and found that they were insensitive and obsessed with money, and treated her like dirt. At one point, she welled up with tears explaining how her own father had been overly focused on his career instead of the emotional well-being of the family, and she "could never marry someone like that!" In the end, Rosemary wanted—needed—someone who was different from all the hard-asses she hung out with at work, which is why she married Sal in the first place. This was something Rosemary often overlooked, as her frustrations with Sal grew.

Along these lines, I suggested to Rosemary that, rather than dwell in her state of anger and disappointment with Sal, she consider how much she needed him for emotional support. I also suggested that Rosemary acknowledge that she had her own struggles and that she would likely be faring much worse if Sal had a tougher emotional and behavioral composition.

Over time, Rosemary came to realize that the reason why Sal was so badly affected by 9/11 was the same reason she fell in love with him: he is an emotionally sensitive guy. She learned to recognize that his idiosyncrasies were part of his personality that she needed, and in the end she was happier with Sal than she would be with anyone else.

Rosemary's situation—and that of almost every couple I've ever worked with—makes me think of the classic Rolling Stones song "You Can't Always Get What You Want." As the song continues, "if you try sometimes, well, you might find, you get what you need."[11] Sal might not be the one Rosemary thought she wanted, but in him she got what she needed.

The Value of Differences

There is a widespread concept that can be found in many religious traditions: *things happen for a reason*. In the Jewish religion, it's understood that relationships are not accidental—people are brought into one another's lives at a certain place and time in order to teach us what we need and to help us become better people.[12] A similar belief is common in New Age circles, which holds that there are no coincidences, and certain souls are destined to work with each other in this lifetime. Even in the secular world, the concept of a "soulmate" is very widespread.[13]

We've discussed that connections with others are inherently difficult because they involve the coming together of differing and often contrary perspectives. But the clash of those perspectives can make us into better, stronger, more well-rounded, and, most of all, more accepting people. Put another way, a soulmate isn't someone who does our bidding all the time. A soulmate is someone who helps us to become a better person. Just like the unpleasant feelings of anxiety can enhance our self-knowledge, self-acceptance, and resilience, so, too, the struggles and lack of control we experience in relationships can be a blessing.

If you're with someone totally similar to you, neither party is likely to be moved to grow or expand their horizons. By contrast, most successful business relationships are between leaders who have complementary but opposite roles. One partner might be a hothead who is extremely well-organized, while the other is not so organized but is more chill. The first serves as the driving force who makes sure the company reaches its goals; the other makes sure people are happy and don't quit when things go awry in the office.

Getting back to romance: A young couple who were not married but had been dating for some time came to me because their differences were starting to get in the way. Jon was the quintessential "bad boy" in high school through his early twenties, when he went to a prominent art college on the East Coast. He always seemed to get into trouble and had plenty of girlfriends, most of whom were as wild as he was. But his current girlfriend, Marta, whom he met after graduating, was relatively demure. They loved each other, but the contrast of their natures and temperaments created major issues for their social life and sex life.

Marta wanted to stay home and was reserved in the bedroom. Jon liked to party with his friends, most of whom were artists or musicians, and Marta didn't feel comfortable in those situations. Over time, distance grew between them. Jon didn't want to alienate Marta by going out, so he would smoke pot and stay at home. Marta hated when Jon was stoned and she would recoil even further, curling up on the couch to binge Netflix when he got high. Meanwhile, Jon could get pretty adventurous in bed. Marta loved his passion but sometimes felt he went too far.

Tensions grew, and they came in for some couples' sessions. Jon identified that he had *fun* in college but, despite his enthusiasm for partying, he often found his carousing to be empty and meaningless. By contrast, he loved feeling connected to Marta but couldn't stand that she was such a *killjoy*. Marta identified that she was attracted to Jon's "bad" side but also nervous that they could get into trouble or that they would end up doing things she would later regret. Marta recalled that her paternal uncle was also a "bad boy" and he once ended up throwing himself off a balcony because he was so drunk, and almost died. These conversations were challenging for both Jon and Marta. Simply discussing their differences required putting the relationship first and relinquishing some degree of control. It required keeping catastrophic thinking and judgments at bay in order to process what was going on.

But something amazing happened during our sessions. Through discussing their differences, Jon recognized that Marta was primarily *afraid*—not inherently reserved. As such, he would simply have to help her come out of her shell. Jon needed to go more slowly in the bedroom, emphasize his feelings of tenderness, and warm Marta up until she reached his level of excitement, which took her longer. Marta recognized that Jon wasn't a *dangerous* guy, just a tad wild, and that his love for her was genuine. As she wrestled with a sense of shame at some of his hijinks, she admitted that they also turned her on. Jon didn't have much to teach those bad girls he used to run with, but he also felt they were just in it for fun and didn't take him seriously. And, while he enjoyed sharing his amorous skills with Marta, he liked even more that she truly loved and cared about him. Once Jon and Marta took this renewed approach to their relationship, they were both amazed and delighted at how enjoyable their relationship became.

The Limits of Acceptance

For all his wildness, Jon was never abusive to Marta, and he always took care not to hurt her. As for Sal, he wasn't the most ambitious man in New York, but he also was no deadbeat. What happens if a partner is physically or emotionally abusive—or genuinely dangerous?

There *is* a line: it's called *psychopathy*.[14] Characterized by an egocentric, antisocial personality, and a lack of remorse, the hallmark feature of a psychopath is malicious intent—the desire to hurt others. Psychopathy (or sociopathy—both terms amount to the same) is flat-out dangerous.

Typically, the roots of psychopathy stem from narcissism, which ironically tends to come from *low* self-esteem, usually developed in childhood. Psychopaths are truly sad, broken people, most of whom suffered from abuse, neglect, or both early in life, and need to prop themselves up by abusing others.

Empathizing with a psychopath is not advisable, since we need to protect ourselves from them. When people feel so negatively about themselves, they lose the capacity to think about anyone else, and the only option is to avoid such people completely. Case in point, it is extraordinarily rare that psychopaths come for therapy, since they have no sense that anything is wrong with them.

Fortunately, in the general population—and even in clinical populations—true psychopathy is rare. I can recall only one such case that I was involved with. A patient of mine was married to a man who was clearly engaged in sociopathic behavior. He blackmailed her with sexual photos he had taken surreptitiously, and he seduced his sister-in-law into a complex emotional and physical affair, with absolutely no remorse. When his wife found out, he gaslighted her—somehow convincing his wife that *she* was insane and the entire story was due to *her* mental health concerns. And when his wife (naturally) became depressed in the context of this emotional abuse, he used that as confirmatory evidence that his wife was insane, admitted the affair, and then blamed his wife for not being able to support him because of *her* depression. It was a sickening situation! Out of hundreds of couples I've worked with, this is the *only* marriage I've ever encouraged a patient to end.

Malicious intent is always the key factor when identifying the limits of acceptance. Recently, a newly married woman who came to me said that her husband was "abusive." When I asked how her husband abused her, she replied that he had told her, "You're immature!"

I validated that was not a nice thing to say, and then I asked, "Did he hurt you? Or did he say that in front of people to shame you?"

"No," she said. "He did it in private. But it's abusive behavior."

"I see how that could be upsetting to hear," I said. "In addition to that comment, did he ever physically hurt you? Did he try to force you to do things that you didn't want?"

"No."

"Did he shame you or put you down just to make you feel bad?"

"No. Nothing like that."

The picture was starting to come together, but I needed to confirm. "Do you think he was trying to hurt you when he called you immature? Was his intent malicious?"

The woman didn't pause for a second. "No, he isn't a bad guy. I think he is in pain and he was trying to get my attention—to be understood. I don't believe he meant to hurt me emotionally."

"I've got news for you," I said. "Your husband has issues. Maybe even serious issues, for all I know. But he doesn't have malicious intent. He's not dangerous, and he's not abusive."

When we discussed the situation further, it came out plainly that the young woman had many issues of her own, but she was refusing to acknowledge them. She was excessively focused on herself; for example, spending lavishly when they couldn't afford it. Further, when her husband tried to engage with her about emotional topics, she would change the subject and even start laughing or teasing him. This left him feeling frustrated, so that he was emotionally lonely. It actually seemed to me that they were a pretty even match for each other and had a lot to offer each other. He was good for her in the sense that being in their relationship required facing some of her immaturity. And she was good for him in that he needed to be more strategic in addressing issues in the marriage.

Despite my assessment, she asked for a divorce about a month later. I was saddened for two reasons. First, I felt she had overreacted and ended a potentially successful marriage. Second, if being married to someone with good intentions—albeit negative impact—was something she could not tolerate, I was deeply concerned for her future relationship prospects. Yes, it is sometimes too painful to remain in a relationship, even when others don't have malicious intent. But in such cases, ending things is generally like going from the fire to the frying pan.

The Disconnection Spiral

In discussing the *anxiety spiral* in chapter 2, we saw that most people are unaware when they are falling into a downward pattern because it occurs as a series of gradual steps. Similarly, people tend to habitually and unknowingly allow disagreements with others to devolve into altercations or chronic discontent. I can't tell you how many times I've asked a patient what happened when they had an altercation with a loved one—a spouse, parent, child, or sibling—and they respond, "I don't know. It just happened!" That may be an accurate perception, but it's an incomplete description because there are clear discernible steps in the process of accelerating a mild disagreement into a major impasse. People feel as if they have no control over a sudden onrush of anger, but when you slow things down there are often many points at which one can take action and avoid falling into intense emotions.

Let's observe the stages of what I call the *disconnection spiral* in order to understand how fights unfold and learn how to slow or stop the process before it gets out of hand. In effect, the *anxiety spiral* and the *disconnection spiral* are similar in that both of them involve the same four steps: a trigger, catastrophizing, judgment and blame (of both the other person and oneself), and escalation into a full spiral.

The trigger of the disconnection spiral can be anything someone else does that doesn't fit with our preferences, wants, or needs. It can be something that a person says, or the way they behave, that creates discomfort, pain, even inconvenience. Or it can be something that another person *doesn't* do that we were expecting or relying on them for. Triggers can also result from miscommunications and misunderstandings; sometimes nothing at all is fundamentally wrong in the moment, but as human beings we may incorrectly perceive a reason for grievance or stress. Along these lines, sometimes the intent of the other person is positive, but the impact on us is negative. As with the anxiety spiral, triggers are nothing to be concerned about. They happen because *life is messy* and people are not perfect. However, triggers only *initially* set off the spiral—it's the following steps that play a much more formative role.

The next step is catastrophizing. As with the anxiety spiral, our thoughts ramp up quickly and start running a mile a minute in the direction of excessive worry, apprehension, concern, or other negative thinking patterns. Often, people jump to think, *He doesn't appreciate me* or *She doesn't respect me*, even though the facts on the ground don't fully add up to that conclusion. Alternatively, we may think about the future more than the present. We may interpret what someone says as having *global* instead of just *local* consequences. We project that the person will *always* act that way and question the viability of the relationship altogether. We get caught up in negative thinking. Catastrophizing is often subconscious, but it's relatively easy to access and become aware of when you slow down your thinking and pay attention to the chatter in your mind (before getting sucked into the full spiral).

The subsequent step involves feelings of blame. We denounce not only the *behavior* that the other person is exhibiting but their *character*. We feel frustrated with the person and lose our tolerance for their idiosyncrasies and struggles. We forget that the other person has his or her own history, and that imperfection is part of being a human. Most of all, we forget to acknowledge that all people—including ourselves!—are imperfect, and we lose patience for the other as a whole.

There is another corollary of this step, which is usually buried more deeply within our subconscious. This involves feelings of self-blame for the other person's actions. When someone treats us badly or neglects to do something that we find important, only part of our response is, "Shame on them!" Another part of us—and again, this is generally not something we are aware of—says, "Shame on *me!*" *Why are they treating me badly? Does it mean I'm not important? Does it mean they don't respect me? Is it because I'm unlovable?* These responses threaten our self-esteem, which inflates the meaning of the other person's infraction. It's precisely for *that* reason, this contributes to the disconnection spiral. When we judge the character of others and take on the internal responsibility for their negative actions, the cacophony of criticism and shame raises our temperature rapidly, often without much awareness at all.

Catastrophizing and Blame in Action

A newly married couple came to me complaining that they kept having the same fight over and over. Ginger and Carlos lived in a tiny one-bedroom apartment, where they would mostly sleep, eat, and watch television. Needless to say, there was no room for guests. Ginger's main complaint was that Carlos didn't pick up after himself. Her mind was off and running before she could even realize it. *What will happen when we have a bigger place and want to have people over? What will happen when we have kids? Where is our relationship going? Don't I matter to him?* This line of thinking exacerbated Ginger's frustrations and negative emotions, and she would routinely lash out at Carlos in anger. His response was to go dead quiet, which angered Ginger further since she viewed his inactivity as confirmation that she and her protests didn't truly matter to him.

The act of not cleaning up—a *local* concern about a messy house—was turning into a *global* catastrophe of a disintegrating new marriage. Before even pausing to let Carlos respond or address the mess, Ginger's mind was racing toward the future—about hosting guests in their next home and what their life would look like with little people to clean up after. But what tipped Ginger over the edge was her judgment of Carlos for being a slob. She failed to recognize that his lack of tidiness was mostly an artifact of growing up in a home that was disorganized—it wasn't personal in any way. Ginger's judgment of Carlos's behavior led to inner questioning of whether she truly mattered to him. At some level, she was internally blaming herself for Carlos's messiness. During one of our sessions, she articulated, "If I were a better wife, he would pay more attention to my needs and clean up the kitchen!"

It's worth noting that in this case, Ginger had a tendency to think and speak quickly and passionately. True to her name, she was a bit of a hothead. This tendency made things worse, given Ginger's dissatisfaction about the state of the home, but it also made it easier to identify her tendency to descend into the disconnection spiral since she was very consistent in her patterns of thought. Before Ginger could even process her thoughts, she would catastrophize about her future with Carlos. Then she would quickly race off down the road of judging him and feeling unloved and uncared for. Ironically, and unfortunately, the more Ginger's mind headed in these directions, the more sensitive she became to Carlos's mess, and the more likely she was to catastrophize and judge (both Carlos and herself) the next time he made a mistake.

Full Disconnection Spiral

The more you add blame to relationship dynamics, the more likely you are to focus on negative things and then catastrophize further. This increases the likelihood of blame—whether subconscious or conscious—which in turn creates more negative interactions within the relationship and additional fodder for catastrophic thinking. This momentum is similar to the downward descent of the anxiety spiral: something triggers anxious feelings, and you begin to catastrophize; you judge yourself as if it were all your fault, and your anxiety heightens, providing more fuel for the fire. By now the spiral is in full swing.

However, since the disconnection spiral involves *two* people and not just *one*, there is another important effect. Catastrophizing and blaming creates a lot of stress, tension, and anxiety for the other person as well. Being on the receiving end of global negative deductions from challenging interpersonal interactions releases adrenaline into our bloodstream, which intensifies our fight-or-flight response. Once activated, the fight-or-flight response will lead us either to escalate, as Ginger did, or to withdraw, as Carlos did. *This* is why many people get angry without explanation: the interplay of two people rapidly escalates things before we can even realize what's going on. In most relationships, the more *one* party becomes activated and fights or flees, the more likely that the *other* party will become activated and fight or flee. We will discuss these patterns in greater detail in chapter 6.

This is what the four stages of the disconnection spiral look like in sequence:

1. **Trigger.** The spiral starts with an individual saying or doing something that we don't like, or *not* doing something that we want or need them to do. They may act in a way that is objectively ill-considered or obnoxious, or it could be that they simply did something that inadvertently rubbed us the wrong way.

2. **Catastrophic thinking.** Then, we catastrophize. We interpret what they did as having not just local but global consequences. We envision the worst, that all their future decisions will take a similar tack, and that this problem will leave us vulnerable and uncomfortable in perpetuity.

3. **Blame.** We blame the *person*, as opposed to simply looking at their actions. Furthermore, often subconsciously, *we blame ourselves* for what the other person did. This creates *shame* on our part since our role in the other person's behavior is called into question in our minds.

4. **Full spiral.** The more we catastrophize and blame (ourselves or the other), the more likely we are to feel tension, stress, and anxiety, and focus on other negatives within the relationship. As a result, we may "suddenly" become aggressive (*fight*) or disengage (*flight*). This usually elicits a *fight-or-flight* response in the other person, thus creating a new set of triggers, which leads to even more catastrophizing and blame. At this point, the full spiral takes over, often before we are even aware of the (many) steps that contributed to our getting into such an agitated state.

The Gift of Anxiety

We can use the experience of anxiety to improve our relationships with others. Anxiety tends to worsen when the disconnection spiral gets triggered (as above). However, we can avoid getting caught in the disconnection spiral if we listen to what our anxious feelings are telling us. When we do this, our relationships become more resilient to triggers such as annoyances, grievances, insults, and injuries.

Having anxiety doesn't mean we are fundamentally broken. As we saw in chapter 2, we can use the experience of anxiety as a reminder that there are natural ebbs and flows in our emotional states. A surge of anxiety is nothing to catastrophize about—it simply means you are human. Furthermore, when anxiety strikes, your body is asking for more acceptance and compassion. If you provide those—even if you don't think you deserve them—you can turn the initial trigger of anxiety into an opportunity for self-love.

We can use a parallel set of strategies to avoid the *disconnection spiral* within our relationships. *Let's begin by recognizing and accepting that no relationship is perfect.* Whether you're in a romantic relationship, maintaining a friendship, interacting with work colleagues, or even have a teacher-student bond, it's only a matter of time until one party will disappoint or rub the other party the wrong way. If you spend any length of time with others, at some point an issue *will* come up that you disagree about. Even the simplest of relationships is prone to disappointment. For example, if you hire someone to remodel your kitchen or repair your car, they will likely disappoint you by not following your directions to a T, taking too long to get the job done, or having cost overruns. When we keep these ideas in mind, we are less likely to catastrophize when others act in unexpected ways. Sometimes—oftentimes—people are simply imperfect, and their own imperfections warrant acceptance and not a worry-fest.

Let's also practice compassion toward others. All human beings are imperfect. I would even say that in the current day and age, all human beings have significant character flaws. These may be readily apparent upon a first encounter, or they may only be revealed over time. However, make no mistake: *all of us have some internal struggle of great significance that we are on this earth to contend with.* Note that compassion is not about being kind when people deserve it—that's called reward, or even fairness. Compassion is about dropping *warranted* judgments and blame, by practicing kindness *specifically* when others are legitimately in the wrong. When we recognize that everyone needs permission to struggle or fail since we are just human beings, the only logical response is to provide copious amounts of kindness and support along the way.

You may question why I insist that anxiety is a blessing when it comes to relationships—it may seem to only make it harder to tolerate others' idiosyncrasies! I say this because, without experiencing the discomfort of anxiety, you might not realize the need to practice acceptance and compassion when things seem off-kilter. But if you've been blessed with anxiety and worked on it using the strategies in part 1 of this book, then you have experienced what it's like to accept that you might not be firing on all cylinders all the time. You also know what it's like to recognize how important it is to give yourself *more* of a break—*not less*—when you're struggling. *These exact same processes—acceptance and compassion—are integral to maintaining thriving relationships with other people.*

In this regard, having anxiety can help us to implement the steps needed to defuse the disconnection spiral, which I outline below. *Our own internal experience of anxiety can make it more intuitive and less challenging to accept and show compassion to others.* With the rare exception of psychopathy, you cannot provide too much acceptance or compassion in a relationship.

The Connection Spiral

In chapter 2 we described how to convert an anxiety spiral into a positive spiral. Once we experience anxiety symptoms, we can choose to accept them and be kind to ourselves. If we do this, not only will we feel less anxious, but we will also develop a closer relationship with ourselves and turn our anxiety into a resource for thriving.

We generally do not have a choice about experiencing the initial symptoms of fear or the onset of our body's fight-or-flight response. Anxiety happens! But we can choose not to catastrophize and blame ourselves for feeling anxious. Instead, we can accept our feelings and be kind to ourselves. When we do this, we grow in confidence and resilience as we convert the initial fearful cues of anxiety into assets.

We can do the same thing in our interpersonal relationships. When a person we are in a relationship with says or does something that triggers our fight-or-flight response, we can follow the steps of the connection spiral below:

1. **Trigger.** The trigger here is the same as in the disconnection spiral, since people are imperfect and even the best relationships will experience miscommunications or discord from time to time.

2. **Accept the imperfection.** Instead of catastrophizing, recognize that all humans are imperfect. Why would you expect any relationship to be perfect, when you consider that interpersonal connections involve *two* people's idiosyncrasies? To this end, don't fight your differences with others. *Accept them and let it ride.* Wait for the conflict to pass since all relationships go up and down. Don't delude yourself into thinking that relationships should be perfectly harmonious all the time—that's a lie.

3. **Have compassion.** Recognize that *all* people in *all* of your relationships are limited human beings who are imperfect. When we blame others, we neglect to recognize their histories and contexts in which their issues developed. Be humble and recognize that you have plenty of issues too. More important, do not blame yourself for others' issues. They are not your fault! Everyone comes into life with something to resolve, and viewing their struggles as nefarious is where blame and shame creep in, which is how people get into serious relationship trouble.

4. **Reduce disconnection.** When we accept the natural vicissitudes of relationships and practice compassion to all, then our sense of disconnection lessens over time and sometimes even subsides.

A Place for Assertiveness?

Some of you may be wondering, *When people do something I don't like, should I do nothing else aside from accept their idiosyncrasies and have compassion (for them and for myself)?* Is it inappropriate or unwise to assert oneself by stating our needs? We will discuss this more in chapter 6, but for now the answer to this question is: obviously not!

Acceptance and loving-kindness do not preclude gently or even firmly clarifying what we need of others. We can also simultaneously practice acceptance and compassion while taking actions to ensure that our needs are met. *Positive attitudes do not require us to put up with everything that others may do to us.* However, being assertive from a position of anger, irritation, and a lack of awareness of our tendency to catastrophize and self-blame is ill-advised and often ineffective. Put differently, without a firm base of acceptance and compassion, assertiveness is generally not a good idea.

This dynamic played out in Miriam's frequent struggles with her younger sister, Bessie, who was jealous of her. Their mother had died when they were both still young, and as the elder sister, Miriam felt responsible for taking care of Bessie when their father was busy with his job as a sanitation worker, often putting in overtime hours to make up for the lack of a second income. Although Miriam was conscientious, her sister resented being "controlled" as a child by being told not to come along when Miriam would go out with the older girls in their neighborhood. Years later, it was Miriam who bitterly resented that Bessie took possession of a number of family heirlooms, especially some prized photo albums, after their father passed away.

When Miriam came to see me, she was consumed with anger at her sister's "confiscation" of the family photographs. In her mind, she had cared for her sister while growing up in very strained circumstances, and she felt that Bessie didn't appreciate her sacrifices. Miriam was so angry that she took the step of "unfriending" and blocking her sister from her social media accounts—a clear protest against Bessie's unrightful pilfering.

I initially suggested that Miriam consider meeting with Bessie in person to share her feelings, but I quickly realized that Miriam was still steaming with rage and not fully aware of her emotions. So we spent a few sessions speaking about her perspectives on the relationship with Bessie, across their long history through the current circumstances. We identified that Miriam did love Bessie and wanted a relationship with her, but she felt incredulous that Bessie took the photo albums. "How could she do this to me, after all we've been through?" Miriam said with scornful judgment. "How can I trust her again?" she catastrophized, with palpable emotion in her voice.

I then asked whether Miriam blamed *herself* for Bessie's theft. "You're right, Dr. Rosmarin," she said. "I *do* blame myself! I should have set better limits with Bessie. She is self-centered and never appreciated me, so it was just a matter of time before she crossed the line. I should have put her in her place a long time ago—this never would have happened!"

Throughout our sessions, I tried to cultivate more acceptance and compassion. I encouraged Miriam to think about Bessie's life experience as a very young girl who had lost her mother, and how she may have felt that Miriam was an inadequate replacement. We also discussed how Bessie may have felt that Miriam was overly controlling, and although this was well-intentioned, the impact might have been negative for Bessie.

Miriam realized, perhaps for the first time, that Bessie might have taken the albums out of resentment, and while these feelings might not have been rightful or just, they made some degree of sense given the circumstances. Miriam also recognized that Bessie's taking of the family photograph albums might have been an attempt to mentally re-create some positive memories from the childhood that she never had. Miriam came to see that both she and Bessie were shortchanged, having lost their mother at such a young and vulnerable stage in their lives. She had entered the connection spiral.

A few sessions later, Miriam was in a much better place emotionally, and we revisited the idea of having a conversation with Bessie—about their relationship history, the present, the future, and also the issue of the "stolen" photo albums.

TOOL #5: THE CONNECTION SPIRAL

Regarding friends and loved ones, the saying goes, "You can't live with them, and you can't live without them." But in reality, only the last part is true: *we can't live without them.* So we need to learn how to weather the vicissitudes of interpersonal connections. Of course, there are some limits to this. If we find ourselves in genuinely abusive relationships with individuals who show no remorse or care for others' well-being, we need to protect ourselves. However, in the absence of malevolent intent, we generally benefit by learning to get along with people who are different from us. We can learn diverse perspectives, become stronger people, and, most of all, learn to be more accepting and compassionate toward ourselves and others. So when you feel irritated by others' idiosyncrasies, or when you are struggling with what other people are doing, engage in the connection spiral by following these steps.

STEP 1

Recognize that it's simply not true that relationships should be perfect. Remember that differences are often a great catalyst to connection and inner growth. *Life is messy!* So it is impossible to have rich relationships with others unless we learn to accept their idiosyncrasies with love and patience.

STEP 2

Catch yourself catastrophizing before things escalate. Recognize and accept local issues without going global. Miscommunications and errors happen all the time, especially when two people are close with each other. Interpreting people's actions as nefarious (when they may not be) makes it impossible to respond with equanimity. When issues arise, take a breather and remain in the present.

STEP 3

Accept that all of us are fallible human beings, and it's not helpful to blame others or yourself when people make bad decisions. As professional athletes like to say, *you can only control what you can control*—for example, if you're pitching a good game and one of your fielders makes a costly error, that's not on you. Along these lines, provide copious amounts of compassion to yourself and to others. Doing so will *not* make the situation worse! All of us have baggage to carry and issues to face, and everyone needs *more*—not less—compassion and love.

STEP 4

Continually practice acceptance and compassion toward others, just as you would do with yourself when it comes to your anxiety. Use the opportunities of interpersonal differences to strengthen bonds with others and love them for who they are.

• •

CHAPTER 6

TRANSCENDENCE IN RELATIONSHIPS

Anxiety Can Help Us Deepen Our Connections with Others

We saw in chapter 4 how human beings thrive more when we are connected to others. Then, in chapter 5, we discussed how there is no perfect option when it comes to relationships; the idea of a relationship that is *always* in equilibrium is fantasy. Once we accept that all relationships are imperfect, we have taken a huge step forward and can focus on the need to keep cool, avoid catastrophic thinking, and refrain from blaming or judging ourselves and others when faced with human idiosyncrasies. We have also seen how having anxiety—and dealing with it by using the strategies in part 1 of this book—can make it *easier* to recognize the patterns of catastrophic thinking and blame that undermine relationships. Still, what we've learned in chapters 4 and 5 will only take us so far. If we wish to truly connect with others, *we need to go a step further by recognizing, accepting, and expressing that we are inherently vulnerable and needy when it comes to our closest relationships*, both personal and professional. We all need others, and we also need to be needed. This is not easy to acknowledge! But when we do, we can transcend to levels of emotional closeness and connection that would otherwise be unattainable. The present chapter will show you how to use your anxiety to generate greater closeness, intimacy, and connection within your relationships.

The Paradox of Relationships

There is an inherent paradox in human relationships. On the one hand, interpersonal connection gives us tremendous fortitude. On the other hand, we derive the *most* strength when we acknowledge a weakness—our vulnerability and resultant need for others—and when others do the same.

For example, in an employee-employer relationship, maximal benefit—on both sides—occurs *when both employee and employer recognize and express their reliance on and need for the other.* Harvard Business School has long extolled the virtues of gratitude in the workplace.[1] Beyond the basics of being considerate and polite, when managers express gratitude, it conveys the message that the employees' contributions at work are valued and needed. This, in turn, tends to *increase* employee loyalty and devotion, and job satisfaction. Similarly, when employers feel that their staff are dedicated, grateful, and reliant on the company (for professional identity or pride, social connections, a sense of purpose, financial security), this creates psychological space for managers and executives to reinvest into company policies that improve the employee experience. And so, paradoxically, the most stable, productive, and thriving human relationships in the workplace are founded on a platform of acknowledging—in some way—their need for the other. *All of us need to be needed, and the best relationships articulate needs on both sides.*

Several years ago, one of my patients shared with me some significant work-related distress that highlights how *not* valuing others, or feeling valued, has deleterious effects. As an exceptionally wealthy and internationally renowned whiz within the financial services sector, Oscar could have comfortably retired without any need for him or his children (and probably even his grandchildren) to ever work another day for payment. With that backdrop, over the past decade or so, his firm had grown very large and taken on a number of junior and midlevel partners, and Oscar was struggling to find meaning and purpose at work. His opinions were often disregarded during meetings, despite the fact that his thirty-year track record for finding profitable ventures was impeccable. He told me that he felt *overcompensated*, and that his partners were keeping him around simply because it would have been too costly to get rid of him. Oscar felt he didn't need his partners, and they didn't need him, and this was taking *all* the joy out of Oscar's working life, even though he was exceptionally wealthy and making a hefty salary. More money than Oscar could ever spend in several lifetimes was *not* enough to compensate for the lack of meaning and purpose that came from a complete absence of vulnerability at work.

Therein lies the relationship paradox. *The strength we extract from our connections with others is never based on receiving more out of relationships than we invest.* On the contrary, our connection depends on (1) the extent to which we are needed by others, (2) how much we rely on others, and (3) expressions of dependence by all parties. Note that I'm using employee-employer and business relationships only to illustrate this general point about human relationships. Indeed, symbiosis and exploitation are insufficient to explain human dynamics even on Wall Street! This is all the more true within social domains, such as families, friends, communities, and romantic relationships. Almost nothing is more degrading than being in a romantic relationship with a partner who doesn't value the contributions you make to their life. Conversely, when romantic partners feel that they need each other, it is one of the most precious experiences we can have. *It may even be the pinnacle of love.*

Independence Vs. Interdependence

Unfortunately, the paradox of relationships is rarely mentioned within academic circles or in the popular media. This occurs for a revealingly simple reason: it goes against the grain of Western individualism to recognize and value our mutual interdependence on one another. Particularly in American society, the individual rights of each person as a separate entity generally surpass those of the group or collective. Our educational systems espouse the same value: from elementary through university level, students are assessed almost entirely based on their individual accomplishments, as opposed to group work.

At the current juncture of human history, however, it is clear that we have pushed well beyond the psychological limits of healthy independence. Our overvaluation of *rugged individualism* is now counterproductive in many ways. Divorce rates are soaring, birth and marriage rates are plummeting, and mental distress is in the stratosphere.[2] Perhaps worst of all, our *do-it-alone* approach to life has led to an exponential increase in anger and violence. Long before the COVID-19 pandemic set in, road rage incidents increased nearly 7 percent *each year*.[3] Today, it's become increasingly common for motorists to pull out firearms when aggrieved by other drivers!

In truth, we can accomplish a lot more with *interdependence* than *independence*. Interdependence occurs when we need other people—and they need us. Interdependence recognizes that we are stronger together than we are apart, since competition and individuality are healthy only to a point, after which they generate rapidly diminishing returns. Interdependence also fosters humility: everyone has their day, and no one is dispensable. As Princess Diana succinctly put it, "Everyone needs to be valued. Everyone has the potential to give something back."[4]

Fortunately, in the modern world, it's not hard to recognize that we *are* dependent on others. We can't even get dressed in the morning, eat breakfast, and operate a computer without using things that have been touched by many other hands—grown, manufactured, shipped, processed, and sold by *hundreds* of people around the globe. I might even go as far as to say that there are spiritual implications here: *we are all interconnected and needed in this world for some purpose.* This notion has been taught by any number of teachers from many of the world's religious traditions.[5]

Years ago, when I was privileged to spend a summer at Boston University's Center for Anxiety and Related Disorders, I managed to swing an "exit interview" with its famed director Dr. David H. Barlow, and I asked him the secret of his success. To my surprise, he shared that *the primary factor*—in addition to hard work, persistence, and luck—*was having a stable relationship with his wife*, whom he married in 1966. As my own academic career has developed over the past two decades, I've gone back to that telling moment in my mind on a number of occasions. Indeed, among my many colleagues—most of them far more brilliant, creative, and well-funded than I ever will be—those who split up with their partners or had significant interpersonal disconnection have struggled with their careers compared to those in successful long-term romantic relationships.

To put it simply, independence is overrated. I vote for interdependence.

What About Codependency?

We need to distinguish between *interdependence* and *codependence*. The latter involves relationships in which one person with low self-esteem and a desire for approval has an excessive emotional or psychological need to provide support for a partner or family member, who in turn is *negatively impacted* by the support. Interdependence, by contrast, is the *opposite* of codependence because the mutual reliance on each other makes both parties stronger, not weaker.

A classic example of codependence involves adult children who have an addiction (for example, to alcohol, substances, gambling) and whose parents *enable* the pathological behavior due to their own low self-esteem. In this scenario, the parents may throw money at the situation, which almost always results in making the addiction worse. What is truly needed is a professionally guided intervention in which the family withholds resources until the addiction is dealt with. This clinical approach treats both parties: it stops the child from using and makes the family face their own dependency for being needed.

Clyde, an eighteen-year-old college student, had been using and dealing the party drug ecstasy for some time before his parents became aware that he had a problem. When they did, they were upset but also *unwilling* to insist that he go into treatment or to cut access to family funds that he was using to purchase large supplies of the drug. His mother, Mathilde, believed she could win his confidence through long, late-night conversations, making dinner for him when he came home from raves, and generously giving him money whenever he asked. Having no experience or understanding of ecstasy, she didn't realize that his desire to talk endlessly was simply an effect of the drug. She felt that he was sincerely trying to connect with her, and that this would help him overcome his addiction, but it only reinforced his maladaptive behavior.

For his part, Clyde was unmotivated to change and didn't think his life would be any better if he stopped using ecstasy, but at some point he agreed to come see me for a few sessions. After realizing that I wasn't getting anywhere with Clyde in treatment, I had a frank conversation with his family. Mathilde already felt like a failure and didn't want to see her son hit rock bottom, so she was not willing to insist he go into rehab or stop enabling him. Clyde's father saw that Mathilde's approach was falling short, but he wasn't willing to rock the boat or expose the family to the "shame of having a son in rehab."

I shared with Mathilde that I thought she and Clyde had a codependent relationship: she wouldn't do what was within her capacity to get him off ecstasy, even though this was what Clyde truly needed. As Mathilde provided more and more support, Clyde just used ecstasy more often. Soon, he had his friends coming over to the house at all hours, creating noise and disruption for his younger siblings, and even safety concerns. All those late-night talks with her son were leaving Mathilde worn out, and she deluded herself into thinking that she was sacrificing for her son's sake, which became a huge part of her identity.

Unfortunately, the family was not willing to change their approach. I therefore backed off the case and said that when the parents and/or Clyde were ready to do what was needed to break their codependency, we could resume treatment.

Bringing It Together

Barring circumstances of codependency, which are relatively rare, we are much stronger together than apart. More specifically, we are stronger to the extent that we are *interdependent* by mutually recognizing our vulnerability and need for one another. Acknowledging and navigating interdependence is all the more important today, when we live such exceedingly disconnected lives in general.

As we will see throughout the rest of this chapter, *we can harness the power of anxiety in our relationships to bring us closer to others by recognizing and expressing our vulnerable needs.* When we do this, our relationships transcend to higher levels of intimacy and closeness, and our anxiety (and anger) fade into the background as we become more connected.

Anxiety and Anger

We are social creatures, and others' behaviors affect us. Precisely *because* of this, we naturally get tense and anxious when we feel that others are doing things (or *not* doing things) that negatively affect our lives. This in itself isn't a problem; it's simply an artifact of being in a connected relationship with people, and as we've seen, this is part and parcel of interdependent living.

However, people often do not express—or even allow themselves to experience—feelings of anxiety when they occur in an interpersonal context. Instead, we tend to convert (or sublimate) our anxiety into anger. Seemingly spontaneous eruptions of anger are generally immediate and subconscious, but make no mistake: *the root of anger toward others, in almost all cases, is anxiety.* After all, anxiety is mediated by the fight-or-flight response.

In chapter 4, I spoke briefly about primary and secondary emotions, but I will go into more depth here. *Primary emotions* occur directly and spontaneously as a result of some external cue. In classic psychology, the four main primary emotions are joy, sadness, fear, and anger, although many now add disgust and surprise to the list. *Secondary emotions* involve feelings that we have in response to our primary emotions. For example, as we learned in chapter 1, we might feel shame when we experience anxiety. We may experience guilt as a secondary emotional response to feeling joy about something that had mixed consequences (such as a benefit for us that involved someone else getting hurt).

Although anger is considered a primary emotion in the animal world, in clinical practice I've seen that it functions more often as a secondary emotion. Anger can take various forms, ranging from mild petulance or irritation to dangerous outbursts or violence. Across this entire spectrum of anger, however, I've found that it rarely occurs without the presence of anxiety, fear, or stress. The research literature has borne this out. My dear colleague Dr. David Moscovitch found many years ago that anger and aggression are elevated for individuals with various anxiety disorders, compared to control subjects without anxiety disorders.[6] When we unconsciously convert anxiety into anger and lash out, this allows us to avoid dealing with our own anxiety, to put the blame on someone else, and to essentially transfer the stress off our plate onto another's.

These patterns were particularly clear during various stages of the COVID-19 pandemic. One day, after mask mandates had been lifted, I went out for a run (maskless) around a local reservoir in Boston. Despite the fact that I kept a healthy distance from all passersby, I got yelled at by an older woman. "Put on your mask! Put on your mask!" She was irate. I politely apologized from a distance, ran off, and that was that. Two days later, I went for another run in the same location, but this time I donned a sports mask since I didn't want to upset anyone. To my surprise, I got yelled at *again*—this time by a younger woman. "Enough with the masks—you don't need to wear that stupid thing! Why are you making everything so much harder?" I took the same approach of briefly apologizing and running off, but this time I went back home and asked myself, *What on earth is going on?*

I concluded that the driving emotion of *both* people who yelled at me was not anger but anxiety. The first woman was trying to convey, *I'm scared. I've been reading that the virus makes me particularly vulnerable, and I don't want to die. I also don't want to infect others.* As for the second woman, she was trying to share her anxieties about freedom. She probably felt that government policies were already overstepping, and that excessive adherence to rules beyond that line would impinge on her social liberties. Ironically, in some ways, both women had the same concerns. They were both thinking, *I want the coronavirus to go away. I want this nightmare to be over. I don't want my stress level to be so high because it's affecting my physical and mental health.* Either way, it was clear to me that *anxious* thoughts were behind the anger. With this perspective in mind, I recalled both incidents and could almost see fear peering out from beneath the veils of rage.

The unfortunate consequence of converting anxiety into anger is that we don't deal with our anxiety at all (or our anger, for that matter). When we take this tack, years or decades go by before we even recognize the need to address our anxiety. And yet, once we realize that anger is the end product of anxiety, we not only get more control over our anger and anxiety, but we can radically create more connection in our lives.

Not Turning Home into a Battlefield

Zoe and Dwayne, a married couple in their midthirties with three kids, came to see me because Dwayne had been acting out in anger around the house. They were both concerned that this would have negative effects on the children. Dwayne confessed that he was struggling with anger, and he felt a good deal of shame and guilt about this, especially because he wasn't able to articulate what was setting him off. "It's like I have a powder keg inside me. I just fly off the handle and start yelling! I feel terrible and really want to change."

The context of Dwayne's anger was, sadly, an all-too-common story in America today. He had recently returned from several tours of duty in Iraq, where he had witnessed horrific scenes of injury and death. Worst of all were things that he had done as a soldier, which were all under orders but still left him questioning his sense of morality as a human being. Regretfully, it remains a common practice among military commanders to advise soldiers *not* to discuss their war experiences with their families upon return to civilian life, and Dwayne fell victim to this bad advice. The talk therapy he received through Veterans Affairs had helped only a bit; he remained plagued by flashbacks, shock, guilt, and shame about the horrors of war, without the capacity to share his inner world with his wife.

Being unable to discuss his feelings with Zoe, Dwayne often exploded at the least little thing. He blamed himself for this and interpreted his failure to control his temper as a sign that he wasn't cut out for civilian life. When he was deployed in Iraq, he had enjoyed the camaraderie with his fellow soldiers, which helped him process his feelings of guilt and shame, as these were shared by many of them. At home, by contrast, so much of Dwayne's cognitive and emotional energy went into managing his feelings that minor changes threw him for a loop.

One time, dinner was called for seven o'clock, and plans changed so that Zoe told him dinner would be at six-thirty because she had to drive one of the kids to soccer practice. Dwayne blew his lid and could not for the life of him explain what made him so upset. When we slowed down that situation in therapy, however, it became clear that Dwayne's anger was really coming from a place of intense anxiety. He was a good soldier and wanted to follow his commander's orders of not sharing his war experiences with his family. Along these lines, he wanted to protect them from his inner turmoil; he wouldn't allow Zoe or the kids to see him struggling with sadness, pain, or guilt. And so, when the schedule was suddenly moved up by a half hour, Dwayne freaked out because he realized that he would have thirty minutes less to prepare himself emotionally to make it through dinner without breaking down.

I explained to Dwayne that he needed to acknowledge his vulnerability, both to himself and to Zoe. I conveyed that I thought Zoe wanted to support him, and that she would prefer that he show his softer feelings like sadness, shame, and tension, rather than his scary side. In speaking with Zoe, she confirmed these impressions and added that she would feel great about herself for "taking care of a big, strong soldier like Dwayne." I encouraged the couple to speak about this openly: Dwayne's need for more support, and Zoe's need to provide that support (in other words, their *interdependence*).

Flipping that switch turned everything around. Dwayne learned to tell Zoe when he was feeling anxious about being able to regulate his emotions. This simultaneously calmed him down, abated some of his anger, and pulled him into a state of deeper emotional connection with Zoe, as opposed to his previous patterns of anxiety suppression, anger outbursts, and interpersonal disconnection. Over time, Dwayne was even able to express his need for physical affection. He recognized that Zoe's hugs and snuggles were deeply soothing for him when he felt triggered, and Zoe was all too happy to provide Dwayne with more physical touch. Once they discussed this openly and brought such conversations into their daily repertoire, things continued to improve.

Most of all, though, Dwayne eventually confronted his deepest fear by conveying to Zoe that he wasn't sure whether he was truly cut out for family life after all he had seen—and done—in Iraq. I encouraged Dwayne to carefully share *some* details of what he had endured during deployment, and Zoe patiently listened to his war stories. This fundamentally shifted Dwayne's perspective about himself: he realized that Zoe was not put off by what he had done in Iraq. On the contrary, she valued her "military man" for what he had endured. This simple shift was all it took for Dwayne to realize that he could indeed be a wonderful husband and father at home, just as he had been a steadfast and reliable soldier serving his country overseas.

Anger and Avoidance: Two Sides of the Same Coin

We've seen that anxiety often triggers anger (the fight response). Previously, in chapter 3, we saw that anxiety can also trigger avoidance of situations that make us uncomfortable (the flight response). In the interpersonal realm, avoidance is similar to, and often no less significant than, anger, but its presentation is more subtle. When people engage in avoidance within the context of relationships, they typically *turtle* into their shell in an attempt to stay clear from confrontation and negative emotion. *Turtling* has many forms, such as changing the topic when potentially contentious issues come up, simply not expressing our true feelings, or even "ghosting" by essentially cutting off contact.

When we compare anger and avoidance, one of these responses isn't necessarily better than the other; both can be equally destructive to any number of human connections in the workplace, family, and of course romantic relationships. Another commonality between these approaches is their impact. While both anger and avoidance are typically used to gain or maintain control over interpersonal relationships, they usually create more emotional distance and make it harder to correct dynamics. Anger disrupts relationships because it scares others from engaging, which can bring all communication to a halt. Avoidance thwarts emotional connection because it makes it impossible to engage or address issues that are creating stress within a relationship.

Cycles of Interpersonal Distance

Dr. Sue Johnson—one of the leading figures in the field of couples therapy—has taught us that three problematic patterns commonly emerge.[7] *All three stem from maladaptive attempts to manage anxiety.* When someone causes us irritation or distress, we tend to respond with anger (fight) or avoidance (flight). The other party, in turn, also chooses anger (fight) or avoidance (flight). The resulting dynamics tend to repeat in a cyclical pattern, creating more interpersonal distance and suffering along the way.

What is missing from all three patterns that follow—on both sides—is acknowledgment of our vulnerability and need for the other party. Instead of creating a transcendent relationship by recognizing and expressing our vulnerability and relying on others, both partners are effectively saying, "I don't want to be dependent on you, so I'm going to cause you pain—or shut you out." Here are the three patterns:

1. Fight-Fight (Approach-Approach)

In this pattern, both partners take an aggressive approach. Even if plates and cutlery aren't whizzing through the air, fights tend to take the form of a mutual blame game, which grows intolerable pretty quickly. In truth, each side feels vulnerable because of some fear—either they don't feel valued in the relationship, or they feel threatened in some way. They typically catastrophize about these fears and blame the other party (and, subconsciously, themselves) for the problematic dynamics. But the fear of accepting and expressing raw vulnerabilities seems more terrifying compared to lashing out and blaming. The result is usually that both sides lock horns, dig in their heels, and continue fighting until one or both retreat to their respective corners, injured, more afraid, and more distant from each other. As you can imagine, these relationships generally don't last very long because the atmosphere becomes too toxic.

2. Fight-Flight (Approach-Avoid)

This is the most common pattern, and by contrast with the first pattern, it often goes on indefinitely. In the approach-avoid dynamic, one person strives to deal with the issue directly even if it requires aggression, and the other *turtles* by avoiding decisive action. As the first escalates in protest, the latter goes increasingly silent, changes the subject, or makes promises but doesn't come through. In order to avoid confrontation, the avoidant partner doesn't come out and say directly that they have no intention of actually addressing the issues being raised by the aggrieved and angry partner. As a result, the anxiety of the angry partner is never fully quelled since the fundamental issues are never addressed, and they feel that the avoidant party doesn't truly care. As for the avoidant partner, their anxiety is also perpetual, since they live in fear that they will be attacked at any moment. Around and around this cycle goes, often for an entire lifetime, with one partner raising issues too intensely (due to anxiety) and the other avoiding discussing those very issues (also due to anxiety). The result is perpetual distance, punctuated by fleeting moments of connection during which the aggressive partner vainly hopes the other will change, and the avoidant partner hopes the other will give up and stop arguing, which is equally vain. The fundamental reason they never make progress is because of a lack of *interdependence*. Neither side articulates that they *need* the other—the aggressive one *needs* assurance that their preferences matter, and the avoidant one *needs* the aggressor to settle down so they can live together in peace.

3. Flight-Flight (Avoid-Avoid)

This pattern is the worst of the three. Typically, things start out with the fight-flight (approach-avoid) dynamic, until the aggressive party gives up and comes to the conclusion that the other person will never change. At that point the music stops, and both parties essentially disconnect from each other in perpetuity. While this may seem on the surface to be a more peaceful resolution relative to the other two forms of conflict, in practice the partners experience much more distance, disconnection, isolation, and sadness. In 100 percent of the couples I have seen where there was marital infidelity, or family relationships where there were years—or decades—of silent treatments, *this* was the pattern at play. I've also seen it manifest within business relationships in which there was surreptitious theft or skullduggery. Once one party concludes firmly that the other is behaving unfairly and there isn't anything that can be done to change their behavior, it's all too common to *take what's rightfully mine* without telling one's partner.

Converting Anxiety into Love

Interestingly, these three patterns tend to happen consistently and repeatedly within relationships, irrespective of what people might be arguing about. In fact, Dr. Johnson's research and clinical work have taught us that the content of disagreements makes almost no difference at all! Colleagues, friends, partners, couples, and families that have fight-fight dynamics will be explosive whenever either party is triggered with anxiety about any topic. Those who have fallen into fight-flight patterns are likely to shift into approach-avoid patterns automatically when stress occurs about any matter. And when flight-flight has become an ingrained pattern, both parties will habitually recede to their respective corners whenever things get challenging. For these reasons, relationship therapies aimed at conflict resolution to address specific issues routinely fail, unless they also address the underlying dynamics.[8]

The crux of addressing interpersonal dynamics involves *converting anxiety to love*. Granted, this is unrealistic, but suppose for a moment that the women who yelled at me during the pandemic would have taken a different approach. What would have happened if the first one had said, "Hey, I noticed you're not wearing a mask. I'm not angry. I'm not gonna yell at you. I just want to let you know that I'm high risk [or I live with someone who's high risk], and it makes me really anxious to think about getting sick or infecting someone, so would you mind putting on a mask?" I would have gladly complied, and we might even have become friends! Similarly, had the second one conveyed, "Excuse me, are you aware that the mask mandate was lifted? I get it that a lot of people are nervous about the coronavirus, but I'm even more concerned that the government and our society are overreacting. It makes me anxious to see you wearing a mask even though the mandate was lifted, because I start to wonder if this nightmare will ever be over so we can all go on living!" I would have apologized in earnest, taken off my mask, and we could have struck up a great conversation.

Both of those messages are substantially different from basically yelling, "You jerk!"

The reality is that we cannot control other people. But by showing our vulnerability, we can draw them close. Paradoxically, this maximizes the likelihood of their compliance with our wishes (though there is never a guarantee that we will get our needs met; more on this to come). When we show anger, we are trying to convey *I'm strong, I can do whatever I want, and you must listen to me!* But in reality, all we are doing is showing our weakness because, short of calling the police or pulling out a weapon, the other person doesn't truly *need* to do anything.

By contrast, in the rephrased examples of my encounters with the two women regarding mask-wearing, two critical elements are being expressed: (1) an acknowledgment of one's anxiety, and (2) a need for the other party. When we do this, we create more interpersonal closeness and circumvent anger and irritation. *We turn our anxieties and vulnerabilities into a force that brings us closer to others, instead of pushing them away and perpetuating distance and isolation.* Converting anxiety into love involves accepting and expressing that we need other people, and that their decisions affect us for good or ill. Doing so starts with staying away from anger and avoidance, and recognizing our tendencies to try to control people instead of acknowledging and expressing our anxious feelings.

Recall Miriam and Bessie, the sisters from chapter 5. After several sessions, Miriam came to a place of compassion and understanding for Bessie's feelings of being controlled. She decided to talk to Bessie about the purloined photo albums. "Hey, those albums meant a lot to me," Miriam said. "So when I saw they were gone I started to panic. I felt super anxious because I thought they were lost. And then, when I realized that you had taken them, it made me scared that if you took one thing, you might take another. Because you're my sister, I need to have a trusting relationship with you—and the fact that I'm questioning that trust makes me feel so sad and concerned. I'm not blaming you or saying you're dishonest. I just want to tell you how it felt that you took the albums without talking with me about it first."

Miriam's acknowledgment of her vulnerable feelings opened Bessie right up. "To be honest," Bessie said, "I was afraid to ask if I could have the albums because you're my older sister and I didn't know if you would let me." Miriam validated and acknowledged that she hasn't always been the most compassionate or *chilled out* sister, and the two of them connected emotionally more than they had in many years. In the end, Miriam suggested that Bessie keep the albums in her apartment so that Bessie would be able to go through them whenever she wanted to take a trip down memory lane.

Three Steps to Acknowledging Our Vulnerability

In practice, what should we do when we feel ourselves getting angry or turtling with someone, whether it's a friend, coworker, boss, family member, or romantic partner? Let's break down how to acknowledge our vulnerability into three concrete steps:

1. Recognize what you're anxious about.

When anxiety is experienced in the context of relationships, it is our body's way of alerting us to our lack of control over others. This is not a bad thing. In reality, we are generally *not* in control, because other people have the agency and autonomy to make their own decisions. They have their own wants and needs, which may or may not align with ours, and they may or may not place our needs before theirs when there is a conflict. So we must start out by identifying: What are we truly concerned might happen if someone doesn't do what we want and expect? This is generally uncomfortable to even think about, since it necessitates acknowledging that we are vulnerable and reliant on other people. In fact, it tends to be even more unpleasant than recognizing aspects of anxiety that we focused on in the first part of this book (chapters 1, 2, and 3).

Many people will initially say, "I don't *need* you!" But when pushed to admit the truth, it becomes clear that they *do* need others—in a big way. This is one of the chief reasons why forging a romantic relationship can be so overwhelming and even scary at times: *the closer we get to others, the more we will need to rely on them—and they truly might not come through for us!* People are free to choose and, once they are embedded into our lives, we are—to some degree—stuck with the consequences of their choices.

Therefore, friends and coworkers need to feel they can trust and rely on one another. Kids in school need their teachers and peers to be understanding and compassionate. Adult children often need their parents to let up a bit. Spouses and partners need more from each other than they're often willing to acknowledge. *It's virtually impossible to escape our vulnerability in relationships across the entire lifespan.*

If we always take care of things ourselves—instead of learning how to rely on others—we become distanced in our relationships, and if we take it too far, we can end up alone. As discussed in chapters 4 and 5, and earlier in this chapter, people are less likely to thrive when they are *independent* versus *interdependent* and collaborative. Our need for others can be hard to accept, but it is easier to deal with once we do accept it. *All* of the alternative options to relying on other people—such as pretending we don't need others, trying to control them with anger or avoidance, or withdrawing from relationships completely—tend to be worse than recognizing and dealing with our vulnerability and discomfort. To that end, the first step in relying on others is recognizing what about that makes us anxious.

2. Guard against anger and avoidance.

This step is difficult to achieve without making strides with the first: unless we are aware of our anxiety as it relates to relying on others, we are sitting ducks for anger and avoidance. As we have discussed, aggression and turtling both stem from unconscious anxiety. The underlying emotion that impels us into antagonism or shuts us down into silence is generally some form of stress, anxiety, or fear. Once we're aware of our true concerns (for example, *Will they come through for me? Can I rely on them? What if they keep doing that thing that's driving me crazy?*), we can start to manage our fight-or-flight responses.

For those of us who readily slip into anger or aggression, we need to recognize when our temperatures start to rise and take a page out of the handbook of our "turtle" counterparts by stepping aside and waiting for our emotions to settle down before expressing how we feel. Anger is a complex emotion, and it clouds our judgment and decision-making; people can make egregious errors when feeling angry—errors that they would *never* make with a clear head and heart. However, the good thing about anger is that it subsides over time; many proverbial hotheads who quickly get angry settle down just as fast. The age-old advice to "count to ten" when you feel angry is actually sage counsel. This is because it is rarely productive to speak with anyone until your anger has settled down. Go for a walk—or a run—and let yourself simmer down before you open your mouth.

On the other side of the spectrum, turtles need to guard against avoidance by standing up and speaking up. Those who avoid dealing with emotionally complex interpersonal situations typically do so, at least in part, because they are afraid of hurting the other party. Yet it is generally more painful to be shut out by a loved one who tends to turtle than to have them openly share their feelings, even if the latter are hurtful. Unlike their aggressive counterparts, those who avoid are generally at low risk for causing actual damage to the relationship by sharing. On the contrary, the biggest risk for these individuals is shutting down, by *not* saying their piece or sharing what they truly think and feel.

3. Express your needs from a place of vulnerability.

And finally, having realized what we are anxious about and having guarded against disconnection, *we need to dig deep and express what we need from others*. In order to do this, we must accept that being in relationships with others means that sometimes—oftentimes—we are not going to be in control. We need to accept that we are vulnerable, and hope to God that others will come through! Acknowledging that we need others is humbling—and terrifying—but is a necessary step in the process of accepting our interdependence and transcending our anxiety. If you don't let go, you'll be short-changing your relationships forever because you're not playing *your* part.

Once we're clear that we need others and that trying to control them is futile, we can express our actual needs and our raw emotions behind those needs—not distaste, judgment, sarcasm, or other secondary emotions but sadness, anxiety, fear, or other primary emotions that are arising. *The goal is to communicate how we feel so the other person can recognize our needs and how the decisions they make may affect our well-being.* When we express anger or silence to someone, the conversation stalls. But when we describe from a vulnerable place what we need from another person, we can potentially have meaningful conversations about our feelings. People don't like to engage when others are angry or silent, but they usually don't mind doing so when people are anxious. When we express our anxiety, it maximizes the chances that the other person will come through for us.

What If They Don't Come Through?

None of this is easy. It's even harder than the exposure therapy techniques I discussed in chapter 3. So if you are feeling uneasy or apprehensive about the previous three steps, consider it a good sign that you understand what I'm saying.

The reason this is anxiety-provoking is simple: to have relationships, we need to accept that people have limitations, and they may or may not come through for us. At some point we need to step back and allow the other party to decide whether to be there for us. We need to stop controlling them, to let go and acknowledge that—at the end of the day—*what will be will be.* Yes, we should share our anxiety with others and ask them nicely to help, but beyond that it is up to them.

Only when we follow the steps of recognizing our anxiety, guarding against anger and avoidance, accepting our vulnerability, and expressing our needs can we safely say that we've done everything we can. At that point, if someone doesn't come through for us, it's on them.

The Good News

Much (though not all) of the time, people *will* come through when you express how you feel as honestly as you can. An article in the prestigious and authoritative scientific journal *Nature* recently declared, "Experimental evidence indicates that human altruism is a powerful force."[9] The article goes on to suggest that human beings are naturally preprogrammed with higher-order values such as compassion, grace, kindness, and benevolence. When we see another human being in need, we are naturally inclined to give and do what we can to help that person.[10] For these reasons, in many but not all cases, when you show that you need someone, they come through for you.

In chapter 5, Rosemary ultimately recognized that she *did* need Sal. At a later point in our work together, she even realized the value of expressing her emotional needs to him. As this dawned on her, she went to Sal and opened her heart, tentatively at first, saying, "I know I've been really angry with you, but I realize where that's coming from. I need you—and sometimes I feel like you don't care about me, which makes me feel really sad and alone." Sal saw that Rosemary had dropped her guard, and even though he continued to struggle with depression and trauma, he *really* needed to come through for her more.

As we worked together, Rosemary realized that she was less angry about Sal's career choices and more because she was starving emotionally for Sal to show that he cared about her. As a primary wage earner, Rosemary didn't truly care so much about Sal's salary or professional achievements, but in her mind, those had become a proxy of his love. In truth, Rosemary needed to create a better connection with her husband, but she was pushing him away instead.

The key for her was realizing that showing vulnerability in a relationship is *not* a bad thing; rather it was a positive step forward that she could take. Rosemary had tried being tough and showing him who's boss for over a decade, and it got her nowhere. She realized that she had to try a new approach, which was to transcend her fear of being vulnerable. Rosemary had to learn that appealing to Sal's sense of justice—*You're my husband and you have to carry your share of the burdens*—was *never* going to work. Instead, appealing to Sal on an emotional level—*I feel lonely and need you to show me that you care*—shifted his perception and helped them to connect.

In another case that I saw, Laurie had been married for five years and had one child. She wanted a bigger family and was trying to get pregnant again, but without success despite numerous trips to a fertility clinic. Her husband, Nathan, was overwhelmed at work and felt embarrassed by all the clinical testing and discussions about his sperm count, so he tried to avoid speaking about fertility. This angered Laurie to no end, as she felt that Nathan didn't care about something that meant the world to her. One night, during an intimate moment, Laurie grew furious when Nathan couldn't get an erection and shouted, "What's wrong with you? Aren't you man enough?" Nathan felt emasculated and shamed, and he drew tightly into his turtle shell, shutting Laurie out for nearly a week. Even once the storm had cleared and he started to emerge, he was unable to perform sexually at all.

As I worked with Laurie, it became clear that the root of her anger that night was anxiety. She was afraid that her biological window for having a baby was closing and that Nathan wasn't going to be able to provide her with another child. She was even more terrified that Nathan wasn't fully committed to expanding their family together, and that ultimately he didn't care about her needs. But Laurie wasn't expressing those fears at all. Instead, she was lashing out at her spouse, saying other hurtful things like, "You don't really love me! I feel like I'm doing this alone!"

Laurie loved her husband and knew deep down that he really cared about her, and she thought that having more kids would help to solidify their relationship. She recalled that after their first baby was born, Nathan was much more engaged and lovey-dovey than usual, but as time went on that glow had dissipated. Now, however, by *not* showing her soft side, she kept him from showing his own affection and in effect was actively pushing him away.

Once I helped Laurie to recognize and express her anxiety, she was able to relinquish her control of Nathan a bit. She realized that she wasn't simply angry; she was terrified—of not having a baby and of losing her closeness with Nathan forever. When Laurie asked me what she should do about Nathan's erectile dysfunction, I suggested that she tell him something along the following lines: "It's not about getting pregnant; I just want to be close with you. If you get an erection, that's great, and if you don't, that's also fine. Because this is really not about your erection; it's about my anxiety. My anxiety means I need you, and whatever happens from there is fine either way."

That approach worked for both of them. By acknowledging her vulnerability to Nathan in a way that he could respond to, as opposed to barking out orders, Laurie was able to relinquish her need to control him. Feeling reassured that Laurie loved him no matter how he performed, Nathan was able to relax and focus on enjoying their physical intimacy. And hearing that Laurie needed him gave Nathan more confidence, which got him more excited.

I kid you not: thirty days after my conversation with Laurie about how to approach her husband, she was pregnant! I almost couldn't believe it when she called to tell me, because it happened so fast, but apparently that is the power of surrendering our need to control others and accepting them instead.

The Bad News

In some situations, the other person may not be ready to come through for you right away, so it may take time. In other circumstances, they may never come through. Oftentimes, this isn't because the person doesn't *want* to come through; they simply cannot do it, either because of practical considerations, neuropsychological factors (such as lack of focus or distraction), or because of an emotional block. However, in some cases, they just don't want to help. Even in such instances, though, it's critical to remain aware of our anxiety instead of being sucked into the vortex of anger or avoidance, so we can accept the reality of the relationship without falling prey to the fight-or-flight response.

Because of these factors, expressing our needs from a place of vulnerability does carry some risk. It can be truly challenging to do all the internal work in this chapter, only for the other person not to respond. But in our closest relationships, it's critical to know where the other person stands and to be clear that their maladaptive patterns are not a function of missteps on our part. In some instances, the best result might be that there will be some degree of distance in the relationship going forward. As painful as that is, it's better to acknowledge the limitations of others, having done our part to deepen the relationship, than to get perpetually caught in cycles of disconnection.

A young man named Chen, born to parents who emigrated from Asia, was having a hard time with their expectations for his academic success. Chen, who was born in New York, wanted to take time off from college to volunteer with the Coast Guard and expand his life experiences. He wasn't as concerned about success as his family was, and he resented that they wouldn't let him broaden his horizons. As an only child, Chen was made well aware of his cultural responsibility to his parents and their intention to rely on him throughout their old age, but he felt he would ultimately be more successful in life if he could follow his own dreams.

Chen and I initially talked about accepting his anxiety and not catastrophizing about his relationship with his parents, trying to give them the benefit of the doubt. Having been born in the US, Chen had grown up with different perspectives on life than his parents, who had lived most of their lives in Shanghai before emigrating. We discussed the conversation he hoped to have with them from a place of compassion, including his desire to let them know how much he needed them to let him be. But—as I had anticipated—that conversation did not go as he had hoped. His parents remained narrow in their focus on Chen's success, and they criticized him for sacrificing productivity. "We sacrificed so much to come to this country," they said. "You are our only son, and we have so much hope for you. We just want you to have a bright future." The implication was clear: the only way Chen could have a bright future was by toeing the line, staying in school, working for an advanced degree, and becoming a big earner.

Chen's response was, "This is a different country from where you grew up, and there are so many more options. I'm going to graduate and get a job, but that's not the be-all and end-all. Don't worry—I'm going to be there for you and will take care of you when you are older." But Chen's parents were so focused on having him follow their game plan that they couldn't even hear what he was saying. It was a very painful conversation for Chen, but as we talked about it over time, he was able to recognize that he had done his part, and his parents' limitations were not his fault. Chen wasn't entirely at peace, but he was able to accept that although they might not give him their blessing, he would have greater calm if he stopped insisting that they see things his way.

A similar thing happened between Marcus and Sheila. When they were first married, they were partiers, gallivanting around, drinking and drugging and hanging out with friends. Eventually, they settled down to have kids, and they were now raising two children under the age of four. Marcus devoted himself to creating a healthy environment for their family and frequently shared thoughts from self-help books that he read. Sheila feigned interest at first, but over time she found herself responding more to calls and text messages from old drinking and drug-using friends, most of whom were still single. Sheila started going out and partying again, leaving Marcus home with the children, and coming home "blitzed out of her mind," as Marcus put it.

Over time, the couple became increasingly distant. Sheila felt that she had made enough "concessions to adulthood," like giving up drugs and not drinking when she was pregnant. Marcus, meanwhile, grew frustrated with Sheila for abandoning him with the kids while she partied through the night with her friends. During the pandemic, things came to a real head. Sheila continued to go out of the house, and Marcus saw this as a safety concern for their family. To keep the peace, I initially encouraged him to accept who Sheila was and not catastrophize. He did a good job of that and was quickly able to share his profound anxiety that Sheila wasn't ever going to be a responsible enough adult to co-parent with him. I encouraged Marcus to express his needs to Sheila and accept that she might or might not come through for him. We practiced in session, and he got misty-eyed when he said how vulnerable he felt.

Unfortunately, though, when Marcus shared his feelings with Sheila from the depths of his soul, she just could not be there for him. It was essentially a marriage of convenience for her, and it became clear through their conversation that she had been having sex with other men during her partying nights. To his great credit, Marcus did not protest, fight, or withdraw from the relationship. He simply stated to Sheila that he was looking for more connection and more of a family life, and he would respect her decision if she didn't want that. In the end their marriage did not survive, but Marcus's emotional strength grew by leaps and bounds through the process of navigating the situation, as did his capacity for future relationships.

. . . .

TOOL #6: ACKNOWLEDGING AND EXPRESSING OUR VULNERABILITY

If you're feeling anxious in a relationship of any kind (for example, friendship, business, family, or romantic), consider it a good sign! When we connect with others, we become vulnerable since their decisions and activities affect us. As such, it's natural to feel tense, stressed, anxious, or fearful. In some ways, anxiety in a relationship is an indication that the connection is solid: if you don't feel any anxiety at all, it's likely that you don't care that much about the relationship.

Anxiety therefore presents an opportunity to make our relationships more intimate. We can choose to share our concerns with other people and give them an opportunity to understand how we feel, comfort us, and come through for us. As I've discussed, in most situations, sharing our vulnerability is a catalyst for others to bring themselves more fully to our relationships and provide what we need. However, in some cases they may not come through for us, which is hard to accept and deal with. Even in such instances, it's better to know where we stand, and to have the satisfaction that we have done our part to maintain connection.

That brings us to our tool. You can thrive with anxiety by acknowledging and expressing your vulnerability to another person, for the purposes of enriching your connection. You could do this with a coworker, boss, friend, family member, or romantic partner.

STEP 1: BUILD AWARENESS

Start by becoming more aware of your anxiety. Be fully aware of what your wants and needs are in the relationship and how they may not be met by the other person. Think vividly about how your life would look different if the person doesn't come through for you, or if they were to do some form of behavior that drives you up a wall. If you feel uncomfortable while thinking about this, you are on the right track!

STEP 2: GUARD AGAINST ANGER AND AVOIDANCE

Next, be careful to guard against anger and avoidance. If you tend to get angry in general, be super attentive to focus on your anxiety and maintain awareness of that primary emotion. With that in mind, take the time to mentally count to ten if you feel yourself getting agitated, and simmer down before moving on to step 3. If you tend to avoid and retreat into your proverbial turtle shell (for example, by changing the topic when potentially contentious issues come up, not expressing your true feelings, or "ghosting"), take the opposite approach: recognize that the dangers of shutting down include losing closeness with others, and that there is a cost to not saying your piece.

STEP 3: EXPRESS YOUR NEEDS

Finally, dig deep and express what you need from others, from a place of accepting that you need their help. Utilize your anxiety to convey that you need the other person to come through for you or to stop doing whatever is causing distress. Remember that the goal is not to control the other person; rather, it's to provide information about your emotional state so they can make an informed decision that accounts for how their actions affect you. Take the time to communicate your needs, even though it's humbling and terrifying, in order to do your part in bringing about a higher level of connection.

PART 3

ENHANCING SPIRITUAL CONNECTION

CHAPTER 7

KNOWING
OUR LIMITS

*Anxiety Can Help Us Recognize the
Limits of Our Knowledge and Control*

First, a few general words on spirituality. As I shared in the intro-duction, spirituality is "the search for the sacred,"[1] which involves transcending the material world. For many, this involves religion, but for others it can reflect *any* aspect of life that is transcendent in some way, such as developing a greater sense of humility, patience, gratitude, kindness, and compassion. Another aspect of spirituality, which we will discuss in chap-ter 9, involves recognizing the human capacity for greatness, mustering the courage to face adversity, and pursuing our goals and dreams. Since spirituality is such a broad domain, I encourage members of any or no faith at all to remain open to the following pages and to learn about how anxiety can enhance our spiritual connection in surprising ways. With that said, some readers may not resonate with part 3 of this book, and that's okay.

The present chapter brings us back to the themes of certainty and control, which we discussed in the introduction. As I've shared, the chief reasons why we are so anxious today are our cultural intolerance for uncertainty and our inability to withstand any lack of security. We are struggling with unprecedented levels of anxiety in large part because we (erroneously) assume that life is supposed to be fully predictable and controllable. Along these lines, we tend to criticize and blame ourselves when things go wrong, even when this is due to factors well beyond our control. And so, when the complexities of life inevitably unfold and the paucity of our knowledge and capabilities is revealed, the mirage of predictability and control dissipates, and we are seized with anxiety. *In this chapter, I will show you how the intrinsic relationships between anxiety, uncertainty, and uncontrollability can be a catalyst for thriving.* We can learn to view our anxiety as an indicator that we are bumping against the limits of our knowledge and control in the world, and that there is no reason to judge ourselves when things go wrong—sometimes life just gets complicated and challenging. When we recognize these aspects of being human, we emerge with less anxiety and with enhanced spiritual virtues, such as humility.

The Limits of Human Knowledge

In the current age of digital information and rapidly expanding scientific knowledge, it can seem that we know everything. Just ask Siri or Alexa and they will tell you pretty much any piece of information you may want to know, in a matter of seconds. At the same time, ironically, our expansive technology and science have shown how much we do *not* know!

For example, quantum physics calls into question even the most basic assumptions that we hold about matter and energy. Artificial intelligence shows how the human capacity for processing information is dwarfed by that of a machine. Modern neuroscience has revealed that the human brain is far more complex than we can presently comprehend—many of its functions are governed by dynamic and ever-changing interactions of multiple networks, as opposed to distinct regions.

At an even more basic level, scientific knowledge today remains incredibly limited. To take just a few examples, scientists do not know why we cry, why we laugh, why we fall asleep, or even how general anesthesia works.[2] When we look into the night sky, our lack of knowledge is even more palpable. Astronomers estimate between one hundred billion and four hundred billion stars are in the Milky Way alone, of which the sun is a relatively minor one. And that's not much compared to the estimated two hundred billion trillion stars in the known universe.[3] In a nutshell: when you compare what we know to what we don't know, it's clear which side tips the scale.

Recognizing these and other limits of human knowledge can make us anxious, unless we are able to tolerate uncertainty.

Being intolerant of uncertainty is a bit like having an allergy. When people who are intolerant of (that is, allergic to) uncertainty encounter it, they also have a strong reaction: they worry and do everything they can think of to get away from, avoid, or eliminate the uncertainty.[4] If you are extremely intolerant of uncertainty, that can lead to even bigger problems, such as expending many hours of the day, and a fair amount of physical and psychological energy, engaging in repetitive behaviors and dealing with the stress and anxiety those behaviors generate.

Allergic to Uncertainty

Bill Wilson, the cofounder of Alcoholics Anonymous, had a major breakthrough when a physician named William D. Silkworth, who was treating him for his addiction, told Wilson that he had an "allergic reaction" to alcohol. Once he took a single drink, he couldn't stop drinking until he either passed out or was hospitalized.

Dr. Silkworth likened chronic alcohol dependence to hay fever, in that one could be free "for many years from any susceptibility to pollen. Year after year, however, there gradually develops a sensitivity to it in certain individuals, culminating at last in paroxysms of hay fever that persist indefinitely when the condition is fully established."[5]

Likewise, many of us have an allergy to uncertainty. Among a certain subset of the population, this may become greatly exacerbated over time, taking the form of obsessive-compulsive disorder (OCD), as we shall explore in this chapter.

The curious thing is that if you are among the unfortunate few who have an allergy to pollen, you can simply avoid exposure to it or take antihistamines. In the case of alcohol, you can eschew it entirely. However, uncertainty is omnipresent and cannot be avoided, so being allergic to uncertainty is much more complicated.

One common coping mechanism to deal with uncertainty is *worry*. As we discussed in chapter 3, worrywarts avoid having a truly overpowering and uncomfortable emotional response—they keep their minds busy thinking superficially about the future so they don't need to think about how deeply uncertain things are in the present. As a result, the worry *reinforces* the anxiety instead of alleviating it.

Other behaviors we may use to alleviate our intolerance of uncertainty include the following:

- seeking excessive reassurance from others
- making long, detailed to-do lists, sometimes several times each day
- calling loved ones repeatedly to "make sure" that they are okay
- double-checking, such as by rereading emails several times before sending to ensure they are perfect
- refusing to delegate work: not allowing others at work or home to do certain tasks—because you cannot be certain that it will be done correctly unless you do it yourself
- procrastination or avoidance[6]

The Classic Worrywart

Madelaine, a sixty-three-year-old divorced, recently retired woman living in a rent-controlled apartment on Manhattan's Upper East Side, came to see me for a consultation. Despite her desirable address, Madelaine didn't have a lot of income, but she remained in New York since her kids lived nearby on Long Island, and she was actively engaged in the local social circuit.

For all that, she had intense general anxiety disorder, characterized by uncontrollable worries about multiple matters, as well as significant physiological signs of stress, such as shortness of breath, muscle aches and pains, difficulty concentrating, and fatigue. In short, Madelaine was a "worrywart" of the highest order.

One of Madelaine's adult children had a pool in the backyard, and she could fixate for days on the possibility of a grandchild falling in and drowning. When the COVID-19 pandemic happened, she became consumed with worry about her own health. Even after she got vaccinated and boosted as many times as possible, she still had difficulty sleeping because of high muscle tension from being keyed up all day.

What really threw Madelaine off and brought her in to see me, though, was that one of her friends from the neighborhood mentioned that her apartment had recently lost its rent-controlled status. Madelaine realized that if she also lost rent-control, she would no longer be able to afford her apartment and would have to move. This disturbed her sense of peace to no end because it was something she had never even thought of. Madelaine realized that if she had reason to worry about an issue that had *never* crossed her mind, *there could be any number of threats and concerns lurking in the shadows.* She became increasingly apprehensive and concerned about uncertainty in general, and started to feel substantially more anxious day-to-day.

When Madelaine came to my office, she expected me to reassure her that everything was going to be fine, that the odds of all the things she was afraid of happening were vanishingly small, and that in reality there was much less to worry about than she had recently come to realize. But I didn't—because I couldn't.

"Every single one of your concerns is legitimate and might happen," I said. "Not only that, but have you considered that you might get stuck in the elevator on your way home today? If you do electronic banking, your account could get hacked. The reality is that *anything could go wrong at any time.*"

Madelaine shot me a look of exasperation. "Why are you making my anxiety *worse?*"

"That's not my intention," I said. "I am trying to point out that there are limits to human knowledge, and we really don't know what's going to happen even in the next hour, let alone in the next day, month, or a year from now. I'm trying to help you to recognize that uncertainty is part of the human condition, instead of fighting against that."

At first Madelaine struggled with this idea, since it made her feel more anxious. At one point during our initial consultation, she even became quite angry with me. But as we continued talking, she slowly began to recognize that, during rare moments of calm in her life, the notion of accepting uncertainty had crossed her mind. She also had no real rejoinder to my comments. When push came to shove, Madelaine recognized that we cannot know the future because there are limits to human knowledge—it's just a fact of life.

Three Options

At first glance, there are just two options for how to deal with the fact that something unexpected and potentially devastating could happen at any time.

Option #1 is to be an ostrich and hide our heads in the sand, pretending that we have certainty. The upside of this approach is that we don't need to think about uncertainty on a regular basis. The downside, however, is that it's not grounded in reality. As a result, it's just a matter of time until we get overwhelmed with reality. This leads to episodic spikes in anxiety that we're ill-prepared to handle.

Option #2 is to live day-to-day with the recognition that nothing is ever certain. This is an accurate approach, but it comes with a hefty price tag: living with full realization that we are constantly in a state of uncertainty seems to be a surefire way to live a panic-stricken life all the time. Indeed, anxiety disorders tend to increase commensurately with actual levels of uncertainty. When nothing is certain, we are at risk for behavioral paralysis, since life just gets too intense.

Fortunately, there is a third option: *we can thrive with anxiety.*

Option #3 is to understand that worry is our mind's way of reminding us that uncertainty is a part of life. While intolerance of uncertainty leads to anxiety, uncertainty in itself does not need to make us anxious or uncomfortable. It is possible to make your anxiety work for you, by recognizing that we are only human, that we don't know everything, and that we don't even need to know everything. When we respond this way to our anxiety, we can convert it into humility, and use our anxiety to live a more meaningful, fulfilling, and ultimately calmer life. Other valuable virtues can also emerge, such as patience when we experience delays, and gratitude for what we have.

Over time, Madelaine (who had been choosing option #2 prior to therapy) learned to be more comfortable with these ideas, which I shared during our sessions, and she experienced a precipitous drop in anxiety. She remained a classic New York worrywart in many respects, but her physiological activation dropped from the severe to the medium range, and she was able to sleep again at night.

Summing up our sessions, Madelaine remarked, "I came to psychotherapy with the hope of achieving certainty so I could be calm again. Now I realize that I don't need to be certain, and I feel less anxious than ever."

College Anxiety

Frank was a high school senior who was anxious about getting into college. Before we met, he managed his anxiety with option #1. He took a lackadaisical approach by pretending that he'd have no problem getting accepted into a college of his choice, regardless of his qualifications. Frank would ignore the unsolicited advice of his parents and guidance counselors, who told him that he had to know what he wanted, have a plan, and put more effort into his studies.

But then, his friends—all of whom applied themselves much more consistently to their studies—started getting acceptance letters, whereas Frank was invited for nary an interview. His anxiety mounted to the point of panic, and he realized that the ostrich approach had not served him well.

As Frank and I discussed his reasons for choosing option #1, Frank said that he didn't want to be a neurotic worrywart like his older sister, Maribel, who tended to choose option #2. She had made it into the college of her dreams, but at a high personal cost. She was popping pills to handle her severe anxiety, and Frank didn't want to do that, nor did he want to work like a madman.

I suggested option #3: to realize that anxiety is our mind's way of reminding us that life is uncertain. Frank could be realistic about the uncertainties in life. He could work hard while recognizing that we don't know what the future holds. He didn't have to be like his sister, but he didn't need to choose option #1 either. "You have to find somewhere in the middle," I said.

And he did. Frank saw that he needed to apply himself more than he had been, beginning by working out a plan with his college guidance counselor, choosing a few realistic colleges to apply to, and spending time on his application essays. As Frank accepted that—despite all his efforts—life remains uncertain, he was able to put in additional effort, since the pressure was within a manageable range. When Frank got into one of the colleges, he was genuinely happy to be there and not anxious about the next uncertain matter—unlike his sister, who was also in college but not happy at all.

Pregnancy Anxiety

After five challenging and anxiety-filled years, including several rounds of in vitro fertilization and multiple miscarriages, Ruby and her husband, Brian, conceived a baby that survived past the first trimester.

Understandably, Ruby was anxious about the viability of her pregnancy. Although she was excited about the prospect of becoming a mother for the first time, this was overshadowed by her daily worries and significant tension about the health of the baby. *How would he develop? Will my body have the strength to carry him to term and go through delivery without complications?* Ruby was also worried about Brian and their relationship. *Will having a baby bring us closer together?* Or, as she had seen in a few other marriages, *Will becoming parents make it harder for us to connect emotionally and physically once the daily stress of caring for a newborn sets in?*

Ruby's approach to anxiety was option #2: she was coping with uncertainty by maintaining constant awareness of the potential pitfalls that could occur in her life. She had developed *overinflated responsibility*, in which a person feels that they are responsible for doing more than what is realistic. She wanted to avoid any potential fault if something happened to her baby. Specifically, Ruby was concerned that if she didn't prepare for *every* possibility by making sure she was 100 percent aware of her health and her baby's health, it would be *because of her* if something happened.

I told Ruby that no amount of worrying or preparation would ever protect her child or her relationship with Brian. I repeated what I've said earlier: if you take all the information in the world that you know for certain, and all the information that you're *not* sure about, the latter is greater by a fair margin.

I also explained to Ruby that there was a very low correlation between knowledge and eventual outcomes. "Let's be honest that Google searching will probably not help your baby," I said. Ruby freaked out initially because she had bought into option #2 so wholeheartedly. But the more we talked, and the more she reflected on her own, the more she settled into the truth of option #3 and calmed down. In the end, Ruby gave birth to a healthy baby boy, and by the end of her pregnancy she was much calmer.

"Initially, when I went into labor, I completely freaked out!" she told me during a follow-up session. "But once my contractions started coming hard and fast, I realized how the whole birth process was completely beyond my control. I remembered our sessions and what you had told me, and I focused on being okay with my human limits. Some things are just out of our hands. From that point, I was able to focus on giving birth instead of being in my head."

The Doubting Disease

If most anxiety stems from our neurotic need for certainty in a highly uncertain world, then perhaps the purest manifestation of this need is obsessive-compulsive disorder (OCD). In the nineteenth-century, OCD was known as "the doubting disease," aptly named because people with OCD are perpetually in doubt, and the many "precautions" they take, on a painfully repetitive basis, never fully resolve their concerns.

Naturally, when a person is as doubtful as OCD sufferers tend to be, the natural solution is to somehow find perfect certainty. The problem, as we've been discussing, is that this is impossible to do, since the world is so uncertain. And so, OCD sufferers often go to extraordinary lengths to determine whether they have done something wrong, or whether something bad is going to happen to them.

My patient Jerry focused on germs to the extent that he was afraid to touch *anything* that might have been touched by someone else. This was before COVID-19, and yet his reasoning was that he just didn't know whether something had been contaminated, so why take the chance?

I went through the data with him, showing that there are traces of urine and fecal matter almost everywhere. This initially made Jerry much more anxious and uncomfortable, since he was trying to live with perfect certainty that he would not get sick. The first stage of treatment, therefore, was to help him realize that uncertainty is intrinsically part of life, and that certainty is never going to happen. "If you're looking for certainty, you're in the wrong place," I said to him. Once he got that, he was able to move forward.

OCD has two components. The first are troubling, "obsessive" thoughts. These are distressing and unwanted but keep coming back no matter what. Usually obsessions are anxiety-related, though sometimes they focus on disgust or simply perfectionism. But across the board, obsessions are always characterized by intolerance of uncertainty. Furthermore, even though the thoughts typically don't make sense, and the person may not even wholly buy into them, the person becomes obsessed with them.

Often these obsessions involve the kind of overinflated responsibility that Ruby experienced during her pregnancy. The sufferer feels responsible way more than anyone should realistically feel, and that's what is making them anxious. Their need to reduce uncertainty stems from the idea that if they don't know what's going to happen next, it will be their fault if things go awry.

Other patients may be obsessed by having thoughts of a sexual or violent nature, and they feel hyper-responsible to eliminate them. Interestingly, psychological science has revealed that it is extremely common for people to have occasional violent or sexual thoughts pop up in their minds.[7] Most of us briefly recognize these and immediately let them go, not giving them much thought at all. But people with OCD can get obsessed about such thoughts because they interpret them as a sign of danger. Most times, they worry that they might act on them—and they think it *would* be their fault that they didn't take corrective action. They obsessively worry that maybe they'll harm someone or do something immoral, and that would be a terrible catastrophe.

The second component of OCD is "compulsions," which are repetitive behaviors that are intended to reduce the anxiety caused by obsessions.[8] For example, a few years back, I saw a patient named Josh in his early twenties. Josh had an obsessive fear that an electric plug might be incorrectly inserted into an outlet in his home and cause a fire. (With today's polarized plugs and sockets this would be almost impossible, but the nature of obsessions is that one can never be sure.) To deal with the anxiety created by this obsession, before leaving the house Josh would check *all* the plugs to make sure that every one was securely in its socket. The thing is, he had already checked them five minutes ago, and again three minutes before that! But he was afraid that he might have missed one. Josh knew full well that the plugs were fine and there was no real risk of fire, but he still went back and checked multiple times to be sure. Unfortunately, this often made him late for appointments. It also disrupted his sleep, since he would repeat all these procedures at night for fear of starting a fire while he was in bed, *and it would be his fault for not checking.*

Other compulsions may include washing one's hands excessively to get rid of germs, replacing distressing and upsetting thoughts with non-threatening images, or engaging in excessive religious rituals that are intended to create a sense of certainty. The problem with all compulsions is that they only reduce one's obsessions and anxiety in the short run. The obsessions and distress *always* come back—with a vengeance! And the more one performs compulsions over time, the worse their obsessions and anxiety get. This is because compulsions make it impossible for people with OCD to do the one thing that could help them: recognize and tolerate the fact that certain things in life are uncertain, and there is nothing human beings can do to change that fact.

Along these lines, OCD treatment starts by helping patients to tolerate uncertainty and peacefully accept our limited knowledge. In reality, houses do occasionally burn down because of faulty wiring. Germs are omnipresent and, as we know all too well, they can spread diseases that are not easily controlled. Every once in a while, a person truly might act on a violent thought or impulse, as the alarming number of mass shootings in this country bears out. But all these situations are far less common than OCD.

Furthermore, *excessive corrective action in the context of uncertainty never helps*. On the contrary, it's just a pathway to being more intolerant of uncertainty, more worried, more anxious, and ever more obsessive over time.

Hit and Run

A surprisingly common form of OCD is known as *hit and run*. As the name rather dolefully implies, this involves an obsessive concern that a driver has hit, and possibly killed, a pedestrian, a child, a bicyclist, or an animal—even though there is no evidence that this has happened. In many cases, the driver will circle back and drive around the same streets again and again just to be sure, or check the newspapers the next day, to see whether there were any hit-and-run accidents in the area they were driving through. They may inspect their car many times over, looking for dents or bloodstains that would indicate that they hit someone, even though they felt or heard no actual impact. They often drive extra slowly on populated streets, avoid driving at night or in crowded areas, or stop driving altogether because of their obsessions.

Marco came to my office with hit-and-run OCD, and the core of his fear was *overinflated responsibility*—if he hit someone with his car and left them dying on the street, it would be his fault. Marco's belief was that since life is uncertain, you have to try extra hard. *"No!"* I insisted. Life is uncertain, period. But that doesn't mean you have to try extra hard. It just means that you have to accept the uncertainty of life as it is.

At first, I suggested exposure therapy, as discussed in chapter 3, but Marco flat out refused to go driving in crowded areas. I realized I had to take a step back, so I had a conversation with him about the fact that we humans cannot ever be fully certain about anything. This approach helped Marco to accept that as a human being, we can never fully know a large degree of information for sure, so he needed to be humble and recognize the limits of human knowledge. Once he grasped that on a cognitive level, he was able to go through exposure therapy. *Marco saw this as a way to work on his humility—a spiritual enterprise.* For Marco, driving became an act of letting go of his need for total certainty and acknowledging that he was simply a human being.

Incredibly, within just one week of our discussions about uncertainty, Marco was driving on the busy streets of Manhattan *during rush hour*, with tons of traffic and pedestrians. He even took up my challenge to drive in the morning when he was tired, without having coffee, and to go out for a drive when he was feeling distracted—all without checking back to look for bodies! Marco saw this as a way of chipping away at his hyper-responsibility, and he ended up thriving through the process.

The Limits of Human Control

So far, we have discussed the limits of human knowledge. We have identified that while recognizing the paucity of our knowledge can be anxiety-provoking at first, it can also be liberating to let go of taking responsibility for everything. In the remainder of this chapter, we will examine something potentially even more terrifying: *the limits of our control.*

The good news is that when we recognize this aspect of life, our humility increases by leaps and bounds, and our anxiety also drops significantly because we stop judging ourselves every time something goes wrong.

Dr. David H. Barlow, from whom I learned so much about exposure therapy (as described in chapter 3), had some formative attitudes about control. In his highly influential academic book *Anxiety and Its Disorders*, which was first published in 1988 and remains a must-read for any clinician-researcher who studies anxiety disorders, Barlow dedicated the text to his children with the line, "May you continue to maintain your illusion of control." I imagine that, at some level, he intended this to be humorous. But at another level, Dr. Barlow was sharing two fundamental insights about life: (1) human control of life is, in fact, an illusion, and (2) maintaining that illusion is one way to avoid struggling with anxiety.

The conundrum the latter point presents, however, is that—similar to the limits of human knowledge—the limits of human control occasionally penetrate the veil of illusion. Hence, it's only a matter of time before we are compelled to recognize our inherent inability to control the world around us. Without sufficient preparation to cope with this recognition, we will end up experiencing anxiety.

The spiritual teacher and bestselling author Pema Chödrön has written insightfully about the inability to control things in our lives. She has brilliantly suggested that, when we recognize our inherent lack of control, we become spiritual warriors—"Not warriors who kill and harm, but warriors of nonaggression" who are emotionally and spiritually resilient to manage the vicissitudes of life.

A warrior accepts that we can never know what will happen to us next. We can try to control the uncontrollable by looking for security and predictability, always hoping to be comfortable and safe. But the truth is that we can never avoid [being out of control]. This . . . is part of the adventure. It's also what makes us afraid.[9]

I share these paradoxical sentiments. On the one hand, recognizing our lack of control is a surefire way to feel afraid. On the other, when we embrace that safety, security, and predictability are a facade—when we voluntarily relinquish the illusion before life penetrates through it—we emerge infinitely stronger as human beings.

Counter to Western Culture

The above ideas are profoundly at odds with what Western culture espouses and teaches. Several years ago, I gave a talk to Harvard College students, which I began by asking them a series of rhetorical questions, such as, "Who in this room chose whether, where, or when to be born? What would your lives look like had you emerged into a different century instead of today? Or had you ended up studying in Russia, Japan, the Congo, or Sri Lanka, as opposed to America? Did anyone here have control over the intellectual or physical abilities that you received at birth? What about your financial situation? What would life look like if you were born an indigenous native of this land during the seventeenth century?"

I went on to say, "It's true that you do have some degree of agency in the world, and you can affect certain opportunities that come your way in life. But let's be intellectually honest and acknowledge that almost all the most important factors that shape your experience and your capacity to make a difference in this world are not in your control: time, geolocation, culture, family, friends, intellectual capacity, socioeconomic status, personal health. *All* of these factors are outside the scope of human choice, and any one of them indelibly shapes virtually the entirety of your life experiences."

At the end of my introduction, I stared out at a sea of blank faces, awash in deafening quiet. Nobody said anything or even asked me a single question! On the one hand, I was proud to have silenced a group of Harvard students. At the same time, I felt deeply concerned about those students, since I realized that most, if not all, of those present had never for a moment entertained the possibilities I posed. They were light-years away from recognizing their lack of control over the world.

When I went home that night after the talk, I reflected on what a precarious situation the students were in. My clinical experience has taught me how *emotionally dangerous* it is not to recognize our lack of control. Granted, this was a bright and super-capable group of individuals who had habituated to high levels of success and achievement. And yet, what would they do—*how would they feel*—if and when they came up against a situation that was beyond their capacity to influence or control?

My concern was that they would blame themselves for not being stronger, better prepared, or for failing, even though they might have done everything they could along the way. I wished they could understand that despite our capacity and best efforts, sometimes things just don't work out the way we want—and that's not necessarily our fault.

A famous line often attributed to Thomas Edison goes, "Genius is one percent inspiration and ninety-nine percent perspiration."[10] This is the philosophy that is promulgated within Western educational institutions. In one sense, the perspective is admirable in that it recognizes the value of hard work and persistence. However, Edison did *not* recognize that genius—as well as innovation and success—often occurs spontaneously and *despite*, not because of, human efforts.

Hard work is insufficient for progress. Just consider the infinite number of outside factors that could generate success or failure, irrespective of human efforts. Many people strain and struggle for years, even decades, without achieving their goals, whereas others may inherit or stumble upon favorable outcomes regardless of, or even despite, their actions.

Besides, a person can be immensely successful in one area of life while riddled with difficulties and shortcomings in others. Edison himself is a notable example. As early as seven years of age, his constant questioning and self-centeredness led his teacher to say that he had an intellectual disability.[11] On another occasion during his childhood, Edison burned down his father's barn because he was "experimenting" with fire, and he almost died![12] All the "perspiration" and hard work in the world wouldn't have mattered had Edison been more unlucky. In other words, so many factors can go askew despite our best efforts. In reality, there are always elements that we cannot control.

There is another concern with attributing success and failure to our hard work alone. As we will discuss in chapter 9, living a balanced and emotionally healthy life necessitates ensuring that we are grounded in our relationships with ourselves and with others, in addition to professional and other pursuits that bring out our unique potential. Focusing on persistent work at the expense of self-care and interpersonal connections is usually not a great long-term strategy.

In this vein, it is notable that Edison's children—who grew up in the lap of luxury—became hopelessly entitled, and some developed alcoholism. One of his sons became so dysfunctional that Edison paid him to change his last name, just to avoid embarrassment to the family.[13] Overly dedicating ourselves to work—and perceiving that our efforts are the primary ingredient in success—can have disastrous consequences.

The Curse of Success (and Blessing of Failure)

At this point in my career, I have more patients for anxiety and related concerns than I care to count. Bar none, the most challenging cases have had the following characteristics: they are brilliant, wealthy, good-looking, and often people of notoriety. Even more often, they are the children of brilliant, wealthy, good-looking, and famous parents. What is it about success that can be such a curse when it comes to emotional and behavioral health?

Nick had made a fortune in the furniture business. He had a large family, and he was athletically gifted, having won the state championship in amateur tennis. Then, in his midforties, he developed a rare autoimmune disorder, which led to extreme weight gain that affected his ability to work and his general health and athleticism.

Nick was overwhelmed by the sudden disparity between certain aspects of his life—his successful business, which he felt he could control, and the health crisis, which he recognized he could not control despite all his wealth and hard work. He became anxious and depressed. He gained 150 pounds, could no longer play tennis, and eventually he could barely walk or get around. It was such a rude awakening for him not to be in control that he wanted to take his own life.

The only thing that got Nick through this crisis was his coming to McLean Hospital, where his treatment team got to work. I was privileged to be involved in his care, and Nick slowly came to recognize the real grace and freedom of realizing that we cannot truly rely on *any* of our own resources to control our lives.

Nick originally attributed his success to "perspiration" (as Thomas Edison would have put it)—that is, hard work and persistence. However, before his health crisis, he was a pretty intense guy who, by his own admission, was *not* a lot of fun to live with. At that time, Nick's work and his athletic exploits consumed him and left little time for his family. He often ignored his three kids, and he would become irate when he *did* spend time with them. He cheated on his wife, largely because his business took him away from her for travel, and he wound up expending his pent-up sexual energy with women to whom he felt no emotional connection at all. For all his financial rewards, he was not living a healthy, balanced life.

After his health crisis struck, Nick had an epiphany. He realized that no amount of work can ever guarantee success, since illness can come at any time. He came to the (correct) conclusion that his success had little to do with his brilliant ideas or his hard work, but rather with the support of his loving wife and family, an athletic constitution, and having been born in a country where entrepreneurs can amass a fortune under the right circumstances.

Most of all, he recognized that a good amount of luck went into his success; so many times he had "caught a break" in ways that were completely out of his control. Had the stars not aligned he would never have been so successful. This humble approach gave Nick a new lease on life. He came to recognize that, far more important than financial success and a few trophies on the mantelpiece, was his relationship with his family, and his character.

Nick got to work battling his crippling depression, rebuilding a relationship with his family, and refocusing on higher-order values. Summing up our work together, Nick said: "I'm going to do the best that I can. But I know that I'm not fully in control, and I'm going to accept that. I'm going to enjoy the relationships that I have to the fullest extent possible. I can't just be a workhorse my entire life because there's more to life than work."

Without question, Nick's autoimmune disease was a blessing in disguise.

From the Ivory Tower to the Real World

My talk to those Harvard students made me rethink my own experience of struggling to bring my dream of Center for Anxiety to fruition. In the ivory tower of academia, I found plenty of challenging work to do, but most of it was fairly manageable, predictable, and relatively low-risk. Academics love to make people jump through hoops: my professors created various criteria by which to evaluate my performance; my department similarly subjects me to periodic reviews with various achievement metrics; and the peer-review process requires adhering to certain standards before my papers are accepted for publication. Across the board, though, the risks are relatively low because professors don't like to have their students fail, departments need faculty members to teach and do research, and editors need to fill the pages of their journals with academic contributions. In the end, those who keep at it eventually see some degree of success, and while I have certainly had my challenges as an academic, my risk-tolerance profile has been high enough to weather storms along the way.

However, when I set out to create an anxiety treatment center in New York while teaching and doing research in Boston, all of a sudden I plunged into a situation where I was out in the real world, and it was sink or swim. For the first time in my life, I faced a truly risky and uncontrollable predicament with real consequences. My approach, as I mentioned in the introduction, was to strategically surge forward. I increased my self-care, spoke to my wife and my mentors, and got the support I needed to embrace unprecedented levels of uncertainty in my life.

But there was another critical piece, which I didn't mention before. Initially, when I saw that things weren't going well, I was kicking myself. *How could I have been so stupid to open up an anxiety clinic in a different city?* Quickly, though, I recognized that whether I would be successful in New York was well beyond the limits of my control. Whether I would turn the corner was largely independent of my efforts and decision-making.

Of course, I was going to try my best within my capacity—I was going to push beyond my comfortable limits and give it my all. My anxiety dropped when I recognized a simple fact: people would either come to my office for help, or not. The market is what the market is. The outcome of the situation would not be fully due to my efforts, for good or otherwise. That recognition helped me immensely.

Yes, it was a challenging reality to come to, since thinking about my lack of control made me palpably more anxious in the moment. But every day since—after I came to the understanding that *human efforts and outcomes are not one and the same*—I have been calmer and less self-critical.

. . . .

TOOL #7: DECOUPLING OUR
EFFORTS AND OUTCOMES

As we've discussed, the primary purpose of worry is to avoid thinking about the fact that, ultimately, life is unpredictable and uncontrollable. Worry gives us a *false* sense of control. This leaves us vulnerable to self-criticism in the wake of life stressors and setbacks, since we tend to blame ourselves when things go wrong.

So if you are feeling worried about an outcome, take the opportunity to recognize that uncertainty and uncontrollability are a part of life. *There is nothing wrong with you or anyone else if you are not able to predict or control the future.* All it means is that you are a human being—a creature with limited knowledge and capacity to influence the events of this world.

Along these lines, consider that, while human efforts are important (as we will discuss in chapter 9), they are ultimately insufficient to control the outcomes of life. This is because of the following fact: in every situation, any number of events could occur that would interrupt the usual sequence of an outcome following from our intentions and actions.

Our tool, therefore, is to *decouple human efforts and outcomes by recognizing that what we do in day-to-day life may or may not lead to the result that we are striving for.*

Even basic acts like turning on a light could be thwarted: the switch may not catch the connecting wires, the electrical circuit may malfunction, the fuse or lightbulb may blow out, or other mishaps may occur, none of which are related in any way to our ability to flip a light switch!

Similarly, the act of standing up from a chair could be interrupted by factors beyond our knowledge or control. The chair may spontaneously collapse, or our muscles and ligaments may not work as we expect them to, or there may be a sudden change in atmospheric pressure or gravity that makes it impossible to stand up. Granted, some of these situations are more far-fetched than others, but none of them is out of the realm of possibility, and all are beyond the scope of human control.

When we look for this on an everyday basis, it is readily apparent. As the great Hindu holy book *The Bhagavad Gita* says, we should focus not on the results of our actions but on the actions themselves.[14]

To these ends, once per day while engaging in a mundane task, briefly consider that the effort you are expending may not result in the outcome you are expecting.

For example, before you open the refrigerator door to get some milk for your breakfast cereal, consider that the door may be sealed shut, or the fridge may not be working, or the milk may be gone or have soured. Consider as well that none of those possibilities reflects poorly on you as a human being—sometimes things occur beyond our control. Stuff happens!

Over time, try this approach when you are feeling anxious or worried. Consider that the efforts you are expending to reduce uncertainty may not pan out. Most of all, recognize that whether or not things go our way, it has a lot less to do with our efforts than we tend to think.

When we take this approach, we can thrive with anxiety by embracing our humble human position and by recognizing that our knowledge and strength are inherently limited.

. . . .

CHAPTER 8

ACCEPTING OUR LIMITS

Anxiety Can Help Us Accept the Limits of Our Knowledge and Control

We learned in chapter 7 how anxiety typically occurs when we are out of the know or out of control, since such situations butt up against our intolerance of uncertainty. We discussed how there are two typical approaches to coping with uncertainty: pretending we have more knowledge or control than we do, or living in perpetual fear. We also discussed a third approach, in which we utilize anxiety to thrive: when we feel anxious, we can take the opportunity to recognize that we have encountered a natural limit to our knowledge and control. *This is not a bad thing; it is a fact of life.* One that fosters humility, which also can lead to a drop in anxiety since it helps us recognize that we are only human and will *always* lack some degree of knowledge and agency. There is nothing wrong with us or the world when things are uncertain or uncontrollable!

In this chapter, we will work on internalizing these concepts—not only recognizing our limits but accepting them. This entails being prepared to face situations in life that we do not wish to occur. The well-known Serenity Prayer asks for divine help "to accept the things we cannot change, the courage to change the things we can, and the wisdom to know the difference." Developing a serene attitude requires fully embracing what we cannot change, even if that might be something we don't want to materialize.

Heads up that this chapter will not be easy; it can be painful to dig deep and prepare to accept unfortunate outcomes. At the same time, going through the mental process of envisioning and accepting misfortune can create a sense of inner strength and resilience, which can engender more courage to face whatever life may bring. Additionally, accepting our limits can be a catalyst to feeling transcendentally connected through the most widely practiced spiritual activity on earth: prayer.

The Inevitability of Threat

When Aileen came to my office, she had been married for six years and was the mother of two young kids. Her family history of cancer led her to develop significant health anxiety (hypochondriasis). She continually surfed the web for medical research, and she went from doctor to doctor looking for reassurance that she didn't have cancer. Eventually, from therapy, Aileen came to recognize that her knowledge and control are limited; no matter how many times she checked, she could not know for sure whether she had cancer. And yet she remained stuck on one point: "I don't want to get cancer!" she said. That is, although she recognized that there were no guarantees, Aileen remained plagued by anxiety since no doctor could promise that she would remain healthy. Because of this,

Aileen justified the distraction of medical research, as she saw this as a way of preventing herself from embracing the fact that she had no control over her situation. Aileen was struggling to accept that she may get sick, and that in the end, there wasn't much she could do about it. So she understandably felt a need to occupy her mind with something in order to relieve her stress.

Around the same time, I also worked with Zelena, an Olympic tri-athlete who called my office in a panic. Professionally, everything had been going Zelena's way for the past few years; her training was progressing, even though it was extremely taxing, and she had been receiving a lot of media attention, which led to increased opportunities to help people in need. Zelena loved speaking at inner-city schools and feeling that she was giving back to communities in which she herself had grown up. However, her mother's business had recently taken a major hit, and Zelena became consumed with worry to the extent that she could barely cope. Notably, as is often true of Olympic athletes early in their careers, Zelena wasn't yet earning much money; while she was confident that would all work out in time, Zelena was concerned that her mother might go bankrupt in the interim. She worried all day about her mother's finances and grew depressed about this one aspect of her life to the point that everything else faded into the background. Zelena's Olympic training had given her a good sense of her lack of knowledge and control! But this was throwing her over the edge because she just couldn't stand the thought of her mother failing financially.

Everyone has stressors or sensitive nodes, which I would call *pain points*. These are embedded in our psyches and, when rubbed against, they make us anxious because we want to avoid those particular stressors. Pain points tend to vary based on our life histories; some of us are anxious about health, others about money and career, and still others worry about family or religion—because these domains have heightened meaning given the context of our lives. A person who grew up in a family that valued academic achievement may get totally freaked out about a bad grade but not be so affected by health issues or the financial markets. Someone who lost a parent to cancer at a young age, on the other hand, may be focused on safety and health, but they might not mind when they get a C-minus or when their bank account runs low. One who grew up with a bean counting parent who questioned the value of every purchase might become increasingly tense about finances but not care much about their health. Everyone has *something* that they are sensitive to, something they do not like to think about. When these pain points are triggered, they make us feel supremely anxious.

And let's face it: our pain points *will* get triggered. At some point in life it's inevitable that the facades of certainty and controllability get lifted, and if we're not prepared for such moments, we will become anxious—suddenly staring into an abyss that scares us like no other. Life has an uncanny way of eventually bringing us into circumstances where we are forced to confront our pain points. Threats occur. It's unavoidable! Some may call this *earth school* or *the university of hard knocks*, and those who do are not incorrect, since we often *do* learn a lot in such situations— about ourselves, others, and the world. You will almost certainly be very anxious about some feared outcome during some period of your life. Somewhere along the path, all of us need to confront challenges in the specific domains of life that mean the most.

Is Threat Inevitable?

Is threat an inevitable part of life? Yes. Definitely. Certainty and control are a total fantasy, as we've discussed. It's also a fantasy to pretend that threats to our pain points won't happen. In fact, it's almost guaranteed that we will feel threatened and scared at some juncture.

When we undergo medical tests, we tend to be aware that we are not fully in control and there is a natural uneasiness—call it anxiety—that bubbles up beneath the surface. But when we walk down the street, do online banking, or eat dinner, we lack just as much control. We may not be thinking about it much, since control may not be at the forefront of our consciousness, but when we *do* contemplate the matter, it becomes clear that at any moment, myriad factors could interrupt daily life and radically transform it for the duration of our days on earth!

This goes beyond cancer and financial setbacks. Those two common examples are only the tip of the iceberg. How about a cyberattack leading to a nationwide power outage lasting for several weeks, months, or even a year? Or the collapse of mission-critical satellite systems, wiping out online communications? There is also the possibility of a major solar flare, or an asteroid colliding with the earth, creating the sort of winter that reportedly wiped out the dinosaurs sixty-five million years ago. Given globalization of the world's economies and agriculture, even just a limited nuclear conflict in any region of the earth could affect the world's food supplies for decades to come. We've already seen the havoc that a novel virus—one that spans just a few nanometers—can cause, but what about one that is much more contagious and deadly?

Let's face the music. Each and every one of these concerns is well within the realm of possibility, at any moment in time. To be sure, many of the events have already happened in human history, to one degree or another. When you stop to think about it, isn't it rather miraculous that more catastrophes don't occur? The truth is that human existence is not only inherently uncertain and uncontrollable but also dangerous. Our relative safety and security could be upset at any moment by any number of factors. Security is a complete smoke screen. One of the only things that is certain about the material world is that it is *not* certain or safe.

If you're feeling anxious while reading this, you're on the right track! Just as anxiety can help us recognize when we are lacking knowledge and control, it can help us identify our lack of security and safety. Embracing this fact is terrifying at first, but if we stay the course and *accept* our inherent lack of security, it can be extremely liberating.

Here is an exercise that I personally do every time I step onto an airplane. First, when I enter the threshold from the jet bridge onto the plane, I briefly touch the side of the plane. I then briefly contemplate that, within forty minutes or so, the long aluminum tube I've just entered will be traveling precariously, over thirty-five thousand feet above the surface of the earth, at a speed of more than five hundred miles per hour. Then, as I take my seat, I think about the fact that as a passenger, I have zero control over the plane—from pushback to landing, and at all points in between. Finally, when I fasten my seat belt, I try to *accept* that any and all things that may befall me in flight are simply beyond the scope of my control, and I relish the experience of letting someone else worry about the plane, since it's not my job to do so.

Once we relinquish our (false) sense of security and safety and accept that anything can happen at any moment—that our pain points can be triggered by circumstances beyond our control—we can emerge calmer and less anxious when handling life stressors across the board. This general approach helps us become more prepared to manage almost anything that can come our way. And, given that human life is inherently uncertain, it behooves us to accept the inevitability of bumping into anxiety at some point! We paradoxically become *less* anxious, since we come to a place of acceptance and recognize that it's okay to live on the edge.

Spiritual Benefits of Thinking the Worst

If it's counterintuitive that thinking the worst can make us calmer, it's even more counterintuitive to think that this could have spiritual benefits. After all, spiritual thinking is known for its uplifting, positive, even Pollyannaish vibes. However, *acknowledging uncertainty with a framework of acceptance can help us cultivate humility, patience, gratitude, and resilience to face life stressors.* Indeed, *earth school* has an uncanny way of developing human virtues, since life struggles can help us to expect less and tolerate more. Along these lines, mentally preparing ourselves to accept our lack of control can help our expectations of life to drop to new lows, and that's a good thing. When we envision significant challenges, we are less likely to take it for granted that life should or always will be safe and secure. This, in turn, tends to increase our sense of gratitude for what we *do* have and what *is* working out well.

In addition to generating more humility, gratitude, and resilience, contemplating the ills that could befall us can help us cultivate faith in something transcendent. This happens for a few reasons. First, we naturally rely on *material* supports—such as money, the government, or our social institutions. Accepting that nothing is certain, therefore, tends to open the door to conversations about faith in a more spiritual sense (for example, about a higher power). More important, transcendent faith is not merely about being positive and pretending that we're in control when we're not. At its core, transcendent faith is about recognizing and internalizing that we do *not* have control—and feeling good about that fact. It involves *letting go completely and surrendering fully with the acceptance that we are only human.* We will discuss this topic later on in this chapter.

Preparing for Threat

If threat is inevitable, we would be wise to prepare for it mentally so we aren't unmoored when it occurs. How can we do that?

In chapter 3, I discussed the seminal contributions of Dr. Tom Borkovec to our understanding of worry. To review briefly, worry is a cognitive process that, ironically and counterintuitively, serves as an avoidance strategy from having to confront our worst fears. Worrywarts review the same superficial fears, which maintain perpetual low-grade anxiety, instead of embracing their most catastrophic and disastrous concerns, which would yield substantially greater tension in the moment. Worrying destines us to a life filled with chronic, perpetual anxiety— akin to a Band-Aid tugging uncomfortably on our skin forever.

By contrast, mentally considering and ultimately accepting the possibility of catastrophe leads to a temporary spike in anxiety, followed by augmented calm and peace. It's like pulling the Band-Aid off completely, to get it over with! In the cognitive behavior therapy world, this is facilitated by *worry exposure*. In this technique, patients with worry are encouraged to describe their concerns with specific high-level detail, at a greater level of intensity than they have ever thought about before. This allows them to achieve escape velocity from anxiety. They set a thirty-minute worry exposure period that occurs at the same time and in the same place every day, and they spend that time having intense, terrifying worries. Patients create a script in the first person, present tense, and review it mentally until they are literally shaking with anxiety. The goal is to get used to thinking the worst and get to a place of acceptance that—in the final analysis—their greatest fears truly could happen.

In the case of Aileen, who was constantly catastrophizing about cancer, I invited her to think every day about getting sick despite her best efforts to avoid illness. I had her read stories about people who had various kinds of cancer, and watch videos about people undergoing painful cancer treatments, some of which were not successful in the end. I went with Aileen to a cancer ward at a local hospital to visit people who were sick. After all that, I asked Aileen to envision what it would be like for *her* to get sick. I had her write out a script, breaking down detail by detail what would happen as her illness mounted and she had to cope with painful cancer treatments, including multiple courses of chemotherapy, radiation, immunotherapy, and even novel experimental treatments. Her anxiety and distress became almost intolerable: she said it was the hardest thing she had ever done. And for her, the worst part was that she recognized—in her gut—that she could do nothing to prevent it. After several wrenching days, Aileen not only recognized but *accepted* the fact that she is not in control of her health. Worry exposure was such a hard process for her that she felt her insides churning. But in the end, Aileen became much stronger and more resilient, having accepted what she could not control, and feeling more humble, grateful, and faithful throughout her life.

With Zelena, the Olympic athlete whose mom was suffering from a major financial setback, we discussed her worries in detail. It turned out that beneath the surface, Zelena's ultimate fear was related to her mother's health, not her finances—the monetary issue had simply highlighted for Zelena her mother's general fallibility. So I had Zelena envision what it would be like for her mother to have a stroke from all her financial stress, and pass away. At first, Zelena couldn't handle even thinking about her mother's business struggles, let alone a stroke, and discussing her mother's death was completely off-limits as a topic. But eventually Zelena did open up about her fears of her mother's passing—and she lost it! As she sat and talked about what she would wear at the funeral, where her mother would be buried, what she would say to family members at the funeral and afterward, she was bawling. Again, the goal of this worry exposure was to engage in a mental exercise to help Zelena accept what she could not control.

Incidentally, and on a personal note, it was humbling for me to be face-to-face with an Olympian, at the top of her athletic game, as she broke down in tears, sobbing uncontrollably and showing her profound vulnerability. I emerged from that experience with immense respect for Zelena and a palpable realization that everyone on earth, no matter how physically strong, has pain points. We are *all* at risk, at *any* time, of facing challenges that could bring us to tears.

What Are We *Really* Anxious About?

Interestingly, many people, when feeling anxious, aren't fully sure what they are concerned about. They will say "I don't want to get sick" or "I don't want to lose my money," but that is usually just at the surface level. Almost always they are afraid of something much more profound, something that they are unconsciously concealing from themselves. This is a form of *cognitive avoidance*, which we discussed in chapter 3. In a nutshell, we don't like thinking about the most sensitive aspects of our pain points. As a result, we usually don't fully contemplate what we are afraid of; we get so caught up trying to avoid the possibility of the threat occurring that we don't fully know what's driving our fear.

To use exposure therapy effectively when feeling threatened, however, one has to delve deeply enough into precisely what they are worried about. For example, some people with financial anxiety are, in fact, worried about losing their sense of importance in others' eyes. In other cases, people with health anxiety are less concerned about their own health than about leaving behind loved ones without someone to care for them.

I recently saw a young father who was consumed with fear about getting into an accident. When we discussed his fears, he had associations of this from childhood: one of his friends lost her mother at a young age in an automobile collision, and he had a terrible time growing up. My patient was therefore resisting the possibility in his mind of leaving his children in such a situation. Before we started working on his specific fears, he hadn't even recognized this historical root of his anxiety, because he was so obsessed with shutting down the pain that he was superficially only preoccupied with his health. Once we spoke about it, though, he recognized that he ultimately did *not* have control over whether he would live or die, and the well-being of his kids was uncontrollable in this regard. Our work therefore pivoted from worries about various ailments and refocused on embracing the possibility that his kids would be left without a dad. This was a hard possibility to face but, ironically, was easier than trying to avoid thinking about it altogether.

In another case, financial anxiety proved to have nothing to do with money. When Alan came to me, I had him pegged all wrong. A finance manager from Midtown Manhattan, he presented with what seemed like typical worry about the financial markets. But when we explored further, he revealed that he was more concerned about being emotionally unavailable to his wife and children because of the resulting stress from a potential market crash. Then, when I probed even further, we reached the heart of the matter: he revealed that when he was a child, his older brother sexually molested him repeatedly for many years. In addition to intense shame, as well as anger toward his brother, Alan blamed his parents for being too distracted by their own financial concerns to recognize what was going on and protect him. But more than his parents, he blamed the markets: the abuse had occurred during a financial downturn, which left his parents preoccupied with work and created more stress in the home. That was the context in which Alan's brother acted out sexually against him, and it was the crux of what he was trying to avoid by always having financial stability.

It is always critical to integrate a full understanding of individuals' anxiety into their worry exposure. If people are terrified about leaving behind relatives, or not being available to protect them, such themes need to be woven into their scripts and repeated in their minds. If such individuals simply go through the mental process of reviewing their superficial concerns, they won't encounter their anxiety at its root, and treatment typically is not effective since the matter remains unresolved.

In practice, the best strategy to accept our lack of control is to *think deeply about the worst possible outcomes that hit our pain points*. Once we've identified the core fear, we then review it over and over again in order to become mentally prepared for it to actually happen. For example, if you feel anxious while sitting on an airplane, don't just sit and worry lightly on a surface level about random plane crashes. Instead, brace yourself for a few tense moments and recognize the following: Once you're in the air, you cannot even enter the cockpit, let alone have any influence or agency over the plane. You are in a vulnerable predicament, traveling in a tin can at hundreds of miles per hour, thousands of feet above the earth, and any number of conditions could occur at a given moment that could be disastrous for all passengers on board. Then, consider the real ramifications of what would happen if just one critical thing went wrong midflight. Consider your family, your legacy, your untimely death, your funeral, and the meaning of your life. Once we can fully and humbly embrace *that* level of uncertainty and uncontrollability, a serene sense of calm will set in, alongside a boost in resilience to accept any number of circumstances that are beyond our control.

Pain Vs. Suffering

Throughout this book, we've been speaking about uncertainty: our anxiety goes up when a negative situation *may* occur, and acceptance of uncertainty is the key to reducing our apprehension. But what happens when unfortunate events actually *do* materialize—when the threat occurs? It's one thing to concede the limits of our knowledge and control when we are at risk, when the *possibility* of something upsetting looms. Hard as this is, there is something much harder: accepting life challenges when they become reality.

This level of acceptance requires several steps beyond exposure therapy. In worry exposures, we simply think about the possibility of something bad occurring. But what if something bad does occur? What should we do then? How can we avoid falling into paralyzing anxiety when we have finally and actually lost control?

"Pain is inevitable. Suffering is optional." This gem of wisdom has been attributed to the Dalai Lama, twelve-step programs, and other sources, but identifying the person to popularize it is less important than understanding the truth at its core. Pain, including unpleasant situations, emotions, and sensations, *is* unavoidable. No matter how fortunate our birth is in this life, we *will* experience pain. *Is there anyone who doesn't struggle at all?* By contrast, suffering—regretting, complaining, and getting angry or anxious in response to pain—is based on *choices* that we all make. The main question is how to prevent pain from turning into suffering. How can we handle situations that hit our pain points without regretting, complaining, or getting angry and anxious about them?

The answer is a main theme of this chapter: *acceptance*. The more we accept and stop fighting against pain—the more we can learn to live with pain and not change it, to simply experience it and recognize that sometimes nothing can be done—the less we suffer. Of course, this is easier said than done, but another way of thinking about it is that this is something we need to practice. Consequently, we need to prepare ourselves better to accept outcomes that we don't want.

Think about it this way: If pain is inevitable, we have only two choices. Either we can prepare for it when things are going well, or we can get caught off guard when it happens. The latter is a reliable recipe for suffering: when pain strikes suddenly without our being mentally prepared to accept the sting and its consequences, we are sitting ducks. The former, on the other hand, gives us a fighting chance that we will experience only transient pain rather than chronic suffering.

In some cases, the act of identifying and recognizing our limits can lead spontaneously to acceptance of pain. As we discussed in chapter 7, realizing that there is only so much we can do and certain things are out of our hands can be a salve, because we feel less responsible for the pain. But it's not always that simple. When genuinely challenging situations materialize—ones that lead to significant pain—it can be hard to accept them, even if we recognize that we're not in control.

What Causes Suffering?

Our resistance is what converts pain into suffering. Not all battles are meant to be waged, and not all wars are meant to be won. Sometimes the test of life is not to win but to lose graciously.

A former patient of mine in his thirties named Marty suffered from social anxiety. He was a quiet guy who worked as an actuary for an insurance company, crunching numbers to determine the probabilities and financial risks that inform underwriting policies. Although his job may sound mundane, it entailed a huge responsibility since a single mathematical error or miscalculation, multiplied across thousands of situations, could easily cost the company tens of millions of dollars. One day, just such an incident occurred. Several years prior, in conducting more than a hundred independent calculations for a single spreadsheet, Marty had missed a single decimal point. The result was a staggering financial loss in insurance payouts. Marty was told to prepare for an urgent session with his boss—and he promptly scheduled an urgent session with me in advance to discuss. Marty understandably got so clammy and sweaty just speaking about his situation that I could see the perspiration soaking through his shirt. Recognizing his lack of control wasn't the problem, however. He was well aware that this was beyond his control!

Marty's main struggle was that he would now need to face an interrogation with the company heads and be compelled to account for making a grievous error. This wasn't just a possibility; a hearing was already scheduled for the following week. To make matters worse, the company was known to take their anger out on people who were found to have made similar errors, using tactics that were genuinely distressing, such as public shaming through email messages to entire departments.

Marty considered quitting, but he quickly rejected that option for financial reasons. His best alternative was to accept the situation and learn to be okay with it. He prepared himself to be gracious while being torn apart in public—a deep-seated fear, given his social anxiety. After getting to a place of acceptance, he decided to take it on the chin, acknowledge his screw-up and the consequences, offer a sincere apology, and accept any sanctions that his bosses might apply. But at least it would be over at that point. As they say in the world of journalism, it would be "just one news cycle," and then he could get back to his life and move on.

Marty did use some aspects of worry exposure in dealing with this situation. He wrote out a script in the first person about being brought in for an investigation, what the CEO and CFO would say to him, how he would respond, and how they would try to humiliate him. His stomach churned so badly that he ran to the bathroom during our session. But he needed to take one more step: *he had to stop fighting the pain.* Marty accepted that he is human, and he had screwed up. He acknowledged that this was the nature of life, and he decided to move forward. It was painful—but as a result of taking this approach, he stopped suffering.

Why Do We Choose Suffering over Pain?

I've found that many of us catastrophize that we wouldn't be able to handle pain. We see in our imaginations all sorts of things that could happen to us, emotionally and otherwise, if we accepted the situation and its consequences. We think those consequences might drive us crazy, in part, perhaps, because the magnitude of the pain is unknown, and again we are intolerant of uncertainty. So we instead resist pain, repress the thoughts, distract ourselves, and contort our psyches in an attempt to maintain a sense of control, even though this only makes matters worse.

The truth of the matter is, *if we are suffering, it shows that we can tolerate pain, since suffering is harder to manage than pain.* Suffering takes more energy and effort, so it is ultimately more challenging. It's like racing with your car to the side of a multilane highway in the middle of a snowstorm when you're having a panic attack, as we saw with John in chapter 1. To reprise the story: John was afraid he might crash his car because of the panic attack, and he *suffered* through a series of daring driving moves to pull over his car, which only made him panic harder. Through our work together, John learned that tolerating the *pain* of his panic by simply driving in a straight line until it passed was a more adaptive and healthier approach. His initial efforts to curtail his pain resulted in an escalation of his fight-or-flight response, which generated catastrophizing that he wasn't able to handle life.

In a similar vein, despite our belief that we won't be able to cope with pain, in reality we are always able to handle it better if we accept it than if we expend useless energy finding ways to avoid it—the latter of which only prolongs and deepens our suffering. Pain hurts, but human beings are surprisingly resilient and can withstand and manage all sorts of dire situations—and this becomes easier, not harder, when we accept those situations.

From this we learn that *a critical step to avoiding suffering is to recognize that pain is tolerable.* The more people suffer by struggling against pain, the less likely they are to realize that they can tolerate it. They come to associate pain with suffering, and don't realize that these are different from one another. If you fight against pain habitually, you'll have a harder time accepting pain. Conversely, the more we practice pain tolerance, the easier it gets over time.

Another reason most people choose suffering over pain is that they don't think they have a choice. But the truth is that we always have a choice. Some of our choices might not be optimal, but we *always* have some sort of choice. Pain cannot take away our freedom of choice entirely. Marty did have the option to hand in his resignation, if he wanted. He decided he did not want to for financial reasons, so he made an alternative choice to face the music. Being conscious about his decision—making a deliberate and intentional choice—turned his situation from suffering into just pain.

To take a more extreme example, if a person is diagnosed with a terminal disease, they still have a choice about whether to insist on dying at home, to go into hospice care for pain management, or to go into a hospital to be put on a feeding tube and fight until the end. All of those options are unpleasant, but they *are* choices, and making a conscious choice is an unshakable human dignity and privilege.

Making Meaning

In 1940, the Viennese psychiatrist Viktor Frankl was a rising psychotherapist with a focus on depression and suicide, when he and his family were sent to the Nazis' Theresienstadt concentration camp. Frankl spent the next three years in four different concentration camps, where he witnessed unspeakable cruelty and suffering—the specter of death was omnipresent each and every day. During those trying years, his wife, brother, and parents were all killed. In 1945, shortly after being liberated from Auschwitz, Frankl wrote about his experiences in a book that, when translated into English in 1959, became an influential bestseller.

Man's Search for Meaning, as the book is now commonly known, is more of an extended essay than a psychological textbook. Frankl's main theme is that people who found meaning and purpose amid intolerable circumstances fared much better than people who gave up or gave in to what they perceived as meaningless misery. And they did better not just mentally but also physically. Frankl famously observed that those who weathered the unspeakable pain while holding on to meaning in life, and those who maintained awareness of their capacity to make conscious choices, were more likely to survive the concentration camps compared to those who turned their pain into suffering. Frankl famously pointed out that we may lack control over the outcomes in life, but we *always* maintain our ability to choose. Toward the end of the book, Frankl concluded, "The way in which a man accepts his fate and all the suffering it entails, the way in which he takes up his cross, gives him ample opportunity, even under the most difficult circumstances, to add a deeper meaning to his life."[1]

Today, this concept is well established in the scientific literature. When people experience stressful life events, the meaning they attribute to such circumstances has an indelible impact on their coping response, and the resulting emotional and even physical health toll that stress plays on the body.[2] Among individuals with chronic pain, those who find constructive purposes for their discomfort—for example, seeing it as an opportunity to learn or connect with others—experience not only less depression but also less physical pain.[3] Similarly, spinal-cord injury patients who find meaning in their loss experience not only greater psychological resilience and well-being but greater physical functioning, even when controlling for severity of their medical symptoms.[4] During the COVID-19 pandemic, individuals who underwent psychotherapy to help them make meaning in negative situations experienced both contemporaneous and long-term benefit in psychological adjustment.[5]

What are the mechanisms by which making meaning can enhance coping and strengthen our emotional and physical responses to trying life circumstances? Put simply, when injury, loss, and other challenging situations occur, having a sense of meaning allows people to reframe their negative experiences more positively. This, in turn, transforms suffering into pain. *Once pain has meaning, people stop struggling against it and become more accepting, so the suffering decreases—and in some cases dissipates altogether.* If you experience pain seemingly for no reason in your upper arms, it's substantially more distressing than if it occurs at the gym while doing bicep curls with weights in each arm. This is because the latter pain has meaning—it's viewed as constructive and a necessary part of building up muscle mass.

Carl, a businessman in his early sixties, had a long-term business partner who he one day discovered had been cheating him all along, skimming money from the business for years. Once Carl found out, it was too late; almost all the money was gone. Thirty years of work amounted to virtually nothing monetarily. His partner was infuriatingly unresponsive when Carl confronted him; he denied everything and pretended to be a pauper. Things got ugly and they ended up in court, where, to Carl's astonishment, his partner won. The guy showed up in a disheveled suit and didn't even have a lawyer, claiming that he couldn't afford one. In the meantime, Carl's business partner had transferred the missing money to an offshore account. It was a bitter pill to swallow, and one that made Carl very depressed.

In speaking with me initially, Carl struggled mightily to make any sense or meaning out of his loss. He had worked day and night for decades and was left with nothing! Over time, though, he found a few nuggets of meaning that decreased his suffering quotient enough that, at times, he was left with just pain and no suffering. During one emotion-filled session, Carl opened up to me about the many nights he had spent chasing money at the expense of spending time with his children. He spoke about how his kids resented him for being a workaholic and how this had made it all the harder to accept his financial loss: "What did I sacrifice for?" he asked rhetorically. I validated Carl's feelings, and as he spoke more, he seemed to come to a place of greater peace. He remarked that he was grateful to have learned the lesson of valuing family over money from the "school of life" in his early sixties, instead of losing yet another decade focused exclusively on work. Carl did make some fundamental life changes subsequent to our discussions, and he spent much more time and effort creating better ties with his children and grandchildren, using the little finances he had.

The process of meaning-making is highly individualized for each person, but here are a few ways to build a greater sense of meaning when challenges arise. Some of us may view pain as an opportunity to grow in our character. Others may take it as an opportunity to refocus on gratitude for what is going well. Still others may see their primary task as learning to suffer with dignity, as opposed to getting out of the suffering. Another approach is to use challenges as a way of connecting to others. Spirituality may also be a way of making meaning, such as those who develop their faith or contemplate a certain divine or ultimate purpose to the pain that may or may not become apparent over time. Regardless of which of these, or other, methods we may use to make meaning, Frankl summed up the most critical aspect as follows:

> There were always choices to make. Every day, every hour offered the opportunity to make a decision, a decision which determined whether

you would or would not submit to those powers which threatened to rob you of your very self, your inner freedom. Which determined whether or not you would become the plaything of circumstance, renouncing freedom and dignity to become molded into the form of a typical inmate.[6]

From this perspective, our responses to trying life circumstances are not just automatic reactions occurring in the context of various biological, social, historical, political, and other conditions. *Human beings have the gift of being able to make choices.* In this regard, pain can uniquely highlight the greatness of what it means to be human. We can choose to retain our dignity, our character, and even our equanimity, to a far greater extent than many of us realize.

The Power of Prayer

Despite a clear progression toward increased secularism across the globe, prayer remains part and parcel of many cultures. In the 2014 Religious Landscape Survey, a scientific report of 102 countries that examined the prevalence of many aspects of spiritual and religious life, the Pew Research Center found that 55 percent of American adults pray on a daily basis.[7] Similarly, in other wealthy countries, some 40 percent of adults pray daily, and worldwide the number jumps above 60 percent.[8] Why is prayer so widespread? What does it have to offer humanity that makes it such a common practice?

Many nonreligious people think of prayer as a way of manipulating the heavens for blessing—trying to bring down physical healing, prosperity, or success for themselves and loved ones. That may be true. Stories abound of people saying, "Oh look! I prayed, and this miraculous healing occurred! Isn't prayer wonderful?" I'm not saying that those things don't happen; sometimes they do. However, as a psychologist, I personally believe that the most powerful effect prayer can have on our lives is not in the realm of shaping our fortune but rather how it influences our perspectives. *Prayer has inconceivable power to make us more accepting, humble, grateful, and resilient, and thus much less anxious.*

Several years ago, the school-age daughter of a close friend from the Midwest was diagnosed with leukemia. Her family tried everything, including multiple stem cell transplants, which initially helped. But the cancer recurred after each round of treatment. They gave her *all* the medical care they could. Spiritually, they created prayer groups of thousands, if not tens of thousands, across the globe. A coordinated effort was mounted to recite chapters from Psalms literally around the clock, with the hope of petitioning God to heal and spare their beautiful daughter's life. They made their choices valiantly, heroically, and with great love, care, and immense faith. And yet, the girl died short of her eleventh birthday.

At her funeral, something happened that I have never seen before, at any point throughout my life. All the prayers in the world had not saved the girl, but they did have a clear and profound effect. The girl's parents, and all those present, seemed uplifted from the tragedy. Of course, there were many bitter tears. The wailing and crying and sorrow was intense, and the pain was hard to fathom. A beautiful, little innocent girl had passed from this world, and there was nothing anyone could do to change that sad and tragic fact. There was bereavement from an incredible loss. However, simultaneously, there was acceptance and peace.

All along, someone looking from the outside might have said that the purpose of prayer was to help the girl. But that's only one part of the picture. More fundamentally, the parents' valiant spiritual efforts, over many years, had instilled within them the perspective that human beings are not in control. That perspective enabled them to achieve clear recognition that they had done everything in their power—spiritually, emotionally, and physically—yet the result was a matter beyond human knowledge, comprehension, and ability to change. Prayer made it possible for the family to get through the tragedy with enormous dignity and strength. The parents' choice to have this beautiful young child survive was taken away, but that did not take away their choice to be dignified. Prayer provided strength by enabling them to accept that they were *not* in control. All the prayers that had been uttered around the globe enabled them to choose to handle the tragedy with meaning. There was an acute experience of severe pain, but without suffering.

The most powerful aspect of prayer is that it can help us internalize the fact that our power is limited, our knowledge is even more limited, and sometimes we just need to recognize that we are not the ones flying the plane. Twelve-step programs talk about turning our strength over to a higher power. Whatever you conceive that higher power to be, and whether or not you pray with any regular cadence, prayer is a powerful tool to accept in our hearts and souls that we are not in control.

. . . .

TOOL #8: ACCEPTING OUR LIMITS

Worry tends to be a shallow process. It rarely allows us to get to the true depth of what is creating anxiety. Worry therefore makes it harder for us to accede to our natural human limits.

So this tool begins with a self-inquiry process that I've adapted from cognitive therapy, which was designed to help us gain access to our core beliefs that we are so often unaware of. The technique involves continually asking ourselves, *If so, then what would happen?* in order to probe downward into what we are sincerely and utterly afraid of.

For example, if you are afraid of getting sick, ask yourself, *If I were to get sick, what would happen?*

The answer might be, *Well then, I'll have to take a leave of absence from work.*

From there, ask yourself again, *If I had to go on leave, what would happen?* You may respond, *I'll feel ashamed around my work colleagues when I return.*

At that point, ask yourself, *If I felt shame upon my return, what would happen?*

The process should continue until you feel viscerally uncomfortable. If you're imagining yourself feeling embarrassed, depressed, losing your friendships, and ending up utterly alone, you're probably doing it correctly. The goal of this part of the exercise is to recognize what you are fundamentally afraid of, and that should feel very uncomfortable to think about.

Once you are good and anxious, *it's time to completely let go and accept.* Immerse yourself in the reality that whatever you fear may actually manifest. Consider that it's probably not so difficult for a combination of factors to coalesce and bring about the feared outcomes. Embrace your vulnerability, and relinquish the facade of knowledge, control, and security. Recognize that, in the long run, we are powerless to control most of the major factors that shape our fortunes, so letting go is the only logical option.

At this point, you should be even more anxious. Remember that you are to truly accept that terrible outcomes could happen at any moment.

Now, recognize that no matter what happens—no matter what circumstances may befall you—*you will always retain the capacity to make choices.* Consider what your options might be (even if none of them are good options) and what you might choose if your fears do manifest.

If prayer is something that you are comfortable with or wish to try, at this point you can pray in whatever language feels comfortable to avert the outcome you're afraid of. However, don't simply focus on the prospect of divine assistance. Rather, use prayer to deepen your acceptance that, ultimately, your control has limits.

CHAPTER 9

TRANSCENDING OUR LIMITS

Anxiety Can Help Us Achieve Our Life Goals and Dreams

Chapters 7 and 8 discussed how anxiety can help us recognize and accept the limits of human knowledge and control. We have seen how this can enable us to *thrive* by keeping us humble and engendering more resilience during life's vicissitudes, particularly times of uncertainty, threat, and adversity. Ironically, when we accept the limits of our humanity, we emerge emotionally and spiritually stronger, with greater serenity, patience, gratitude, kindness, and compassion. In this final chapter, we will see that the power of anxiety to help us thrive goes much deeper: *Anxiety can help us identify, strive toward, and actualize our unique human potential. We can harness anxiety as a tool to help us identify and fulfill our ultimate purposes in life.* How? The specific things that make us anxious are usually the very matters in which we have immense potential to thrive and succeed—anxiety tends to attach itself to our areas of greatest strength. Furthermore, actualizing human potential—dreaming about what we have to offer the world and heroically pursuing those dreams—inherently conjures up anxiety, since all big plans carry significant risk of failure, and pushing beyond our limits inherently requires facing adversity. Therefore, when we experience anxiety in the context of self-actualization, it is an indication that we are on the right track. This chapter will show you how to use anxiety to identify what you value most, transcend your perceived limits, and achieve your spiritual potential in ways that you may never have thought possible.

Our Potential for Greatness

Western culture has not done an especially noteworthy job of teaching students—children or adults—how to recognize their unique potential or visualize their greatness. In our educational system, we are still taught mostly by rote. We reward students for memorization, and there is insufficient emphasis on learning how to think critically and creatively.[1] Furthermore, students are generally evaluated in a very limited number of domains. College entrance exams and other standardized tests have a known bias of valuing academic success in language and mathematics more than social, creative, or emotional intelligence—not to mention the practical problem-solving skills that we call *street smarts*.[2] Even more problematic, our society tends to have binary views of success and failure; rather than recognizing human growth from the station we are currently in—trying to be our unique best—we view people as either successful or not. So it's no surprise we have a decadent culture that tends to value immediate gratification over character development, and that we give precedence to *quantitative* rather than *qualitative* results (for example, having lots of money instead of making a significant impact on the lives of others).

These cultural values make us fiercely competitive. The metaphor of a "rat race," popularized in the 1950s, was based on the image of lab rats being manipulated and rewarded with food for traveling through a series of meaningless mazes. The term was applied to the state of rampant competition in corporate America, in which workers would blindly follow their executive masters like creatures with no specific meaning or purpose other than to feed themselves as much as possible. Recent years have seen some positive changes within the corporate world that offer a small glimmer of hope that new values are emerging, but the rat race continues to be an apropos description of work life for many people.

Because of all these trends, many today never think of themselves as having a unique capacity for greatness. We don't even know what our individual potential is, since we have always compared ourselves to others. When I ask my patients what they would truly like to accomplish in life, they almost always start by describing generic ambitions to amass significant wealth, comfort, material possessions, notoriety, fame, or even a large number of followers on social media platforms. When I press the issue, however, they typically acknowledge that none of this makes them truly happy, and they actually don't have a real sense of how to express their individuality in this world. Most don't even know themselves well enough to recognize how they can add value to the lives of others with their unique internal constellation of social, emotional, practical, and intellectual strengths.

We have all but lost the perspective that we have an inner potential for greatness to discover and develop! We don't even think about how we can make the world a better place. I believe this is one of the chief reasons why today's society is so badly plagued with anxiety. Almost all of my patients between the ages of eighteen and thirty-five experience significant anxiety when asking themselves questions like: *Why am I here? What's the point of my life? Am I really special? Do I have anything to contribute to this world?* Their existential tensions rise when contemplating these matters because few of them have compelling answers, due to the way they grew up. Indeed, our society shies away from these questions altogether, so they typically go unaddressed.

However, the natural anxiety that we experience when contemplating these questions can be a starting point for *self-actualization*—the process that renowned humanistic psychologist Abraham Maslow described as being "everything you are capable of becoming."[3] Feeling anxious about our identity or the nature of our inner value to the world is the closing salvo in learning to thrive with anxiety. The entire point of the natural discomfort we feel when contemplating our uniqueness is to motivate us to push through and begin to self-actualize. Our latent distress is highly functional—quite literally a tool to thrive—since we can use it to uncover and learn to implement the unique gifts that we have to share with the world. In this regard, we can utilize anxiety to flourish with meaning and purpose.

It's important to note that our unique mission in life could be something we get paid to do, or it could be something we dedicate a lot of time to do *on the side* of our livelihood. One of my friends is a successful lawyer who feels that his real purpose on earth involves running a soup kitchen on the weekends. His legal work helps to pay his mortgage, but what really makes him *tick* is putting food in front of people in serious need. Another friend of mine is a stay-at-home parent and homemaker. He thrives by tending to his children and family, and creating a warm and loving environment to support them in every way he can. He views his primary mission and purpose as being a dedicated dad, even though it doesn't yield financial dividends directly. Bottom line: if there is something we love to do and have the capacity for, and the world needs it, that's our ticket for envisioning and actualizing our unique greatness, regardless of how much it pays.

As discussed in chapters 7 and 8, nothing is certain and our control is extremely limited. But that doesn't mean we cannot accomplish anything.

We have immense divine potential inside us that we are free to unpack during our lifetime. Whether we choose to do so is up to us; that is the primary opportunity of life, and also the risk (particularly if we choose *not* to do so). Having seen thousands of patients, I can attest that it's almost as if we are programmed to be able to identify and actualize our potential in this world. There is something uncanny about the way that each person's highly individualized goals, dreams, and capabilities manage to line up very well with what those around them need. Conversely, I have never seen anyone fully thrive if they don't feel they are fulfilling their unique vision of greatness. In such situations, those connected to such individuals—family, friends, communities, workplaces—also tend to struggle, since *everyone* misses out in some way on having their needs met.

I feel the need to point out the following: in all of my secular education—from kindergarten through college, two graduate degrees, and two years of postgraduate fellowship—I don't recall my professors extolling these virtues. I learned these general concepts from my *spiritual* education. To quote my spiritual mentor, Rabbi Lawrence Kelemen: "You are one million times more unique than your fingerprints; there has never been anyone like you to walk planet Earth, and there will never be anyone like you ever again in the future."[4] To this end, our anxiety can help us identify our uniqueness and courageously strive toward the tremendous opportunities that we have right in front of our eyes.

Anxiety Is a Compass

In my first year as a clinical fellow at McLean Hospital, I completed a rotation at the Obsessive Compulsive Disorders Institute (OCDI), which is one of just a handful of residential OCD treatment programs around the world. As a nascent OCD therapist, I took the opportunity to learn whatever I could about this fascinating disorder. I was shadowing Bob—a veteran clinician who had been practicing at the OCDI for nearly twenty years—and I learned that OCD can manifest in many different domains in life, such as contamination, health, organization, harm or violence, sexuality, and even religion. During one of my first visits to the OCDI, I asked Bob why some patients experience OCD about germs and others about violence or religion. Without missing a beat, Bob responded, "OCD attaches itself to that which a person values the most in life." He went on to explain that when patients have obsessions and compulsions about contamination, they deeply value their physical well-being and health; when OCD manifests in the realm of religion, they have spiritual values that are at the core of their identity.

Since that brief but formative training encounter, I have seen this trend in virtually every patient I've ever met: people tend to get anxious about that which they truly care about. Over the subsequent years, I've come to realize another facet of this basic truth about human psychology. Since anxiety tends to be about what we value the most in life, *anxiety can serve as a compass, providing the key direction of areas to focus on to actualize our potential.*

Marcia, a young, single woman in her early twenties, was plagued by significant health anxiety. She would spend hours on the internet doing research about various symptoms that she thought she was experiencing, and she would visit various doctors every month for tests that invariably came up negative. She could not function during the day unless she took all of her vitamins and minerals and kept a perfectly balanced diet to minimize the chances of her getting sick. These activities were debilitating for Marcia on many levels; she was fired from her job because she was caught spending hours on WebMD while at work, and thereafter her quality of life quickly went downhill. Marcia spent all her new spare time scanning her body for signs of cancer and doing even more compulsive medical research online. She became obsessed about her health to the point that she could not go out with friends or date because it was too stressful to even get dressed. By the time she called my office, her hypochondriasis had left her virtually homebound.

Marcia and I went through the approaches to anxiety from part 1 of this book, helping her to improve her self-care, be more self-compassionate, and accept as well as face her emotions. She engaged in exposure therapy to think intentionally and at length about her health risks without engaging in any compensatory compulsive behaviors. We also implemented strategies from part 2, including connecting with others. I suggested that Marcia prioritize her relationships and open up to her friends about her health anxiety, which was a huge step in the right direction. Marcia's health anxiety remitted considerably with these approaches, but she didn't seem happy yet—she was less distressed but not thriving.

After about ten months of therapy, I asked Marcia what she wanted to do in life, and she said she would love to become a health-care advocate and consultant; she wanted to use her medical knowledge to guide and support others struggling with serious conditions. At first, I was concerned that Marcia was backtracking, as this seemed like a new way of expressing her health anxiety. But I quickly realized that Marcia's anxiety had manifested in the realm of physical health for a reason: she had a unique gift for identifying medical symptoms and treatments. If she were able to utilize her gifts to make the world a better place, she could express her unique capacity for greatness.

I helped Marcia turn her dream into reality. While she was excited at first, she quickly realized that becoming a health-care advocate is a huge undertaking. In addition to being terrified that she might inadvertently do more harm than good, Marcia was concerned that she wouldn't be able to get enough clients to have a successful career in this area. Nevertheless, I encouraged Marcia to pursue her dream. She built a website, made business cards, took some online courses in small-business management, and started to offer her services in helping people who needed guidance about diagnoses, treatment options, and even how to navigate the insurance system. All of this took a *lot* of courage because Marcia was facing adversity, putting herself out there, and taking risks by investing time and money that she didn't know would come back. Within just three months, though, Marcia's health-care consulting practice was up and running. People were thrilled with her work, and she was happier than ever. Meanwhile, Marcia's health anxiety fell completely to the wayside because she was using it to thrive instead of allowing her anxiety to rule her life.

Cases like Marcia's are ubiquitous. Once we build a more connected relationship with ourselves and others using the strategies discussed in parts 1 and 2 of this book, we can circle back to our anxieties and utilize them to actualize good in the world. As I've said, this is because anxiety often attaches itself to areas of central meaning in our lives—areas in which we have unique potential to thrive. Once we've used our anxiety to strengthen our relationships with ourselves and others, we can use anxiety to build a vision of our greatness.

Steps to Building a Vision

Practically speaking, how can we build a vision of greatness for ourselves? Even if we break free from the societal riptide and believe in our capacity for greatness in a unique way, many people fall short of self-actualization because they just don't know what to do.

Creating a vision for our greatness involves two steps:

Step 1: Brainstorm.

Think of something that you are naturally gifted at to some degree, and in which, with a reasonable amount of application and hard work, you could be even more adept. It could be a job, a hobby, or a not-yet-realized passion.

Ask yourself:

- *What do I love to do?*
- *Which job or hobby or activity do I find the most fulfilling?*
- *Are there any aspects of my life that I wish I could do more of?*
- *What are my strengths as a person?*

Note that it's common that what we love to do is also an area of strength. This happens for a few reasons. First, everyone wants to be successful, so we are often drawn to do things that we are naturally good at. Second, and more important, many of the world's spiritual traditions teach that human beings are preprogrammed for excellence in one or more domains. When we are authentic with ourselves and pursue what we truly love, we are destined to be successful. Along those lines, if the above prompts don't help you to generate ideas, ask yourself: *What is my biggest accomplishment to date? What am I the most proud of in my life?* Sometimes thinking about our past successes can help us generate visions of greatness for the future.

You can also ask yourself: *What action or pursuit makes me feel the happiest?* Note that "happiness" is not the same as comfort; typically, what makes us feel happy and fulfilled is actually *uncomfortable*, as we will discuss later in this chapter. Think back to something you've achieved that gave you the purest sense of fulfillment and purpose. It could be a singular one-time achievement, like winning a tennis match, taking a beautiful photograph, or learning about birds you admire. Or it could be a long-term project that you worked on and had a sense of accomplishment once it was finished.

Brainstorming should not stop with simple answers to any of these questions. Once you have something in mind, ask yourself the following:

- *What dreams, hopes, and visions could I accomplish if I were to develop these strengths further in my life?*
- *How could I use this vision of myself to make the world better in some way?*
- *How would my life look different if I were to take this domain of excellence seriously and focus on it more?*
- *What changed in me, or for others, when I previously achieved something in this area?*
- *What was the impact of my accomplishment on the world?*

All these questions, which pertain to the first part of creating a vision of greatness—brainstorming—may or may not be anxiety-provoking. Some people *do* feel anxious when contemplating what they'd like to do, and others may simply feel excited and invigorated thinking about their strengths, interests, and capacity for greatness.

By contrast, the next step *always* requires a healthy dose of anxiety.

Step 2: Think practically about how to pursue your vision.

Ask yourself:

- *What are specific, tangible things I can do to further develop my strengths?*
- *What changes do I need to make in my day-to-day life to bring my vision into reality?*
- *How will others around me react when I tell them what I'm doing?*
- *How will these changes affect my schedule, my social life, my finances, and other aspects of my current life?*

Consider the disparity between where you are today, and the vision that you've started to brainstorm. Think about what would be necessary, in as much detail as possible, to get to where you'd like to be.

Note that this does *not* (yet) involve taking action; no behavior change is required to build a clear vision of greatness for ourselves. However, seriously considering the practical steps to bring our potential into reality should be stressful and even fear-inducing.

If you aren't experiencing any stress or fear when thinking practically about your vision, it's an indication that your vision is missing something critical. It could be that you don't truly care about what you are envisioning. It could also be that you're selling yourself short and not envisioning true greatness. Another possibility is that you don't yet fully realize all the hard work it will entail. Regardless of the reason, if you're not feeling significant anxiety in completing this exercise, go back and do it again! Conversely, once you feel palpably anxious, take it as a positive indicator that you're on the right track.

Everyday Heroes

Achieving our life goals and dreams starts with building a vision of our greatness—brainstorming, and identifying concrete plans to actualize our potential. But at some point, we also need to transcend from theory to practice, which involves pursuing our goals *behaviorally* by taking action, not just planning things in our minds. As we cross over from the internal world of our thoughts to interfacing with the external world through our behaviors, we are no longer simply *visualizing* our greatness. Rather, we exert efforts to bring our dreams into reality.

In today's culture, the word *hero* is used in many ways, so I'd like to take a moment to define what I'm talking about. The physical valor of first responders or military personnel, the moral daring to fight corruption at work or in government, and the personal courage to face life-threatening health challenges, all require heroism. But for most of us who are not face-to-face with an overwhelming physical, political, or societal threat, daring to actualize our inner potential through developing our inner strength and discipline is the kind of heroism I'm affirming here. I am referring to *everyday heroes* who may or may not be recognized by others, and may or may not even be successful in their pursuits. *It is heroic to push through the stress, fear, and discomfort that comes along with bringing our dreams into reality*. What unites all heroes is that they exert significant effort to express their unique potential out in the world; they are engaged in the process of self-actualization.

The happiest people I know are all heroes. They have visions for themselves and the world, and every day they push through the stress and fear associated with those visions. They dream with their eyes wide open. However, all the heroes I know also face significant stress and fear, because all human pursuits of significant value involve facing adversity. This is not by accident. When we push ourselves to achieve some goal, we simultaneously take on risk, which increases our anxiety while engaging our capacity to realize our potential and experience true happiness. You cannot have one without the other; anxiety is a necessary aspect of thriving. As I've said repeatedly throughout this book, anxiety in and of itself is not a bad thing, and it can help us to thrive. I would go as far as to say that heroically pursuing our goals in life necessitates facing stress, adversity, and fear—*anxiety is a critical aspect of human happiness.*

Put differently, if you're not anxious about what you're doing, you probably don't care that much about it, and overall your emotions will be "meh." Either we feel excited *and* we're anxious about the outcomes, or we don't care and we feel neither excited nor anxious—there is no middle ground.

Of course, there is nothing wrong with pushing forward toward a challenging goal and taking a break from time to time to calm ourselves down and reset to equilibrium. We should not strive to have superintense emotions around the clock (as we will see later in this chapter). But if we avoid *all* emotional intensity when pursuing our dreams, we will forever shortchange our heroism—and our capacity to thrive.

Human Beings Need Adversity

The marathoner community has a common phrase: "Running is my therapy." Motorcyclists similarly say: "Biking is my therapy." When you think about it, these are odd phrases. Running is physically stressful, and biking can be outright dangerous such that it elicits a bona fide fear response. How can stressful and fear-inducing pursuits be perceived to *enhance* mental health? Why would anyone think that these activities are a form of therapy? How do they *help* with anxiety?

In chapter 3, we spoke about the amygdala and how blood flows into this area of the brain when we experience distressing emotions, such as fear. A growing body of research suggests that the amygdala is *also* triggered by excitement, exhilaration, and other varieties of intense *positive* emotions.[5] Based on these findings, many theorists now believe that the amygdala not only controls our fight-or-flight response but the *intensity* of our emotional experience in general.[6] Powerful emotions—both positive and negative—are mediated by the amygdala. In other words, *the same brain region that controls anxiety also controls our ability to thrive and be happy.*

You may recall the story I mentioned in chapter 1 about the outstanding National Hockey League goalie Glenn Hall. Besides being considered the best goalie ever to play for the Chicago Blackhawks, Hall was famous in the hockey world for vomiting before every game because of his high level of tension and stress. Was Glenn Hall anxious? Yes! And was he a hero who actualized his unique potential in the world? Undoubtedly. These are not coincidental. Hall built up his inner strength to face hockey pucks being shot directly at him at speeds of one hundred miles per hour or more, under tremendous pressure of his teammates, all while facing public scrutiny for even the smallest movements on the ice. Again, though, being a hero does not necessitate being rich or famous. We do not need to play in major sporting events or be musicians in concerts attended by thousands to be a hero. Bringing any vision we have into reality—persevering through our stress and fear to self-actualize—is heroic.

It is therefore no surprise that when we do *not* pursue our deepest goals and dreams, existential anxiety seeps in and manifests in the form of various worries, social anxiety, panic, phobias, or OCD. Alternatively, and preferably, we can choose to be genuinely and appropriately nervous by dreaming big and exerting heroic efforts to actualize our unique potential. In the former case, anxiety is largely meaningless and feels like a disease because it makes life worse. In the latter case, however, anxiety is not a problem or even a malady. On the contrary, it's an indication that we are on the right track because we are facing the fears associated with self-actualization. In essence, we *will* feel anxiety either way, so we're better off choosing to harness and face our anxiety through the process of self-actualization than experiencing it as a disorder.

Jadyn grew up in the Midwest and always experienced some degree of anxiety, but after he moved to the East Coast in his midthirties, he felt disconnected and aimless, and he was truly suffering. When he came for a consultation to my office, he not only worried every day about all the usual suspects—health, finances, family, politics, climate change—but he was also chronically depressed. Jadyn felt that his entire life was meaningless. He was miserable commuting from Long Island to Manhattan every day to work, but it was paying him so much money that he felt it was the "right and responsible thing to do" for himself and his family.

When I asked Jadyn what he *really* wanted to do, he scoffed at first, as if to say there was no point in even discussing the matter because he was stuck in his job. But we kept meeting weekly, and every so often I would bring up the question again: "Jadyn, what do you really want to do in life? Do you have a vision of your unique greatness? Do you have a talent that can benefit the world?"

After several tries he finally responded, albeit quietly and with a lump in his throat, "I want to be a writer." I asked Jadyn what he wanted to write about, and with an awkward laugh, he responded, "Philosophy."

I was utterly surprised. Jadyn was a sharp and insightful guy; he was the first and only person I had met who worked at a well-respected Manhattan hedge fund and secretly fantasized about creating philosophical writings. I asked Jadyn if he had written anything, and he responded, "Not in a long time." When I pushed for more information,

Jadyn clarified that he hadn't even tried writing in over five years. I reflected to myself how tragic it was that doing what Jadyn thought was "right and responsible" had made it impossible to do what he loved for half a decade!

In an attempt to inch Jadyn along, I suggested that he search through his old computer files for something he felt good about having written, and that he bring it to our next session. The following week, Jadyn presented me with a twenty-page essay that he had penned nearly eight years before. As I flipped through the pages, I could feel Jadyn's tension and fear mounting—this was the first time in nearly a decade that Jadyn was sharing his writing with someone else.

Jadyn's essay was spectacular—it was cogent, coherent, linear yet broadly constructed, and also rather witty—so I didn't need to fudge at all when I remarked, "You are an incredibly talented writer!" Jadyn's face lit up. I hadn't seen him that happy or engaged *ever* before. I encouraged Jadyn to find a philosophy writing project on the side of his finance job. Again, he scoffed, but this time it was more muted, so I could see that he was thinking about it.

Within a few months, after sharing his essay with a friend who happened to work for an independent publisher, Jadyn was invited to write a chapter for a forthcoming anthology on modern philosophy. That was when the challenges amped up signficiantly. As soon as Jadyn had an actual assignment, his distress shot through the roof. He articulated self-doubt, skepticism about the project, and concern that it was a stupid idea to write philosophy when he had a job that "actually paid something." Beneath the surface, though, was unadulterated stress, anxiety, and fear.

Jadyn was consumed with worries about how the chapter would turn out, what the publisher and his friend and readers would think about him. He became obsessed that he might do a bad job, and he worried that he would never be able to balance this side-gig with his professional work. Most of all, he was terrified that his finance colleagues would read his chapter one day and realize that he had other interests, which would affect his clout and standing within the hedge fund firm. As you may have guessed, I encouraged Jadyn to face these fears head-on and persevere through them—to write the chapter, face the uncertainty and adversity, and to go for it with everything he had.

As Jadyn continued to write, his fear and stress kept mounting. Indeed, he was facing a *real* risk—this was new territory for Jadyn, in an area that had a lot of personal meaning, and it was entirely possible that he could fail. I nevertheless encouraged Jadyn to keep pushing, and he heroically worked on his chapter each and every day.

After about two months, Jadyn had completed a draft. He delivered it on time to his editor, who read it with great enthusiasm and remarked that it was the best chapter in the entire book. Jadyn had done a fabulous job, and for the first time in many years, he felt genuinely happy and proud. Furthermore, Jadyn's anxiety and worry about health, finances, family, politics, and climate change had plummeted. When I asked him about this, he remarked, "When I was writing the chapter, I felt more afraid and stressed than ever, but I wasn't anxious about *those* things!" At first, I thought Jadyn was simply overwhelmed while working on his writing project, and he didn't have time to worry. But after some discussion, we both realized something more profound: Jadyn had used anxiety as his therapy. Instead of being passive and letting anxiety control his life, Jadyn had harnessed his anxiety in order to thrive by taking on discomfort and distress to accomplish something of personal value. In doing so, he had conquered his fears. His myriad worries had been vanquished, since Jadyn had channeled his anxiety as a positive force.

Human beings thrive the most when we experience anxiety in the process of self-actualization. Any accomplishment we can be proud of—anything that generates a sense of fulfillment and ultimate happiness—*will* involve a degree of discomfort and distress. *By its very nature, the processes of planning out how we want to contribute to the world, and subsequently mining our internal reservoir of strengths and abilities to bring that dream into reality, are challenging.* However, therein lies the opportunity to turn our anxiety into a strength. Discomfort is necessary to pursue real-life dreams; if we're not anxious, what we're chasing probably isn't that important. Conversely, when we voluntarily accept anxiety, stress, and even fear, in the pursuit of our deepest and most important life goals, we engage in self-actualization and start *thriving with anxiety*.

Let's dive into the nitty-gritty of what typically holds people back from becoming heroes and using their anxiety to thrive. From my vantage point, there are two major impediments (in addition to the ones described earlier in this chapter): (1) fear of failure, and (2) the need to achieve balance. I would like to suggest that embracing, as opposed to avoiding, our anxiety can get us over both of these hurdles, and doing so can be a catalyst to spiritual growth.

Fear of Failure

We naturally fear failure. No one likes to set out on a path only to turn around midway, unable to complete their journey. As such, when we venture beyond our comfort zones into risky territory, our emotions protect us by ramping up our level of anxiety. The aversive feelings of anxiety are our body's natural way of telling us that risk is increasing. However, as we've discussed, without risk we cannot thrive—no pain, no gain! For this reason, it is common for us to experience a cacophony of internal doubting when we are aiming for heroism. This is particularly the case at the beginning stages, when one has only initially started exerting efforts to achieve their visions.

Fear of failure is multifaceted. Much of the time it takes the form of doubts regarding the external world. Once we start pursuing our goals, new impediments become visible—ones we didn't fully expect or envision—and these naturally generate stress and fear. "What? I didn't realize it would take so much effort!" we say. "There are unexpected challenges here that I need to overcome," we tell ourselves. Such concerns are scary, but not nearly as pernicious as those pertaining to our internal worlds. The latter involve questions and concerns regarding our capacity for success. "What did I get myself into?" we may ask, calling into question the very decision to pursue our goals. "This is beyond my ability!" we may think, when the intensity of our stress and fear reaches new heights. As the noises of self-doubt reverberate, it can seem as if we don't have internal reservoirs deep enough to make it through the struggle.

Most of the time, if we stay the course and keep pursuing our goals, the voices and impediments will fade away, and we will achieve what we set out to accomplish. At times, though, the external or internal pressures are genuinely too much for us and things don't work out the way we hoped or planned. In such cases, we need to confront our fear of failure head-on. One spiritual perspective that can carry us through when such situations materialize is to recognize that failure is not always a bad thing. First of all, failure can keep us humble by helping us to recognize that as humans, we inherently lack knowledge and power.

More important, failure is an integral part of becoming a hero. Sometimes, heroic people set out on a pathway and the realities of life grind them to a halt; this is just the way the cookie crumbles. If you're going to exert serious effort in life, you will undoubtedly fail at points along the way, but that isn't a bad thing. All it means is that you're pushing past your limits, and you have reached a wall, which brings a learning opportunity that will make you stronger and more resilient to face the next challenge.

Finally, sometimes failure is a blessing in disguise. When we are self-actualizing by pushing our limits and exerting heroic efforts to bring our dreams into reality, setbacks and challenges present opportunities to grow and to redirect our efforts. Embracing failure when it occurs—as well as the anxiety that comes along with it—can be a catalyst to thriving.

Do you remember Carl from chapter 8? He had suffered a life-altering business setback when he discovered that his longtime partner had been embezzling money from their company and stashing it in an offshore account. After recovering emotionally from the enormous shock and disillusionment, Carl realized that he was still in his early sixties and had time to make some important life changes. Carl chose to spend much more time creating better ties with his children and grandchildren, and developed a new business based on what he had learned from his unfortunate losses. He started a consulting firm focused on helping businesspeople deal with challenging business partnerships. A key feature of his new service was teaching entrepreneurs to recognize the warning signs of partners and employees who were ripping them off. Needless to say, this required heroic efforts on Carl's part, perhaps the most challenging of which was confessing his own failings and naivete. However, this paradoxically became an attractive calling card, because entrepreneurs took confidence in knowing that Carl had been through the trenches of a difficult partnership, and he had firsthand experience of what he was talking about. It turned out that Carl's previous *failure* became a priceless experience that enabled him to flourish along a new path in life.

Another spiritual perspective that may be helpful is that exerting heroic efforts has value in and of itself, regardless of the outcomes. When human beings dig deep to bring their unique internal potential out into the world—when we try and try again, in the face of stress, fear, and impediments—we are self-actualizing, whether or not we achieve our goals and dreams. Yes, this flies in the face of Western culture that narrowly defines achievement and success, and values nothing else. Ask yourself, though, *Which of these perspectives is more psychologically adaptive? Which is more likely to generate resilient human beings who flourish over the long run?* Is it better to value the pursuit of our inner visions despite the outcomes? Or should we (continue to) favor material success, even if it involves no self-actualization or heroism at all?

Achieving Balance

Another common impediment to heroism comes from the obvious fact that human beings are not machines. *We all need to achieve balance.* In some respects, it's easier to never let up until we've reached our goal than to build a broad base of emotional, behavioral, and social health upon which to exert heroic efforts. Pushing continually in ways that disrupt, disturb, or destroy our relationships with ourselves and others is not only bad advice but counterproductive, and sometimes even dangerous. Many times, people who work exceptionally hard do so on the backs of others around them. They demand too much of others, get irritable, lose their patience, and become narcissistic. They may also abuse themselves by not tending to their own needs for sleep, a balanced diet, downtime, and a social life. The art of being a hero is doing so while respecting ourselves and others in our lives. For that reason, *all the strategies presented in this chapter need to be taken in concert with the information and practical tools offered in all eight previous chapters.*

When she was in her early twenties, Cassandra told me she felt that "everyone is prettier, thinner, smarter, and has more friends" than she did. This set her up to develop self-destructive patterns with guys. She would crave attention and not be nearly selective enough about her partners. Unfortunately, and predictably, many of them would sleep with her and then not even call the next day—or ever—making her feel disposable and even worse about herself. She was driven to seek therapy after a particularly intense bout of depression and anxiety. Cassandra worked extremely hard to increase her self-awareness, self-care, and self-compassion, and also to accept her anxiety about her body image and social standing without resorting to old patterns that weren't working for her. She also developed closer and more emotionally intimate relationships with friends, both men and women. These enabled her to utilize her depressive and anxious tendencies to understand and provide support to others, and to recognize and express her relational needs. After several months of work, Cassandra started to think about her life's purpose, and she began to push herself toward realizing a vision of becoming an actress. That was when things took a precipitous turn for the worse.

Cassandra started to experience intensified stress and fear—all of which was warranted given her strivings to self-actualize. However, Cassandra pushed herself too far, and her wheels began to come off. Her self-care tanked as she pushed way past reasonable limits—staying up too late, waking up too early, and skipping meals. Her friendships deteriorated since she was too busy working to connect with others in the acting world, and when she did eventually catch up with her friends, she seemed too distracted and even self-absorbed with her projects to fully engage with them. All of these factors led Cassandra into another dark period filled with self-criticism, negative social comparisons to others—especially in the area of body image—and significant anxiety. Fortunately, she did not succumb to previous maladaptive patterns with men, but her anxiety ultimately made it impossible to sustain her heroic efforts in the realm of acting, and she had to pause in pursuing her dream.

Unfortunately, Cassandra's pattern is all too common. Countless patients of mine have pursued their higher-order values and visions at the expense of their well-being, only to find themselves needing to retreat and rebuild. In extreme cases, I've seen patients experience manic episodes—involving extreme changes in mood for days—when they attempted to actualize their potential. One patient became so obsessed with building her music career that she started to have anger outbursts at strangers and dangerous bouts of road rage!

Honing and pursuing a vision of greatness is like a double-edged sword. On the one hand, wielding this powerful tool in the context of a balanced life—supported by self-love and rich connections with others—is the key to human thriving. But at the same time, plowing ahead with our plan to be a hero at the expense of other areas of connection is an epic recipe for destruction. As already mentioned, pursuing our dreams without considering our relationships with ourselves or others can be dangerous. In Cassandra's case, after a few tumultuous weeks, she fortunately chose to accept the fact that she had bumped up against her personal limits. She decided to slow down and put her acting career on pause while she reset her balance internally and interpersonally.

An important spiritual perspective can help us maintain balance while pursuing our dreams with heroic efforts. In chapters 7 and 8, we identified that we are inherently limited in our knowledge, control, and scope of influence, leaving us at the mercy of umpteen factors that can sideline our plans. Yet, here in chapter 9, I've extolled the virtues of having a vision and exerting significant efforts to bring our dreams into reality. On the surface, these concepts seem contradictory: Why would we kick ourselves into gear to improve the world when, in truth, our efforts cannot accomplish much unless the stars align?

One potential answer is as follows: spiritually speaking, one of the most powerful effects of exerting heroic efforts is that doing so can increase our awareness of how *little* is in our hands. Stress and fear mount as we surge forth to realize our dreams because of the *true* perception that our efforts could get toppled at any moment, and we could easily be left with nothing to show for them. Ironically, the more we push to achieve our dreams, the more we can recognize the limits of our control, as it becomes crystal clear that we are not invincible or impervious to risk and failure. Viewed in this light, exerting heroic efforts is not simply a prerequisite material enterprise to accomplishing our goals. Rather, it has the potential to be a spiritually laden process of exerting our freedom of choice in the world, while surrendering to the fact that ultimate outcomes are beyond the scope of our control. When we view our efforts this way, they can become a catalyst to increasing our resilience and faith. These perspectives are critical to achieving balance and harmony while pursuing our dreams. If we can internalize our limits, yet simultaneously recognize the spiritual value of pursuing our dreams, we are much more likely to take breaks when needed, practice self-compassion, and take the necessary time to connect with others.

After a three-month pause from any acting-related work, Cassandra felt more stable and ready to try again. But this time, she was careful to create and stick to a daily self-care schedule of eating healthily, exercising regularly, limiting her use of electronics at night, and getting sufficient and restful slumber. When her stress increased because of her career, Cassandra *increased* her self-care to make sure to stay balanced. She also reconnected with her friends and took it upon herself to never go more than forty-eight hours without meaningful social contact. Again, her heroic efforts slowed because of these choices. And yes, it felt like a hassle for Cassandra to prioritize her self-care and interpersonal connections at some points, given her intense acting schedule. But she realized that thriving with anxiety requires a firm base. More important, Cassandra redirected her intentions such that her heroic efforts were not merely a means to an end of changing the world. Instead, she came to view them as an end in themselves, with the ultimate goal of changing just one thing: herself.

. . . .

TOOL #9: TRANSCENDING OUR LIMITS

Anxiety can help us to identify, strive toward, and actualize our unique human potential. When we thrive with anxiety in these ways, it helps us fulfill our ultimate purpose in life. This tool will teach you how to use anxiety to thrive by transcending your limits.

First, recognize that *anxiety is inherent and necessary on the path to self-actualization.* When we envision what we have to offer the world and start to implement concrete plans to bring our dreams into reality, we will be facing risks and therefore we *will* feel some anxiety.

To those ends:

- Consider how thinking about one of your dreams—a new job, a new career, a new relationship, even a vacation that you keep postponing—conjures up anxiety.
- Ask yourself: *Am I hesitating or procrastinating to pursue my aspirations because I feel anxious?*
- If that's the case, *face your fears and think about transcending your limits!*

Second, anxiety tends to attach itself to areas of great human strength. This may take some creativity and thought, but consider the following questions:

- What are the domains in your life that make you the *most* anxious and concerned right now (for example, relationships, finances, health, climate change)?
- Now, consider your unique potential in those domains. If you're concerned about relationships, for example, might you have particular talents and strengths when it comes to family and friends? If you're worried about money, could it be that you are particularly adept at managing finances? If health is an area of concern, how could you use that to benefit the lives of others?

Finally, *transcend your limits to actualize your potential.* This will require making heroic efforts by pushing through stress, fear, and discomfort, in order to bring your dreams into reality.

Ask yourself:

- *Might my "anxiety" just be a natural stress or fear response that I am experiencing since I'm pursuing big dreams?*

- *Am I simply feeling anxious because I am investing in something important?*
- *Am I afraid of failure because I am taking on real risks?*
- *If so, might my discomfort be a good thing? Could it be that I am persevering through the challenges of life, and thriving with anxiety?*

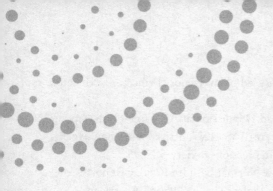

NOTES

Preface

1. Adam Grant, "There's a Name for the Blah You're Feeling: It's Called Languishing," *New York Times*, April 19, 2021, https://www.nytimes.com /2021/04/19/well/mind/covid-mental-health-languishing.html.

Introduction

1. US Department of Health and Human Services, "Any Anxiety Disorder," National Institute of Mental Health, accessed September 30, 2022, https://www.nimh.nih.gov/health/statistics/any-anxiety-disorder.

2. Bridget F. Grant et al., "Prevalence, Correlates, Co-Morbidity, and Comparative Disability of DSM-IV Generalized Anxiety Disorder in the USA: Results from the National Epidemiologic Survey on Alcohol and Related Conditions," *Psychological Medicine* 35, no. 12 (2005): 1747–59, https://pubmed.ncbi.nlm.nih.gov/16202187/.

3. Jill M. Hooley, Kathryn R. Fox, and Chelsea Boccagno, "Nonsuicidal Self-Injury: Diagnostic Challenges and Current Perspectives," *Neuropsychiatric Disease and Treatment* 16 (January 2020): 101–12, https:// doi.org/10.2147/NDT.S198806.

4. "Suicide," National Institute of Mental Health, last updated June 2022, https://www.nimh.nih.gov/health/statistics/suicide.

5. "COVID-19 Pandemic Triggers 25% Increase in Prevalence of Anxiety and Depression," World Health Organization, March 2, 2022, https:// www.who.int/news/item/02-03-2022-covid-19-pandemic-triggers-25 -increase-in-prevalence-of-anxiety-and-depression-worldwide.

6. W. H. Auden, *The Age of Anxiety*, ed. Alan Jacobs (Princeton: Princeton University Press, 2011).

7. Tom Porter, "Anxiety, Stress and Depression at All-Time High Among Americans: Study," *Newsweek*, April 18, 2017, https://www.newsweek .com/recession-mental-health-depression-anxiety-585695.

8. Jean M. Twenge, "Studies Show Normal Children Today Report More Anxiety than Child Psychiatric Patients in the 1950s," American Psychological Association, 2000, https://www.apa.org/news/press /releases/2000/12/anxiety.

9. Karen L. Fingerman et al., "Helicopter Parents and Landing Pad Kids: Intense Parental Support of Grown Children," *Journal of Marriage and Family* 74, no. 4 (August 2012): 880–96, https://doi.org/10.1111/j.1741 -3737.2012.00987.x.

10. Valencia Higuera, "All About Lawnmower Parenting," Healthline, October 30, 2019, https://www.healthline.com/health/parenting /lawnmower-parents.

11. "Number of Lifetime Prevalent Cases of Anxiety Disorders among Adults in Select Countries Worldwide in 2018, by Gender (in Millions)," Statista (chart), April 2019, https://www.statista.com/statistics/1115900 /adults-with-anxiety-disorders-in-countries-worldwide-by-gender/.

12. A. J. Baxter et al., "Global Prevalence of Anxiety Disorders: a Systematic Review and Meta-Regression," *Psychological Medicine* 43, no. 5 (May 2013): 897–910, https://doi.org/10.1017/S003329171200147X.

13. Ayelet Meron Ruscio et al., "Cross-Sectional Comparison of the Epidemiology of DSM-5 Generalized Anxiety Disorder Across the Globe," *JAMA Psychiatry* 74, no. 5 (2017): 465–75, https://doi.org /10.1001/jamapsychiatry.2017.0056.

14. Rachael Rettner, "Anxiety Linked to High IQ," Live Science, May 30, 2013, https://www.livescience.com/36259-anxiety-linked-high-iq.html.

15. Amanda Macmillan, "Why People with Anxiety May Have Better Memories," *Time*, February 27, 2018, https://time.com/5176445/anxiety -improves-memory/.

16. A. Kalueff and D. J. Nutt, "Role of GABA in Anxiety and Memory," *Depression and Anxiety* 4, no. 3: 100–10, https://doi.org/10.1002/ (SICI)1520-6394(1996)4:3<100::AID-DA2>3.0.CO;2-K.

17. "Mark Twain—Famous Bipolar Author," Famous Bipolar People, accessed January 24, 2023, http://www.famousbipolarpeople.com/mark-twain.html.

18. *Larry King Live*, "Panel Discusses Depression," CNN, June 12, 2005, https://transcripts.cnn.com/show/lkl/date/2005-06-12/segment/01.

19. Goalcast, "Jim Carrey—Be Yourself," Facebook video, May 30, 2017, https://www.facebook.com/goalcast/videos/1414580435285809/.

20. Kayla Blanton, "Howie Mandel Says Struggling with OCD and Anxiety Is Like 'Living in a Nightmare,'" *Prevention*, June 9, 2021, https://www.prevention.com/health/mental-health/a36673654/howie-mandel-ocd-anxiety/.

21. Locke Hughes, "Selena Gomez Opens up about How Therapy Changed Her Life," WebMD, accessed February 27, 2023, https://www.webmd.com/mental-health/features/selena-gomez-opens-up-about-therapy.

22. Jake Smith, "Adele Reveals She Experienced the 'Most Terrifying Anxiety Attacks' Amid Her Divorce," *Prevention*, November 15, 2021, https://www.prevention.com/health/mental-health/a38254699/adele-reveals-anxiety-attacks-due-to-divorce/.

23. Carly Mallenbaum, "Lady Gaga Shares Mental Health Struggle, Thoughts of Suicide: 'My Inner Voice Shut Down,'" *USA Today*, November 9, 2018, https://www.usatoday.com/story/life/people/2018/11/09/lady-gaga-mental-health-patron-awards-sag/1940329002/.

24. Jacob Stolworthy, "Bruce Springsteen 'Knows He's Not Completely Well' As He Opens up About His Mental Health," *The Independent*, November 30, 2018, https://www.independent.co.uk/arts-entertainment/music/news/bruce-springsteen-mental-health-depression-broadway-netflix-tour-a8660336.html.

25. David H. Barlow, *Anxiety and Its Disorders: The Nature and Treatment of Anxiety and Panic* (New York: Guilford Press, 1988), 12.

26. Kenneth I. Pargament, *The Psychology of Religion and Coping: Theory, Research, Practice* (New York: Guilford Press, 1997), 39.

Chapter 1: Knowing Ourselves

1. National Center for Health Statistics, "Leading Causes of Death," Centers for Disease Control and Prevention, last reviewed January 18, 2023, https://www.cdc.gov/nchs/fastats/leading-causes-of-death.htm.

2. Katsuyuki Miura et al., "Pulse Pressure Compared with Other Blood Pressure Indexes in the Prediction of 25-Year Cardiovascular and All-Cause Mortality Rates: The Chicago Heart Association Detection

Project in Industry Study," *Hypertension* 38, no. 2 (August 2001): 232–37, https://doi.org/10.1161/01.HYP.38.2.232.

3. Robert A. Smith, Vilma Cokkinides, and Harmon J. Eyre, "American Cancer Society Guidelines for the Early Detection of Cancer, 2003," *CA: a Cancer Journal for Clinicians* 53, no. 1 (2003): 27–43, https://doi.org /10.3322/canjclin.53.1.27.

4. Tawseef Dar et al., "Psychosocial Stress and Cardiovascular Disease," *Current Treatment Options in Cardiovascular Medicine* 21, no. 5 (2019), https://doi.org/10.1007/s11936-019-0724-5.

5. Masanori Munakata, "Clinical Significance of Stress-Related Increase in Blood Pressure: Current Evidence in Office and Out-of-Office Settings," *Hypertension Research* 41, no. 8 (2018): 553–69, https://doi.org/10.1038 /s41440-018-0053-1.

6. John D. Hayes, Albena T. Dinkova-Kostova, and Kenneth D. Tew, "Oxidative Stress in Cancer," *Cancer Cell* 38, no. 2 (2020): 167–97, https:// doi.org/10.1016/j.ccell.2020.06.001.

7. Huan Song et al., "Association of Stress-Related Disorders with Subsequent Autoimmune Disease," *JAMA* 319, no. 23 (2018): 2388–400, https://doi.org/10.1001/jama.2018.7028.

8. Leonid N. Maslov et al., "Is Oxidative Stress of Adipocytes a Cause or a Consequence of the Metabolic Syndrome?", *Journal of Clinical and Translational Endocrinology* 15 (2019): 1–5, https://doi.org/10.1016/j.jcte .2018.11.001.

9. Myrick C. Shinall et al., "Association of Preoperative Patient Frailty and Operative Stress with Postoperative Mortality," *JAMA Surgery* 155, no. 1 (2020): e194620, https://doi.org/10.1001/jamasurg.2019.4620.

10. Oleguer Plana-Ripoll et al., "Nature and Prevalence of Combinations of Mental Disorders and Their Association with Excess Mortality in a Population-Based Cohort Study," *World Psychiatry* 19, no. 3 (2020): 339–49, https://doi.org/10.1002/wps.20802.

11. William C. Dement and Christopher C. Vaughan, *The Promise of Sleep: A Pioneer in Sleep Medicine Explores the Vital Connection between Health, Happiness, and a Good Night's Sleep* (New York: Dell, 2000).

12. Sarah L. Chellappa and Daniel Aeschbach, "Sleep and Anxiety: From Mechanisms to Interventions," *Sleep Medicine Reviews* 61 (February 2022): 101583, https://doi.org/10.1016/j.smrv.2021.101583.

13. Heather Cleland Woods and Holly Scott, "#Sleepyteens: Social Media

Use in Adolescence Is Associated with Poor Sleep Quality, Anxiety, Depression and Low Self-Esteem," *Journal of Adolescence* 51 (2016): 41–49, https://doi.org/10.1016/j.adolescence.2016.05.008.

14. National Center for Chronic Disease Prevention and Health Promotion, "How Much Sleep Do I Need?" Centers for Disease Control and Prevention, last reviewed September 14, 2022, https://www.cdc.gov/sleep/about_sleep/how_much_sleep.html.

15. "American Heart Association Recommendations for Physical Activity in Adults and Kids," American Heart Association, last reviewed April 18, 2018, https://www.heart.org/en/healthy-living/fitness/fitness-basics/aha-recs-for-physical-activity-in-adults.

16. Ivan D. Escobar-Roldan, Michael A. Babyak, and James A. Blumenthal, "Exercise Prescription Practices to Improve Mental Health," *Journal of Psychiatric Practice* 27, no. 4 (2021): 273–82, https://doi.org/10.1097/PRA.0000000000000554.

17. Sammi R. Chekroud et al., "Association Between Physical Exercise and Mental Health in 1–2 Million Individuals in the USA Between 2011 and 2015: a Cross-sectional Study," *The Lancet Psychiatry* 5, no. 9 (2018): 739–46, https://doi.org/10.1016/S2215-0366(18)30227-X.

18. "Americans Check Their Phones 96 Times a Day," Asurion, November 21, 2019, https://www.asurion.com/press-releases/americans-check-their-phones-96-times-a-day/.

19. Tzach Yoked, "Arianna Huffington Tells Haaretz: Everyone Should Put Down Their Phones and Keep Shabbat," March 14, 2018, https://www.haaretz.com/us-news/.premium.MAGAZINE-arianna-huffington-everyone-should-keep-shabbat-1.5908269.

20. Larry Rosen et al., "Sleeping with Technology: Cognitive, Affective, and Technology Usage Predictors of Sleep Problems Among College Students," *Sleep Health* 2, no. 1 (2016): 49–56, https://doi.org/10.1016/j.sleh.2015.11.003.

21. Personal communication from Peter Occhiogrosso, September 2022.

22. Michelle Baran, "Why U.S. Workers Need to Step up Their Vacation Game," AFAR, October 18, 2018, https://www.afar.com/magazine/why-us-workers-need-to-step-up-their-vacation-game.

23. Shawn Achor and Michelle Gielan, "The Data-Driven Case for Vacation," *Harvard Business Review*, July 13, 2016, https://hbr.org/2016/07/the-data-driven-case-for-vacation.

24. Laura Giurge and Kaitlin Woolley, "Don't Work on Vacation. Seriously," *Harvard Business Review*, July 22, 2020, https://hbr.org/2020/07/dont -work-on-vacation-seriously.

25. Achor, "The Data-Driven Case for Vacation."

26. "The Danger of 'Silent' Heart Attacks," Harvard Health, November 3, 2020, https://www.health.harvard.edu/heart-health/the-danger-of-silent -heart-attacks.

27. Richard P. Console Jr., "The Most Common Causes of Collision," *The National Law Review*, October 13, 2020, https://www.natlawreview.com /article/most-common-causes-collision.

28. David Haugh, "Today's NHL Makes 'Mr. Goalie' Sick," *Chicago Tribune*, May 21, 2009, https://www.chicagotribune.com/news/ct-xpm-2009-05 -21-0905200907-story.html.

Chapter 2: Accepting Ourselves

1. Aaron T. Beck et al., *Cognitive Therapy of Depression* (New York: Guilford Press, 1987).

2. Sonya VanPatten and Yousef Al-Abed, "The Challenges of Modulating the 'Rest and Digest' System: Acetylcholine Receptors As Drug Targets," *Drug Discovery Today* 22, no. 1 (January 2017): 97–104, https://doi.org/10 .1016/j.drudis.2016.09.011.

3. J. H. Burn, "The Relation of Adrenaline to Acetylcholine in the Nervous System," *Physiological Reviews* 25, no. 3 (1945): 377–94, https:// doi.org/10.1152/physrev.1945.25.3.377; D. Górny et al., "The Effect of Adrenaline on Acetylcholine Synthesis, Choline Acetylase and Cholinesterase Activity," *Acta Physiologica Polonica* 26, no. 1 (1975): 45–54.

4. Laura Campbell-Sills et al., "Effects of Suppression and Acceptance on Emotional Responses of Individuals with Anxiety and Mood Disorders," *Behaviour Research and Therapy* 44, no. 9 (September 2006): 1251–63, https://doi.org/10.1016/j.brat.2005.10.001.

5. Steven C. Hayes, Kirk D. Strosahl, and Kelly G. Wilson, *Acceptance and Commitment Therapy: The Process and Practice of Mindful Change*, 2nd ed. (New York: Guilford Publications, 2012).

6. Kristin D. Neff, and Pittman McGehee, "Self-Compassion and Psychological Resilience Among Adolescents and Young Adults," *Self and Identity* 9, no. 3 (2010): 225–40, https://doi.org/10.1080 /15298860902979307; Karen Bluth and Kristin D. Neff, "New

Frontiers in Understanding the Benefits of Self-Compassion," *Self and Identity* 17, no. 6 (2018): 605–608, https://doi.org/10.1080/15298868.2 018.1508494.

7. Fuschia M. Sirois, Ryan Kitner, and Jameson K. Hirsch, "Self-Compassion, Affect, and Health-Promoting Behaviors," *Health Psychology* 34, no. 6 (June 2015): 661–9, https://doi.org/10.1037/hea0000158; Wendy J. Phillips and Donald W. Hine, "Self-Compassion, Physical Health, and Health Behaviour: A Meta-Analysis," *Health Psychology Review* 15, no. 1 (March 2021): 113–39, https://doi.org/10.1080/1743719 9.2019.1705872.

8. Filip Raes et al., "Construction and Factorial Validation of a Short Form of the Self-Compassion Scale," *Clinical Psychology & Psychotherapy* 18, no. 3 (May/June 2011): 250–55, https://doi.org/10.1002/cpp.702.

Chapter 3: Transcending Ourselves

1. Martin M. Antony and Richard P. Swinson, *The Shyness and Social Anxiety Workbook (A New Harbinger Self-Help Workbook)* (Oakland: New Harbinger, 2018), 153–54.

2. Rebecca E. Stewart and Dianne L. Chambless, "Cognitive–Behavioral Therapy for Adult Anxiety Disorders in Clinical Practice: A Meta-analysis of Effectiveness Studies," *Journal of Consulting and Clinical Psychology* 77, no. 4 (August 2009): 595–606, https://doi.org/10.1037 /a0016032.

3. Lauren Slater, "The Cruelest Cure," *New York Times*, November 2, 2003, https://www.nytimes.com/2003/11/02/magazine/the-cruelest-cure.html.

4. American Psychological Association, "What Is Exposure Therapy?" Clinical Practice Guideline for the Treatment of Posttraumatic Stress Disorder, July 2017, https://www.apa.org/ptsd-guideline/patients-and -families/exposure-therapy.

5. Norman B. Schmidt et al., "Dismantling Cognitive–Behavioral Treatment for Panic Disorder: Questioning the Utility of Breathing Retraining," *Journal of Consulting and Clinical Psychology* 68, no. 3 (2000): 417–24, https://doi.org/10.1037//0022-006x.68.3.417.

6. Alessandro Pompoli et al., "Dismantling Cognitive-Behaviour Therapy for Panic Disorder: A Systematic Review and Component Network Meta-Analysis," *Psychological Medicine* 48, no. 12 (2018): 1945–53, https:// doi.org/10.1017/S0033291717003919.

7. Beryl Francis, "Before and After 'Jaws': Changing Representations of Shark Attacks," *Great Circle: Journal of the Australian Association for Maritime History* 34, no. 2 (2012): 44–64, http://www.jstor.org/stable/23622226.

8. Jess Romeo, "Sharks Before and After *Jaws*," *JStor Daily*, August 14, 2020, https://daily.jstor.org/sharks-before-and-after-jaws/.

9. "Sharks: Half (51%) of Americans are Absolutely Terrified of Them and Many (38%) Scared to Swim in the Ocean Because of Them . . . ," Ipsos, July 7, 2015, https://www.ipsos.com/en-us/sharks-half-51-americans-are-absolutely-terrified-them-and-many-38-scared-swim-ocean-because-them.

10. Edna B. Foa, "Prolonged Exposure Therapy: Past, Present, and Future," *Depression and Anxiety* 28, no. 12 (December 2011): 1043–47, http://doi.org/10.1002/da.20907.

11. Antony and Swinson, *The Shyness and Social Anxiety Workbook*, 160–61.

12. Fritz Strack, Leonard L. Martin, and Sabine Stepper, "Inhibiting and Facilitating Conditions of the Human Smile: a Nonobtrusive Test of the Facial Feedback Hypothesis," *Journal of Personality and Social Psychology* 54, no. 5 (1988): 768–77, https://doi.org/10.1037/0022-3514.54.5.768.

13. David Ropeik, "How Risky Is Flying?" PBS: *NOVA*, October 16, 2006, https://www.pbs.org/wgbh/nova/article/how-risky-is-flying/.

14. T. D. Borkovec, "The Nature, Functions, and Origins of Worry," in Graham C. Davey and Frank Tallis, *Worrying: Perspectives on Theory, Assessment and Treatment* (Oxford, England: Wiley, 1994), 5–33.

15. National Institutes of Health: Office of Extramural Research, "Notice of Special Interest (NOSI): Limited Competition Administrative Supplement to the US Deprescribing Research Network to Support Feasibility Clinical Trials of Complementary and Integrative Approaches for Deprescribing Benzodiazepines," Notice Number: NOT-AT-22–012, February 17, 2022, https://grants.nih.gov/grants/guide/notice-files/NOT-AT-22-012.html.

16. Matej Mikulic, "Number of Alprazolam Prescriptions in the U.S. 2004–2020," Statista, October 17, 2022, https://www.statista.com/statistics/781816/alprazolam-sodium-prescriptions-number-in-the-us/.

17. Robert Whitaker, *Anatomy of an Epidemic: Magic Bullets, Psychiatric Drugs, and the Astonishing Rise of Mental Illness in America* (New York: Crown, 2011), see especially chapters 7 and 14.

Chapter 4: Knowing Others

1. Emiliana R. Simon-Thomas, "Do Your Struggles Expand Your Compassion for Others?" *Greater Good*, November 18, 2019, https://greatergood.berkeley.edu/article/item/do_your_struggles_expand_your_compassion_for_others.

2. Daniel Lim and David DeSteno, "Past Adversity Protects Against the Numeracy Bias in Compassion," *Emotion* 20, no. 8 (December 2020): 1344–56, https://doi.org/10.1037/emo0000655.

3. "Biography," biography of Marsha Linehan, University of Washington, accessed November 24, 2022, https://blogs.uw.edu/linehan/biography/.

4. Benedict Carey, "Expert on Mental Illness Reveals Her Own Fight," *New York Times*, June 23, 2011, https://www.nytimes.com/2011/06/23/health/23lives.html.

5. Emma C. Winton, David M. Clark, and Robert J. Edelmann, "Social Anxiety, Fear of Negative Evaluation and the Detection of Negative Emotion in Others," *Behaviour Research and Therapy* 33, no. 2 (February 1995): 193–96, https://doi.org/10.1016/0005-7967(94)e0019-f.

6. David A. Fryburg, "Kindness as a Stress Reduction–Health Promotion Intervention: a Review of the Psychobiology of Caring," *American Journal of Lifestyle Medicine* 16, no. 1 (2022): 89–100, https://doi.org/10.1177/1559827620988268.

7. John Bowlby, *Attachment and Loss* (New York: Basic Books, 1969).

8. John Bowlby, *Maternal Care and Mental Health*, World Health Organization, Master Work Series, vol. 2 (1951; reprint Northvale, NJ: Jason Aronson, 1995), 355–533.

9. Harry F. Harlow, Robert O. Dodsworth, and Margaret K. Harlow, "Total Social Isolation in Monkeys," *Proceedings of the National Academy of Sciences* 54, no. 1 (1965): 90–97, https://doi.org/10.1073/pnas.54.1.90.

10. Harry F. Harlow, "The Nature of Love," *American Psychologist* 13, no. 12 (1958): 673–85, https://doi.org/10.1037/h0047884.

11. Phillip Radetzki, "Harlow's Famous Monkey Study: The Historical and Contemporary Significance of the Nature of Love," *Canadian Journal of Family and Youth/Le Journal Canadien de Famille et de la Jeunesse* 10, no. 1 (2018): 205–34, https://doi.org/10.29173/cjfy29349.

12. Mario Mikulincer, Phillip R. Shaver, and Dana Pereg, "Attachment Theory and Affect Regulation: The Dynamics, Development, and Cognitive Consequences of Attachment-Related Strategies," *Motivation*

and Emotion 27, no. 2 (2003): 77–102, https://doi.org/10.1023/A :1024515519160.

13. Thomas Insel and Larry J. Young, "The Neurobiology of Attachment," *Nature Reviews Neuroscience* 2, no. 2 (2001): 129–36, https://doi.org/10 .1038/35053579.

14. Katherine B. Ehrlich and Jude Cassidy, "Attachment and Physical Health: Introduction to the Special Issue," *Attachment & Human Development* 21, no. 1 (2019): 1–4, https://doi.org/10.1080/14616734 .2018.1541512.

15. Silke Schmidt et al., "Attachment and Coping with Chronic Disease," *Journal of Psychosomatic Research* 53, no. 3 (2002): 763–73, https://doi.org /10.1016/s0022-3999(02)00335-5.

16. Anthony Bateman and Peter Fonagy, *Mentalization Based Treatment for Borderline Personality Disorders: A Practical Guide* (Oxford: Oxford University Press, 2016).

17. Anthony Bateman and Peter Fonagy, "Mentalization Based Treatment for Borderline Personality Disorder," *World Psychiatry* 9, no. 1 (February 2010): 11–15, https://doi.org/10.1002/j.2051-5545.2010 .tb00255.x.

18. Stephen Covey, "The 90/10 Principle," YouTube (2010), accessed November 24, 2022, https://www.youtube.com/watch?v=cMipyQ5cgyg.

19. Richard Lane and Ryan Smith, "Levels of Emotional Awareness: Theory and Measurement of a Socio-emotional Skill," *Journal of Intelligence* 9, no. 3 (2021): 42, https://doi.org/10.3390/jintelligence9030042.

20. Jeff Thompson, "Is Nonverbal Communication a Numbers Game?" *Psychology Today*, September 30, 2011, https://www.psychologytoday.com /us/blog/beyond-words/201109/is-nonverbal-communication-numbers -game.

21. The main primary emotions are joy, sadness, fear, disgust, and surprise.

22. Although anger is often considered a primary emotion, it can sometimes do double duty as a secondary emotion. We will explore this more in chapter 6.

23. Lionel Giles, *The Sayings of Confucius: A New Translation of the Greater Part of the Confucian Analects* (New York: E. P. Dutton and Co., 1910), https://www.gutenberg.org/files/46389/46389-h/46389-h.htm.

24. John M. Gottman, *The Science of Trust: Emotional Attunement for Couples* (New York: W. W. Norton & Co., 2011).

25. *Merriam-Webster*, s.v. "attunement (*n.*)," accessed February 28, 2023, https://www.merriam-webster.com/dictionary/attunement.

26. Amy Canevello and Jennifer Crocker, "Creating Good Relationships: Responsiveness, Relationship Quality, and Interpersonal Goals," *Journal of Personality and Social Psychology* 99, no. 1 (2010): 78–106, https://doi.org/10.1037/a0018186.

27. Linda Rueckert and Nicolette Naybar, "Gender Differences in Empathy: The Role of the Right Hemisphere," *Brain and Cognition* 67, no. 2 (July 2008): 162–67, https://doi.org/10.1016/j.bandc.2008.01.002.

Chapter 5: Accepting Others

1. "John Wayne: I'm a Nixon Man," Richard Nixon Foundation, May 26, 2015, https://www.nixonfoundation.org/2015/05/john-wayne-im-nixon -man/.

2. Genesis 1:27.

3. Judith S. Wallerstein, "The Long-term Effects of Divorce on Children: A Review," *Journal of the American Academy of Child & Adolescent Psychiatry* 30, no. 3 (May 1991): 349–60, https://doi.org/10.1097/00004583 -199105000-00001.

4. Olga Khazan, "The High Cost of Divorce," *The Atlantic*, June 23, 2021, https://www.theatlantic.com/politics/archive/2021/06/why-divorce-so -expensive/619041/.

5. Richard Fry and Kim Parker, "Rising Share of US Adults Are Living Without a Spouse or Partner," Pew Research Center, October 5, 2021, https://www.pewresearch.org/social-trends/2021/10/05/rising-share-of -u-s-adults-are-living-without-a-spouse-or-partner/.

6. Charles M. Blow, "The Married Will Soon Be the Minority," *New York Times* (opinion), October 20, 2021, https://www.nytimes.com/2021/10 /20/opinion/marriage-decline-america.html.

7. Tami Luhby, "Millennials Say No to Marriage," *CNN Business*, July 20, 2014, https://money.cnn.com/2014/07/20/news/economy/millennials -marriage/index.html.

8. Lisa Bonos and Emily Guskin, "It's Not Just You: New Data Shows More Than Half of Young People in America Don't Have a Romantic Partner," March 21, 2019, https://www.washingtonpost.com/lifestyle/2019/03/21 /its-not-just-you-new-data-shows-more-than-half-young-people-america -dont-have-romantic-partner/.

9. Liz Mineo, "Good Genes Are Nice, but Joy Is Better," *The Harvard Gazette*, April 11, 2017, https://news.harvard.edu/gazette/story/2017/04/over-nearly-80-years-harvard-study-has-been-showing-how-to-live-a-healthy-and-happy-life/.

10. Generation X, born between 1965 and 1980 and currently 41–56 years old (65 million people in the US); Generation Y, or millenials, born between 1981 and 1996 and currently 25–40 years old (72 million); and Generation Z, born between 1997 and 2012 and currently 9–24 years old (68 million). See "Boomers, Gen X, Gen Y, Gen Z, and Gen A Explained," *Kasasa* (blog), July 6, 2021, https://www.kasasa.com/exchange/articles/generations/gen-x-gen-y-gen-z.

11. Keith Richards and Mick Jagger, "You Can't Always Get What You Want," 1969, sung by the Rolling Stones on *Let It Bleed* (US: London Records), 1969, LP, track 9.

12. S. Wolbe, *Kaas O' Savlanus, Vaad Rishon*, Alei Shur (Bais Hamussar: Jerusalem, Israel, 1985).

13. Nathan D. Leonhardt et al., "'We Want to Be Married on Our Own Terms': Non-University Emerging Adults' Marital Beliefs and Differences Between Men and Women," *Journal of Family Studies* 28, no. 2 (2022): 629–51, https://doi.org/10.1080/13229400.2020.1747520.

14. *Merriam-Webster*, s.v. "psychopath (*n.*)," accessed September 29, 2022, https://www.merriam-webster.com/dictionary/psychopath.

Chapter 6: Transcendence in Relationships

1. Amy Gallo, "Giving Thanks at Work: An HBR Guide," *Harvard Business Review*, November 24, 2021, https://hbr.org/2021/11/giving-thanks-at-work-an-hbr-guide.

2. "Mental Health Statistics 2023," SingleCare, updated Feburary 3, 2023, https://www.singlecare.com/blog/news/mental-health-statistics/; "Mental Illness," National Institute of Mental Health, updated January 2022, https://www.nimh.nih.gov/health/statistics/mental-illness.

3. "Road Rage: What Makes Some People More Prone to Anger Behind the Wheel," American Psychological Association, 2014, https://www.apa.org/topics/anger/road-rage.

4. "Princess Diana's 15 Most Powerful and Inspirational Quotes," *The Telegraph*, June 29, 2018, https://www.telegraph.co.uk/women/life/princess-dianas-15-powerful-inspirational-quotes/.

5. See, for instance, Ogyen Trinley Dorje Karmapa, *Interconnected: Embracing Life in Our Global Society* (Somerville, MA: Wisdom Publications, 2017).

6. David A. Moscovitch et al., "Anger Experience and Expression Across the Anxiety Disorders," *Depression and Anxiety* 25, no. 2 (February 2008): 107–13, https://doi.org/10.1002/da.20280.

7. Sue Johnson, *Hold Me Tight: Your Guide to the Most Successful Approach to Building Loving Relationships* (London: Piatkus Books, 2011).

8. Candice C. Beasley and Richard Ager, "Emotionally Focused Couples Therapy: A Systematic Review of Its Effectiveness over the Past 19 Years," *Journal of Evidence-Based Social Work* 16, no. 2 (2019): 144–59, https://doi.org/10.1080/23761407.2018.1563013.

9. Ernst Fehr and Urs Fischbacher, "The Nature of Human Altruism," *Nature* 425, no. 6960 (2003): 785–91, https://doi.org/10.1038/nature02043.

10. Dacher Keltner, "The Compassionate Instinct," *Greater Good*, March 1, 2004, https://greatergood.berkeley.edu/article/item/the_compassionate_instinct.27, 20ter 7:Knowing Our Limits14.

Chapter 7: Knowing Our Limits

1. Kenneth I. Pargament, *The Psychology of Religion and Coping: Theory, Research, Practice* (New York: Guilford Press, 1997).

2. Nicole Haloupek, "12 Common Things Science Still Hasn't Figured Out," Mental Floss, January 7, 2019, https://www.mentalfloss.com/article/567856/common-things-science-hasnt-figured-out.

3. "How Many Stars Are There in the Universe?" European Space Agency, accessed September 29, 2022, https://www.esa.int/Science_Exploration/Space_Science/Herschel/How_many_stars_are_there_in_the_Universe.

4. "Intolerance of Uncertainty," Anxiety Canada, accessed September 29, 2022, https://www.anxietycanada.com/articles/intolerance-of-uncertainty/.

5. William D. Silkworth, "Alcoholism As a Manifestation of Allergy," *Medical Journal* 145 (March 1937): 249, https://www.chestnut.org/Resources/8b7ff2b0-522c-4496-8f0a-ede79be1ddc5/1937-Silkworth-Alcoholism-as-Allergy.pdf.

6. "Intolerance of Uncertainty," Anxiety Canada.

7. Simon McCarthy-Jones, "The Autonomous Mind: The Right to Freedom of Thought in the Twenty-First Century," *Frontiers in Artificial*

Intelligence 2 (2019): 19, https://doi.org/10.3389/frai.2019.00019; Stanley Rachman and Padmal de Silva, "Abnormal and Normal Obsessions," *Behaviour Research and Therapy* 16, no. 4 (1978): 233–48, https://doi.org/10.1016/0005-7967(78)90022-0.

8. Jonathan Grayson, *Freedom from Obsessive-Compulsive Disorder: A Personalized Recovery Program for Living with Uncertainty* (New York: Penguin, 2014).

9. Pema Chödrön, *The Places That Scare You: A Guide to Fearlessness in Difficult Times* (Boston: Shambhala, 2002), chapter 1.

10. "Thomas Edison," Wikiquote, accessed September 29, 2022, https://en.wikiquote.org/wiki/Thomas_Edison.

11. Gerald Beals, "The Biography of Thomas Edison," ThomasEdison.com, 1997, http://www.thomasedison.com/biography.html.

12. Laurie Carlson, *Thomas Edison for Kids: His Life and Ideas: 21 Activities* (Chicago: Chicago Review, 2006), 3.

13. Jake Rossen, "How Thomas Edison Jr. Shamed the Family Name," Mental Floss, April 21, 2017, https://www.mentalfloss.com/article/93390/how-thomas-edison-jr-shamed-family-name.

14. "Therefore one should act without interest in the result of the action, without 'desire or hate.' Indifference is the great desideratum [that which is desired or needed]," Franklin Edgerton, trans., *The Bhagavad Gita* (New York: Harper & Row, 1946), 159.

Chapter 8: Accepting Our Limits

1. Viktor E. Frankl, *Man's Search for Meaning* (1959; reprint New York: Pocket Books, 1984), 87.

2. Crystal L. Park and Susan Folkman, "Meaning in the Context of Stress and Coping," *Review of General Psychology* 1, no. 2 (1997): 115–44, https://doi.org/10.1037/1089-2680.1.2.115.

3. Jennifer E. Graham et al., "Effects of Written Anger Expression in Chronic Pain Patients: Making Meaning from Pain," *Journal of Behavioral Medicine* 31, no. 3 (2008): 201–12, https://doi.org/10.1007/s10865-008-9149-4.

4. Terri A. deRoon-Cassini et al., "Psychological Well-Being after Spinal Cord Injury: Perception of Loss and Meaning Making," *Rehabilitation Psychology* 54, no. 3 (2009): 306–14, https://doi.org/10.1037/a0016545.

5. Ziyan Yang et al., "Meaning Making Helps Cope with COVID-19:

A Longitudinal Study," *Personality and Individual Differences* 174 (May 2021): 110670, https://doi.org/10.1016/j.paid.2021.110670.

6. Frankl, *Man's Search for Meaning*, 86.

7. "Frequency of Prayer," Pew Research Center, accessed November 25, 2022, https://www.pewresearch.org/religion/religious-landscape-study /frequency-of-prayer/.

8. Jeff Diamant, "With High Levels of Prayer, U.S. Is an Outlier among Wealthy Nations," May 1, 2019, https://www.pewresearch.org/fact-tank /2019/05/01/with-high-levels-of-prayer-u-s-is-an-outlier-among-wealthy -nations/.

Chapter 9: Transcending Our Limits

1. Diane F. Halpern, "The Nature and Nurture of Critical Thinking," in *Critical Thinking in Psychology*, eds. Robert J. Sternberg, Henry. L. Roediger III, and Diane F. Halpern (Cambridge University Press: 2007), https://doi.org/10.1017/CBO9780511804632.002.

2. Robert J. Sternberg and The Rainbow Project Collaborators, "The Rainbow Project: Enhancing the SAT Through Assessments of Analytical, Practical, and Creative Skills," *Intelligence* 34, no. 4 (July/ August 2006): 321–50, https://doi.org/10.1016/j.intell.2006.01.002.

3. Abraham Harold Maslow, *Self-Actualization* (Tiburon, CA: Big Sur Recordings, 1987), 64.

4. Rabbi Lawrence Kelemen, personal correspondence with the author, September 2020.

5. Louise Bonnet et al., "The Role of the Amygdala in the Perception of Positive Emotions: An 'Intensity Detector,'" *Frontiers in Behavioral Neuroscience* 9 (2015): article 178, https://doi.org/10.3389/fnbeh .2015.00178.

6. Michela Gallagher and Andrea A. Chiba, "The Amygdala and Emotion," *Current Opinion in Neurobiology* 6, no. 2 (April 1996): 221–27, https://doi .org/10.1016/s0959-4388(96)80076-6.

Appendix: Anxiety Tools

1. "Therefore one should act without interest in the result of the action, without 'desire or hate.' Indifference is the great desideratum [that which is desired or needed]," Franklin Edgerton, trans., *The Bhagavad Gita* (New York: Harper & Row, 1946), 159.

ACKNOWLEDGMENTS

ronically, writing a book about anxiety can cause a fair amount of disquiet. I thankfully managed to *thrive* with my feelings, with the help of many people along the way.

Peter Occhiogrosso was my write hand (pun intended), who masterfully shaped the haphazardly structured outlines I created and delivered by email, together with my long-winded diatribes during our weekly phone meetings, into an initial draft of each chapter for me to expand upon. His persistence and, more important, his patience and good humor kept the project on course while enabling me to simultaneously juggle myriad clinical, administrative, and research responsibilities throughout the writing process. Peter's expertise is apparent on every page, and I could not have written this book without him.

My editors at Harper Horizon, Meaghan Porter and Amanda Bauch, both enthusiastically and diligently pushed this project through its many stages, all while subtly and tactfully softening my academic prose into language that is more accessible and meaningful (that is, intelligible) to a popular audience. I am also thankful to Horizon's Andrea Fleck-Nisbet and Matt Baugher for giving me this opportunity.

Leslie Meredith, my agent, has been a wonderful support ever since we connected on the coattails of a *New York Times* feature piece on anxiety written in the early days of the pandemic, which happened to have quoted me. From day one, it was Leslie who believed the world needed a book on the *positives* of anxiety.

My wonderful team at Center for Anxiety helps hundreds of patients to *thrive with anxiety* every week. I am humbled by their dedication to our mission and values. In particular, my executive leadership team, David Braid, Dr. Marcia Kimeldorf, and Estee Ferris, have grown our program beyond anything I could have ever expected, while ensuring that our team provides a high quality of clinical care. I am also immensely grateful to my clinical leadership team, Drs. Christy Clark, Staci Berkowitz, Lisa Chimes, and Stephen Scherer, as well as Noah Hercky and Thanos Nioplias, for leading our clinicians in supporting our patients each day.

My trustworthy, detail-oriented, and super-responsive assistant, Moses Appel, has also been an incredible support since we started working together six years ago. In addition to his diligence in formatting over 150 references for this book, he helped with more administrative details than I can count or even recall. A shout-out also goes to Alex Campos for her assistance with managing my personal clinical caseload, and to Nicole Drago for introducing me to the wonderful world of social media outreach.

It is an immense privilege to work at McLean Hospital and Harvard Medical School under mentors who are, quite literally, luminaries of modern psychiatry. My primary academic mentor, Dr. Brent Forester, is detail-oriented to the max, never fazed, always exuding warmth, and hysterically funny. I can only hope to emulate his leadership and personal qualities. Equally hard-acts-to-follow are Drs. Scott Rauch, Kerry Ressler, Dost Öngür, Phil Levendusky, Thröstur Björgvinsson, and Diego Pizzagalli. I am grateful to each one of them for unabashedly supporting my novel work on spirituality and mental health, and collaborating with me on various research projects.

My McLean Hospital Spirituality & Mental Health Program colleagues—Rev. Angelika Zollfrank, Rev. Alissa Oleson, Dr. Caroline Kaufman, and my research assistants Mia Drury, Sean Minns, Poorvi Mandayam, Alana Johnston, and Eleanor Schuttenberg—are simply wonderful! I must also thank Adriana Bobinchok and the Media Affairs department for their support and guidance over the years.

Academic work is only possible with funding, and when you study spirituality, that means relying on philanthropy. I am immensely grateful to Lori Etringer, Sue Demarco, Jeff Smith, Jennifer Meyers, and the rest of the McLean Hospital Development Department, for their stewardship and dedication in fundraising for my work. Our incredible donors, including Rev. Dr. Barbara Nielsen, Ann O'Keefe, Joe and Dawn Colwin, David and Susan Fowler, and countless others, have not only provided generous financial support but sage counsel and the wisdom of personal experience, which has indelibly shaped my thinking and approach to research and clinical work.

Transitioning from academic to popular writing is a challenge that would not have been possible without the support of Dave Nussbaum, Joseph Fridman, Jamie Ryerson, and the entire Beyond the Ivory Tower workshop team. I am deeply indebted to each of you, as well as the John Templeton Foundation for supporting the workshop.

It is impossible to describe how my spiritual mentor, Rabbi Lawrence Kelemen of Jerusalem, shaped *Thriving with Anxiety* and all my other work. I will simply share that his influence transcends the spiritual, emotional, and physical spheres in my life.

To my wonderful wife, Miri, I could not do anything without you! You have inspired this book and everything else I have accomplished, both professionally and personally. Perhaps even more important, you help quell my anxiety and show me how to *thrive* with it.

APPENDIX: ANXIETY TOOLS

Psychotherapy involves two main components: cognitive change, which includes inculcating helpful values and perspectives, and behavioral change, which includes developing psychologically adaptive habits and behaviors. Throughout this book, I've used both elements. The mainstay of each chapter seeks to provide a rich conceptual framework of how to thrive with anxiety, and the final element of each chapter—the Anxiety Tools—is composed of behavioral approaches to harness anxiety as a catalyst to living a more connected life.

This appendix includes all the Anxiety Tools from the text. They are collected here as a resource for readers to refer back to during times of particular stress and anxiety.

TOOL #1: IS IT STRESS OR ANXIETY (OR BOTH)?

If we acknowledge our anxiety and learn how to work with it instead of denying or fighting it, our anxiety will end up helping us. But first, we must develop the ability to distinguish anxiety from stress. This requires taking some time to focus on what's going on within ourselves.

STEP 1

In order to use this tool, first choose a time when you are free from distractions for at least five to ten minutes, preferably alone. Sit in a comfortable chair or at a desk. And turn off your phone!

STEP 2

Now look back at the most recent times when you have felt intensely "anxious" (stress, fear, or anxiety)—if you are currently feeling anxious, then focus on the present moment—and inquire of yourself whether you are experiencing significant stress. For example:

- Do you feel that you don't have enough time in the day to get things done that you need to do?
- Do you feel overwhelmed by work, school, or other responsibilities?
- Are you short on time, money, or other precious resources?
- Are you or someone you love experiencing a health concern that is weighing on you emotionally?
- Do your anxiety-like sensations become more intense when your demands exceed your resources?

If you answered yes to one or more of these questions, you are feeling at least some degree of significant stress.

Bear in mind that you can simultaneously feel both stress and anxiety, so the fact that you are feeling stress does not automatically rule out that you may also be feeling anxious. But it's important to recognize each feeling separately so that you do not confuse basic stress with anxiety.

STEP 3

If you are experiencing stress, you have *only* two possible solutions: (1) increase your resources, or (2) decrease your demands (or both).

Increase your resources with the following:

- Improve your sleep quality and quantity. Try to get at least seven to nine hours of sleep per night for the next two weeks.
- Get moving! Physical exercise is critical to maintaining strength. Try to get thirty minutes of vigorous cardiovascular exercise at least five times per week over the next two weeks.
- Get connected by speaking about your feelings with a friend (or a therapist) regularly over the next two weeks.

Decrease your demands with these strategies:

- Take a tech break: every day for thirty minutes, plus a longer break each week, plus no screen time a half hour before bedtime each night. This alone will change your life!
- Say no to others when you are overstressed.
- Accept your limitations by recognizing that you are human, and that's okay.

STEP 4

Now look back again at times when you have felt "anxious" (stress, fear, or anxiety), and inquire of yourself whether you are experiencing significant anxiety. Remember that anxiety involves a fear response when there is nothing truly dangerous to be afraid of. For example:

- Do you have concerns that you may suddenly die when you have panic-like sensations, even though you have no medical symptoms?
- Are you overly concerned by what others think about you, even if they haven't said anything critical?
- Are you more worried than you need to be about everyday events, such as your family's well-being, health, and finances?
- Are you excessively concerned about getting sick?
- Do you feel fearful about coming into contact with spiders, dogs, snakes, or other common creatures?

If you answered yes to one or more of these questions, then congratulations, you have anxiety! Again, be aware that you can simultaneously feel both stress and anxiety.

STEP 5

This book is chock-full of strategies to deal with anxiety, but in this first tool we are focusing on just one: recognizing the blessing of fear and anxiety. Take a few minutes to contemplate and recognize that, just because you're anxious, this doesn't mean that something is wrong with you! On the contrary, anxiety is an indication that your fear response—which is critical to human survival—is intact. Yes, you may need to learn to chill out and take things down a notch, but you're better off having too much anxiety than too little.

Think about how your anxiety

- helps you to be aware when things may go wrong,
- helps you to perform and accomplish things, and
- primes you for leadership roles.

TOOL #2: THE POSITIVE SPIRAL

Anxiety gets out of control when we enter the anxiety spiral and the initial experience of an adrenaline surge leads to catastrophic thinking, self-judgment, and a worsening of anxiety. Conversely, we can utilize the opportunity of the initial fight-or-flight response (whether triggered by a real or perceived threat) to enter a positive spiral, which begets acceptance of our anxiety and self-compassion. When we take this approach, we harness the power of anxiety to increase our self-acceptance, thereby turning anxiety into a strength that can help us thrive. Here are some concrete steps to take when you start to feel anxious, in order to enter the positive spiral.

STEP 1

Remember that your *fight-or-flight* (sympathetic nervous system) response has an equal and opposite reaction called the *rest-and-digest* (parasympathetic nervous system) response. Over time, your anxiety will fade as adrenaline wanes and acetylcholine makes its way through the nervous system.

STEP 2

Do not fight your anxiety! Don't suppress or curtail or try to decrease it in any way. Simply accept it and *let it ride*. Let your anxiety wash over you. Allow yourself to experience anxiety without trying to change it. Simply observe the feelings, even if they are uncomfortable, and wait for them to pass. (Yes, they will eventually pass.) Turn anxiety into a strength by taking the opportunity to accept discomfort in your life.

STEP 3

Accept yourself. Don't judge yourself for feeling anxious. Anxiety is a normal response that all of us have. Furthermore, everyone who experiences anxiety has a reason why they are anxious—that could be something in the past, or a current stressor, or another factor. Don't judge yourself harshly or self-criticize. Thrive with anxiety by learning to be more accepting of who you are.

STEP 4

Practice self-compassion. Doing so does not mean you will become complacent or lazy. On the contrary, when you are struggling, give yourself a break and a hand—just like you would to a friend who's having a hard time. Remember that practicing self-compassion means being kind to yourself specifically when you do not feel like you deserve it! Take the opportunity to become a more compassionate person.

TOOL #3: FACING UP TO ANXIETY

Anxiety is scary, but—as long as we stand up to it and don't let it rule our lives—it's not more powerful than we are. Facing anxiety requires activating strength and courage that we have inside. Further, when we confront our anxiety head-on, we use it for good by searing into our minds that we have deep internal reservoirs of strength. The most concrete step we can take to actualizing this is simple: *start facing your anxieties!*

Consider just one anxiety that you could start to face at this point in your life. Ask yourself: *What am I avoiding because of anxiety? Are there any situations I steer clear of (behavioral avoidance)? Do I stop myself from thinking about certain things* (cognitive avoidance)? Here are some common fears and various forms of avoidance that people tend to engage in.

Anxiety	Avoidance
Spiders	Going camping

Flying	Planes, airports, videos of flying
Shyness	Speaking up in class, meeting new people, parties
Panic (for example, heart palpitations)	Exercising, having sex
Post-traumatic stress disorder (for example, accidents)	Driving, stories or videos of accidents, war films
OCD (for example, contamination fears)	Public toilets, shaking hands
Agoraphobia	Leaving home, situations where you might panic
Medical or dental	Visits to doctors or dentists
Public speaking	Office meetings, conferences, seminars
Financial	Balancing checkbook, credit card statements

- Pick one anxiety from the list (or another if it's more relevant) and identify how you avoid it.
- Now, visualize yourself facing your anxiety by eliminating, or decreasing, the avoidance. Take a moment to envision what it would be like to transcend your anxiety to some degree.
- Then, when you're ready, take a step forward. Face your fear. Allow yourself to feel anxious! And relish the difficult but wonderful process of resetting your thinking and transcending your anxiety.

TOOL #4: USING OUR EMOTIONS TO UNDERSTAND OTHERS

We can thrive with anxiety by harnessing our emotional distress to understand and respond to the pain of others. This will deepen our connection with other people and help quell the fires of our own anxiety so that we consequently reap the physical and mental benefits of having richer connections with others. If you've *ever* felt anxious before, you can use your anxiety to enhance the depth of your understanding of other people, which will help you (and them) in the long run.

Take a few minutes to make a mental inventory for someone in your life. It could be a coworker, friend, family member, intimate partner, or even a complete stranger (for the latter you may need to take some poetic and creative license to complete the exercise).

Provide at least one example of each of the following that the person may be experiencing at present. If you struggle to come up with something in one category (such as a sensation), simply quiet and focus your mind and try again. But if you get really stuck and cannot think of anything after a few minutes of focused trying, just move on to the next category.

1. **Goals:** What are some of the person's current ambitions or objectives? What are they striving to accomplish?
2. **Needs:** What do they want or require in life at this time? What would make their life easier, happier, or even just more convenient in some way?
3. **Sensations:** Do they feel pain, pleasure, warmth, cold? Do they smell or taste something? Or do they have another physical feeling?
4. **Thoughts:** What are some of the things on their mind? Try to pick thoughts that are relevant to how you think they may be feeling emotionally.
5. **Behaviors:** Which behaviors, whether subtle or overt, have they been engaging in recently? Try to identify action tendencies that are instrumentally associated with their emotional states.

6. **Feelings:** Which emotions have they been feeling lately? Which feelings underlie their physical sensations, thoughts, and behaviors? Are they primary emotions (direct responses to situations) or secondary emotions (emotional responses to their feelings)? Are they simple emotions? Do they "make sense" or seem conflictual or complex?

TOOL #5: THE CONNECTION SPIRAL

Regarding friends and loved ones, the saying goes, "You can't live with them, and you can't live without them." But in reality, only the last part is true: *we can't live without them.* So we need to learn how to weather the vicissitudes of interpersonal connections. Of course, there are some limits to this. If we find ourselves in genuinely abusive relationships with individuals who show no remorse or care for others' well-being, we need to protect ourselves. However, in the absence of malevolent intent, we generally benefit by learning to get along with people who are different from us. We can learn diverse perspectives, become stronger people, and, most of all, learn to be more accepting and compassionate toward ourselves and others. So when you feel irritated by others' idiosyncrasies, or when you are struggling with what other people are doing, engage in the connection spiral by following these steps.

STEP 1

Recognize that it's simply not true that relationships should be perfect. Remember that differences are often a great catalyst to connection and inner growth. *Life is messy!* So it is impossible to have rich relationships with others unless we learn to accept their idiosyncrasies with love and patience.

STEP 2

Catch yourself catastrophizing before things escalate. Recognize and accept local issues without going global. Miscommunications and errors happen all the time, especially when two people are close with each other. Interpreting people's actions as nefarious (when they may not be) makes it impossible to respond with equanimity. When issues arise, take a breather and remain in the present.

STEP 3

Accept that all of us are fallible human beings, and it's not helpful to blame others or yourself when people make bad decisions. As professional athletes like to say, *you can only control what you can control*—for example, if you're pitching a good game and one of your fielders makes a costly error, that's not on you. Along these lines, provide copious amounts of compassion to yourself and to others. Doing so will *not* make the situation worse! All of us have baggage to carry and issues to face, and everyone needs *more*—not less—compassion and love.

STEP 4

Continually practice acceptance and compassion toward others, just as you would do with yourself when it comes to your anxiety. Use the opportunities of interpersonal differences to strengthen bonds with others and love them for who they are.

TOOL #6: ACKNOWLEDGING AND EXPRESSING OUR VULNERABILITY

If you're feeling anxious in a relationship of any kind (for example, friendship, business, family, or romantic), consider it a good sign! When we connect with others, we become vulnerable since their decisions and activities affect us. As such, it's natural to feel tense, stressed, anxious, or fearful. In some ways, anxiety in a relationship is an indication that the connection is solid: if you don't feel any anxiety at all, it's likely that you don't care that much about the relationship.

Anxiety therefore presents an opportunity to make our relationships more intimate. We can choose to share our concerns with other people and give them an opportunity to understand how we feel, comfort us, and come through for us. As I've discussed, in most situations, sharing our vulnerability is a catalyst for others to bring themselves more fully to our relationships and provide what we need. However, in some cases they may not come through for us, which is hard to accept and deal with. Even in such instances, it's better to know where we stand, and to have the satisfaction that we have done our part to maintain connection.

That brings us to our tool. You can thrive with anxiety by acknowledging and expressing your vulnerability to another person, for the purposes of enriching your connection. You could do this with a coworker, boss, friend, family member, or romantic partner.

STEP 1: BUILD AWARENESS

Start by becoming more aware of your anxiety. Be fully aware of what your wants and needs are in the relationship and how they may not be met by the other person. Think vividly about how your life would look different if the person doesn't come through for you, or if they were to do some form of behavior that drives you up a wall. If you feel uncomfortable while thinking about this, you are on the right track!

STEP 2: GUARD AGAINST
ANGER AND AVOIDANCE

Next, be careful to guard against anger and avoidance. If you tend to get angry in general, be super attentive to focus on your anxiety and maintain awareness of that primary emotion. With that in mind, take the time to mentally count to ten if you feel yourself getting agitated, and simmer down before moving on to step 3. If you tend to avoid and retreat into your proverbial turtle shell (for example, by changing the topic when potentially contentious issues come up, not expressing your true feelings, or "ghosting"), take the opposite approach: recognize that the dangers of shutting down include losing closeness with others, and that there is a cost to not saying your piece.

STEP 3: EXPRESS YOUR NEEDS

Finally, dig deep and express what you need from others, from a place of accepting that you need their help. Utilize your anxiety to convey that you need the other person to come through for you or to stop doing whatever is causing distress. Remember that the goal is not to control the other person; rather, it's to provide information about your emotional state so they can make an informed decision that accounts for how their actions affect you. Take the time to communicate your needs, even though it's humbling and terrifying, in order to do your part in bringing about a higher level of connection.

TOOL #7: DECOUPLING OUR EFFORTS AND OUTCOMES

As we've discussed, the primary purpose of worry is to avoid thinking about the fact that, ultimately, life is unpredictable and uncontrollable. Worry gives us a *false* sense of control. This leaves us vulnerable to self-criticism in the wake of life stressors and setbacks, since we tend to blame ourselves when things go wrong.

So if you are feeling worried about an outcome, take the opportunity to recognize that uncertainty and uncontrollability are a part of life. *There is nothing wrong with you or anyone else if you are not able to predict or control the future.* All it means is that you are a human being—a creature with limited knowledge and capacity to influence the events of this world.

Along these lines, consider that, while human efforts are important (as discussed in chapter 9), they are ultimately insufficient to control the outcomes of life. This is because of the following fact: in every situation, any number of events could occur that would interrupt the usual sequence of an outcome following from our intentions and actions.

Our tool, therefore, is to *decouple human efforts and outcomes by recognizing that what we do in day-to-day life may or may not lead to the result that we are striving for.*

Even basic acts like turning on a light could be thwarted: the switch may not catch the connecting wires, the electrical circuit may malfunction, the fuse or lightbulb may blow out, or other mishaps may occur, none of which are related in any way to our ability to flip a light switch!

Similarly, the act of standing up from a chair could be interrupted by factors beyond our knowledge or control. The chair may spontaneously collapse, or our muscles and ligaments may not work as we expect them to, or there may be a sudden change in atmospheric pressure or gravity that makes it impossible to stand up. Granted, some of these situations are more far-fetched than others, but none of them is out of the realm of possibility, and all are beyond the scope of human control.

When we look for this on an everyday basis, it is readily apparent. As the great Hindu holy book *The Bhagavad Gita* says, we should focus not on the results of our actions but on the actions themselves.[1]

To these ends, once per day while engaging in a mundane task, briefly consider that the effort you are expending may not result in the outcome you are expecting.

For example, before you open the refrigerator door to get some milk for your breakfast cereal, consider that the door may be sealed shut, or the fridge may not be working, or the milk may be gone or have soured. Consider as well that none of those possibilities reflects poorly on you as a human being—sometimes things occur beyond our control. Stuff happens!

Over time, try this approach when you are feeling anxious or worried. Consider that the efforts you are expending to reduce uncertainty may not pan out. Most of all, recognize that whether or not things go our way, it has a lot less to do with our efforts than we tend to think.

When we take this approach, we can thrive with anxiety by embracing our humble human position and by recognizing that our knowledge and strength are inherently limited.

TOOL #8: ACCEPTING OUR LIMITS

Worry tends to be a shallow process. It rarely allows us to get to the true depth of what is creating anxiety. Worry therefore makes it harder for us to accede to our natural human limits.

So this tool begins with a self-inquiry process that I've adapted from cognitive therapy, which was designed to help us gain access to our core beliefs that we are so often unaware of. The technique involves continually asking ourselves, *If so, then what would happen?* in order to probe downward into what we are sincerely and utterly afraid of.

For example, if you are afraid of getting sick, ask yourself, *If I were to get sick, what would happen?*

The answer might be, *Well then, I'll have to take a leave of absence from work.*

From there, ask yourself again, *If I had to go on leave, what would happen?* You may respond, *I'll feel ashamed around my work colleagues when I return.*

At that point, ask yourself, *If I felt shame upon my return, what would happen?*

The process should continue until you feel viscerally uncomfortable. If you're imagining yourself feeling embarrassed, depressed, losing your friendships, and ending up utterly alone, you're probably doing it correctly. The goal of this part of the exercise is to recognize what you are fundamentally afraid of, and that should feel very uncomfortable to think about.

Once you are good and anxious, *it's time to completely let go and accept.* Immerse yourself in the reality that whatever you fear may actually manifest. Consider that it's probably not so difficult for a combination of factors to coalesce and bring about the feared outcomes. Embrace your vulnerability, and relinquish the facade of knowledge, control, and security. Recognize that, in the long run, we are powerless to control most of the major factors that shape our fortunes, so letting go is the only logical option.

At this point, you should be even more anxious. Remember that you are to truly accept that terrible outcomes could happen at any moment.

Now, recognize that no matter what happens—no matter what circumstances may befall you—*you will always retain the capacity to make choices.* Consider what your options might be (even if none of them are good options) and what you might choose if your fears do manifest.

If prayer is something that you are comfortable with or wish to try, at this point you can pray in whatever language feels comfortable to avert the outcome you're afraid of. However, don't simply focus on the prospect of divine assistance. Rather, use prayer to deepen your acceptance that, ultimately, your control has limits.

TOOL #9: TRANSCENDING OUR LIMITS

Anxiety can help us to identify, strive toward, and actualize our unique human potential. When we thrive with anxiety in these ways, it helps us fulfill our ultimate purpose in life. This tool will teach you how to use anxiety to thrive by transcending your limits.

First, recognize that *anxiety is inherent and necessary on the path to self-actualization.* When we envision what we have to offer the world and start to implement concrete plans to bring our dreams into reality, we will be facing risks and therefore we *will* feel some anxiety.

To those ends:

- Consider how thinking about one of your dreams—a new job, a new career, a new relationship, even a vacation that you keep postponing—conjures up anxiety.
- Ask yourself: *Am I hesitating or procrastinating to pursue my aspirations because I feel anxious?*
- If that's the case, *face your fears and think about transcending your limits!*

Second, anxiety tends to attach itself to areas of great human strength. This may take some creativity and thought, but consider the following questions:

- What are the domains in your life that make you the most anxious and concerned right now (for example, relationships, finances, health, climate change)?
- Now, consider your unique potential in those domains. If you're concerned about relationships, for example, might you have particular talents and strengths when it comes to family and friends? If you're worried about money, could it be that you are particularly adept at managing finances? If health is an area of concern, how could you use that to benefit the lives of others?

Finally, *transcend your limits to actualize your potential*. This will require making heroic efforts by pushing through stress, fear, and discomfort, in order to bring your dreams into reality.

Ask yourself:

- *Might my "anxiety" just be a natural stress or fear response that I am experiencing since I'm pursuing big dreams?*
- *Am I simply feeling anxious because I am investing in something important?*
- *Am I afraid of failure because I am taking on real risks?*
- *If so, might my discomfort be a good thing? Could it be that I am persevering through the challenges of life and thriving with anxiety?*

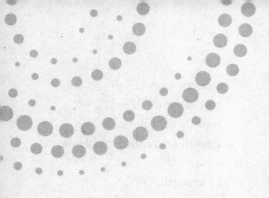

INDEX

B

C

D

E

earth school, 214, 216

Edison, Thomas, 203–204

emotional awareness

    anxiety as enhancing, 105–107

    double-edged sword regarding, 117–121

    learning, 113–117

    measurement of, 114–115

    mentalization and, 113–117

    overview of, 101–102

    people-watching and, 108–110

    understanding others through, 127–128, 287–289

emotions

    abuse and, 140–141

    accepting, 50

    anxiety cycle and, 37

    attachment and, 112

    brain activity and, 70, 247

    demands of, 5–6

    dissociation from, 87–88

    emotional attunement, 121–128, 287–289

    fluctuation of, 117

    intuition regarding, 121–122

    primary, 116–117, 162

    processing of, 72

    responding to, 122–123

    secondary, 117, 162

    statistics regarding, 134

    suppressing, 50–51

    using to understand others, 127–128, 287–289

    See also specific emotions

empathy, 103

everyday heroes, 245–257

exercise, 12

exposure therapy

    barriers to, 86

    behavioral avoidance and, 80–81

    examples of, 96–97

    facing fears within, 68–70

    health anxiety and, 241

    for hit and run, 200

    neurobiology of, 70–72

    overcoming phobias through, 72–74

    overview of, 66–68

    process of, 220

    relinquishing control within, 81–82

    transcending anxiety with, 82–85

    types of, 75–76

    worry and, 89

F

G

H

Hall, Glenn, 23–24, 247
happiness, 115
hard work, 203–206
Harlow, Harry, 111
health, 10, 20, 39–40, 97, 212–213, 240–242
heart attacks, 21
heights, fear of, 81–82, 85–86, 134–135
helicopter parenting, xxiii–xxiv
heroes, 245–257
hippocampus, 70, 74, 89

hit and run, as obsessive-compulsive disorder (OCD) form, 199–200
hole analogy, 51
homelessness, 109–110
Huffington, Arianna, 14
human control, limits of, 200–207
human knowledge, limits of, 188–196
human potential, 236, 258–259, 296–297
hypochondriasis, 20, 39–40, 212–213, 240–242

I

identity, 238, 239
imaginal exposure therapy, 75
imperfection, 134, 150
income level, xxiv
individualism, 158
infants, 111–112
intelligence, xxvi, 188–196

interceptive exposure therapy, 75
interdependence, 158–159, 165
interpersonal distance, 167–169
in-vivo (real-life) exposure therapy, 75
Is It Stress or Anxiety (or Both)? label, 28–31, 282–284

J

Jaws, 71
Johnson, Sue, 167, 169
journaling, xxx

joy, 115
judgment, xx, xxii, 34–35, 37, 38–41, 42, 54–55, 60–61

M

N

O

P

S

U

V

Z

ABOUT THE
AUTHOR

David H. Rosmarin, PhD, is an associate professor at Harvard Medical School, a program director at McLean Hospital, and founder of Center for Anxiety, which services over one thousand patients per year in multiple states. Dr. Rosmarin is an international expert on spirituality and mental health whose work has been featured in *Scientific American*, the *Boston Globe*, the *Wall Street Journal*, and the *New York Times*. He can be reached via his website, www.dhrosmarin.com.